MOBILE APPLICATIONS DEVELOPMENT WITH

ANDROID

Technologies and Algorithms

MOBILE APPLICATIONS DEVELOPMENT WITH
ANDROID
Technologies and Algorithms

Meikang Qiu, Wenyun Dai, and Keke Gai

Pace University, New York City, New York, USA

CRC Press

Taylor & Francis Group

Boca Raton London New York

CRC Press is an imprint of the
Taylor & Francis Group, an **informa** business

A CHAPMAN & HALL BOOK

CRC Press
Taylor & Francis Group
6000 Broken Sound Parkway NW, Suite 300
Boca Raton, FL 33487-2742

First issued in paperback 2020

© 2017 by Taylor & Francis Group, LLC
CRC Press is an imprint of Taylor & Francis Group, an Informa business

No claim to original U.S. Government works

Version Date: 20160512

ISBN 13: 978-0-367-57414-7 (pbk)
ISBN 13: 978-1-4987-6186-4 (hbk)

Visit the Taylor & Francis Web site at
http://www.taylorandfrancis.com

and the CRC Press Web site at
http://www.crcpress.com

Contents

List of Figures

List of Tables

Preface

Mobile applications have dramatically penetrated in numerous fields and have changed people's lives. Developing an effective mobile app has become a significant issue for current enterprises to spread out their services or produces, and build up a direct connection with customers. A mobile application is an option of receiving the full attention of its users, which distinguishes from a desktop that has multitask offerings. The number of mobile app downloads and executions have been rising considerably over years with the rapid development of the mobile technologies. Differentiating from other mobile apps has become an important issue for enterprises to increase the mobile applications' value. Therefore, finding an effective way to maximize the performance of mobile apps creates an urgent demand for contemporary mobile app practitioners. Using advanced techniques of mobile applications is considered an effective approach to making mobile apps stand out in a group of app selections.

This book focuses on introducing advanced techniques of mobile apps and attempts to instruct learners in skills of using those advanced approaches in practical mobile apps developments. The approaches involved in this book address the recent main achievements of mobile technologies and wireless networks. Learners can gain knowledge on a broad scope of mobile apps within the Android framework. The instructional aim is to successfully disseminate novel mobile apps development methods and enable knowledge discoveries in the field. Students will obtain updated mobile techniques and app development skills matching the graduate level studies after understanding the contents of this book. The instructions will cover a few fields, including advanced algorithms, embedded systems, novel mobile app architecture, and mobile cloud-computing paradigms.

There are mainly two concentrations in this book, namely mobile apps development and algorithms. These two concentrations are covered by three sections, which represent three major dimensions in the current mobile app development domain. They are:

1. **Mobile app design and development skills.** This includes Chapters 2 to 4. In Chapter 2, we offer a quick start on Android from introducing Java to running an Android application on a real phone. Chapter 3 provides an overview of key concepts and design in Android mobile applications. Finally, Chapter 4 introduces skills of 2D graphics and UI design as well as multimedia in Android mobile apps.

2. **Advanced mobile app optimizations.** Chapters 5 to 8 focus on this aspect. We provides an overview of mobile embedded system and its architecture in Chapter 5. Chapter 6 introduces techniques of data storage in Android. Moreover, we discuss the knowledge of mobile optimizations by dynamic programming in Chapter 7. Finally, a presentation of mobile optimizations by loop scheduling is given in Chapter 8.

3. **Mobile app techniques in emerging technologies.** This is discussed in Chapter 9 and Chapter 10. In Chapter 9, we discuss the techniques of mobile cloud computing in mobile applications deployment. In addition, we offer the other advanced techniques used in big data in Chapter 10, which focuses on mobile big data storage.

The overall educational objective is to enable readers to cognize the approaches of developing Android mobile apps using advanced techniques for achieving enhanced performances. The emerging technologies impacting on mobile apps are also considered. The instructional concentration targets facilitating students awareness of the knowledge by combining knowledge representations with practical exercises. This book's content has been evaluated by practical instructions in higher education, such as Columbia University (New York) and Pace University (New York).

Acknowledgments

We are enormously grateful to numerous individuals for their assistance in creating this book. First, we gratefully acknowledge those who have provided insights or feedback to this creation and the immeasurable help and support from the editors and anonymous reviewers. We also sincerely appreciate the support given by the Department of Computer Science at Pace University.

Dr. Qiu thanks his wife, Diqiu Cao, son; David Qiu, father Shiqing Qiu; mother Longzhi Yuan; brother Meisheng Qiu; sister Meitang Qiu; and many other relatives for their continuous love, support, trust, and encouragement throughout his life. Without them, none of this would have happened.

Dr. Dai expresses his sincere thanks to his wife, Ana Wu, and parents, Guobin Dai and Bing Wen, for their love and support.

Dr. Gai dedicates this work to his parents, Jinchun Gai and Tianmei Li, who have raised him and scarified so much for him. Dr. Gai could never have done this without his parents' love, support and constant encouragement. Dr. Gai also expresses his special gratitude to his Ph.D. Supervisor, Dr. Meikang Qiu, for his thoughtful supervision. Sincere appreciation to all Keke's family members for their continuous love.

Acknowledgments

Author Biographies

Meikang Qiu earned BE and ME degrees from Shanghai Jiao Tong University, China in 1992 and 1998, respectively. He earned MS and PhD degrees in computer science from University of Texas at Dallas in 2003 and 2007, respectively. Currently, he is an associate professor of computer science at Pace University and adjunct professor at Columbia University. He is serving as a Chair of IEEE STC (Special Technical Community) in Smart Computing at IEEE Computer Society. He had worked at Chinese Helicopter R&D Institute, IBM, etc., for nine years. Currently, he is an IEEE senior member and ACM senior member. His research interests include cloud computing, big data storage and security, embedded systems, cyber security, hybrid memory, heterogeneous systems, mobile and sensor networks, operating systems, optimization, intelligent systems, cyber-physical systems, etc.

Many novel results have been produced, and most of them have already been reported to the research community through high-quality journal and conference papers. He has published 4 books, 320 peer-reviewed journal and conference papers (including 150 journal articles, 170 conference papers, 40+ IEEE/ACM Transactions papers), and 3 patents. He has won ACM Transactions on Design Automation of Electrical Systems (TODAES) 2011 Best Paper Award. His paper about cloud computing has been published in JPDC (Journal of Parallel and Distributed Computing, Elsevier) and ranked No. 1 in Top Hottest 25 Papers of JPDC 2012. He has won another 6 Conference Best Paper Award (IEEE/ACM ICESS '12, IEEE GreenCom '10, IEEE EUC '10,

IEEE CSE '09, IEEE CSCloud '15, IEEE BigDataSecurity '15) in recent years. Currently he is an associate editor of *IEEE Transactions on Computers* and *IEEE Transactions on Cloud Computing*. He is the General Chair of IEEE HPCC/ICESS/CSS 2015, IEEE CSCloud 2015 (Cyber Security and Cloud Computing), and NSS'15 (Network and System Security), Steering Committee Chair of IEEE BigData Security 2015, and Program Chair of IEEE SOSE/MobileCloud/BigData 2015. He won Navy Summer Faculty Award in 2012 and Air Force Summer Faculty Award in 2009. His research is supported by the US government, such as *National Science Foundation* (NSF), the Air Force, the Navy, and companies such as Nokia, TCL, and Cavium.

Wenyun Dai earned BE and ME degrees from Xiamen University and Shanghai Jiao Tong University, China, in 2010 and 2014, respectively. He is pursuing a PhD at Seidenberg School of Computer Science and Information Systems (CSIS), Pace University, New York. His research interests include high performance computing, mobile data privacy, resource management optimization, cloud computing, and mobile networking. He has served as financial chairs in several IEEE conferences, such as HPCC/ICESS/CSS'15.

Keke Gai holds degrees from Nanjing University of Science and Technology (BEng), The University of British Columbia (MET) and Lawrence Technological University (MBA and MS). He is currently pursuing his PhD at Department of Computer Science at Pace University, New York. Keke Gai has published more than 60 peer-reviewed journals or conference papers, 20+ journal papers (including ACM/IEEE Transactions), and 40+ conference papers. He has been granted three IEEE Best Paper Awards by IEEE conferences (IEEE SSC '16, IEEE CSCloud '15, IEEE BigDataSecurity '15) in recent years. His paper about cloud computing has been ranked as the "Most Downloaded Articles" of *Journal of Network and Computer Applications* (JNCA). He is involved in a number of professional/academic associations, including ACM and IEEE. Currently, he is serving as a Secretary/Treasurer of IEEE STC (Special Technical Community) in Smart Computing at IEEE Computer Society. He has worked for a few *Fortune 500* enterprises, including SINOPEC and GE Capital. His research interests include cloud computing, cyber security, combinatorial optimization, business process modeling, enterprise architecture, and Internet computing. He also served as Finance Chair/Operation Chair/Publicity Chair/Web Chair in an amount of academic events, such as IEEE SmartCloud '16, SmartCom '16, IEEE CSCloud '15 '16, IEEE BigDataSecurity '15 '16, and IEEE HPCC/ICESS/CSS '15.

I

Mobile App Design and Development Skills

CHAPTER 1

Overview of Mobile App and Mobile Interface

CONTENTS

Mobile SYSTEM AND MOBILE APP are two fundamental aspects in Android mobile app development. In this chapter, we introduce the overview of mobile system and mobile app, which include:

1. Introduction of the mobile system.

2. Mobile interface and applications in mobile system.

3. Optimization in mobile system.

4. Mobile embedded system.

5. Mobile cloud computing.

6. Big data in mobile system.

7. Data security and privacy protection in mobile system.

8. Mobile app.

9. Introduction of android.

1.1 MOBILE SYSTEM

Mobile system includes mobile device, mobile operating system, wireless network, mobile app, and app platform.

The mobile device consists of not only smartphones but also other handheld computers, such as a tablet and Personal Digital Assistant (PDA). A mobile device has a mobile operating system and can run various types of apps. The most important parts of a mobile device are Central Processing Unit (CPU), memory, and storage, which are similar to a desktop but perform weaker than an on-premise device. Most mobile devices can also be equipped with Wi-Fi, Bluetooth, and Global Positioning System (GPS) capabilities, and they can connect to the Internet, other Bluetooth-capable device and the satellite navigation system. Meanwhile, a mobile device can be equipped with some human - computer interaction capabilities, such as camera, microphone, audio systems, and some sensors.

All kinds of mobile devices run on various mobile Operating Systems (OS), also referred to mobile OSs, such as iOS from Apple Inc., Android from Google Inc., Windows Phone from Microsoft, Blackberry from BlackBerry, Firefox OS from Mozilla, and Sailfish OS from Jolla. Mobile devices actually run two mobile operating systems. Besides the mobile operating systems that end users can see, mobile devices also run a small operating system that manages everything related to the radio. Because of the high time dependence, the system is a low-level proprietary real-time operating system. However, this low-level system is security vulnerable if some malicious base station gains high levels of control over the mobile device [1, 2, 3]. We will discuss the security problem in mobile device later.

Mobile devices can connect to the Internet by wireless networks [4, 5]. There are two popular wireless networks for mobile devices: cellular network and Wi-Fi. The cellular network is peculiar to portable transceivers. A cellular network is served by at least one fixed-location transceiver, called cell site or base station, as shown in Fig. 1.1. Each mobile device uses a different set of frequencies from neighboring ones, which means a mobile device must connect to the base station before it accesses to the Internet [6]. Similarly, when a mobile device using a cellular network wants to connect another mobile device, it must connect to some base stations before it communicates with the target device via the base stations.

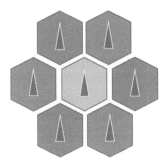

Figure 1.1 Structure of a cellular network.

Figure 1.2 Logo of Wi-Fi.

Wi-Fi is a local area wireless technology, which allows mobile devices to participate in computer networks using 2.4 GHz [1] and 5 GHz radio bands. Fig. 1.2 represents two common logos of Wi-Fi. Mobile devices can connect to the Internet via a wireless networking access point. The valid range of an access point is limited, and the signal intensity descends as the distance increases. Wi-Fi allows cheaper deployment of Local Area Networks (LAN), especially for spaces where cables cannot be run. Wi-Fi Protected Access encryption (WPA2) is considered a secure approach by providing a strong passphrase. A Wi-Fi signal occupies five channels in the 2.4 GHz band. Any two channel numbers differ by five or more. Many newer consumer devices support the latest 802.11ac [2] standard, which uses the 5 GHz and is capable of multistation WLAN throughput of at least 1 gigabit per second.

1. Hz is the unit of frequency in the International System of Units and is defined as one cycle per second. One gigahertz (GHz) represents 10^9 Hz.

2. IEEE 802.11ac was approved in January 2014 by IEEE Standards Association.

A mobile app is a program designed to run on smartphones, tablet computers, and other mobile devices. Mobile apps emerged in 2008 and are operated by the owner of the mobile operating systems. Currently, the most popular digital distribution platforms for mobile apps are App Store, Google Play, Windows Phone Store, and BlackBerry App World, as shown in Fig. 1.3. These platforms are developed by Apple Inc., Google, Microsoft, and BlackBerry Ltd., respectively, and provide different apps, which only can be used on their own operating systems.

Figure 1.3 Four dominate platforms for mobile apps.

1.2 MOBILE INTERFACE AND APPLICATIONS

Mobile devices, to some extent, are much more powerful than desktops. They are highly personal, always on, always with users, usually connected, and directly addressable. Furthermore, they are crawling with powerful sensors with various functions that detect location, acceleration, orientation, movement, proximity, and surrounding conditions. The portability of mobile devices combined with powerful sensors makes mobile interface extremely valuable for using mobile devices.

The User Interface (UI) is the look and feel of the on-screen system, including how it works, its color scheme, and how it responds to users' operation. The interactions include not only users' active operations, but also the passive ones. Users' passive operations include users' locations, movements, and other information that does not need users' active operations. We will take telehealth as an example of mobile interface. Telehealth is the delivery of health-related services and information via telecommunications technologies [7].

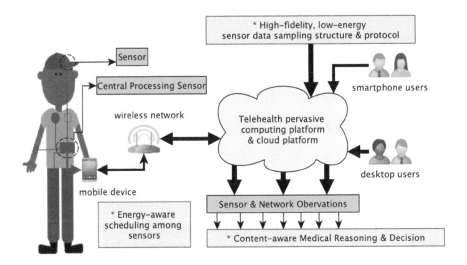

Figure 1.4 Structure of the telehealth systems.

We can separate telehealth system into several modes: store-and-forward, real-time, remote patient monitoring, and electronic consultation, as shown in Fig. 1.4. Each mode finish their job respectively and achieve the whole process of collecting data from users, transmitting this data to medical or clinical organizations, medical reasoning and decision, and sending back to users. In the first step, observations of daily living and clinical data are captured and stored on the mobile device. All the sensors that collect and record data are heterogeneous medical devices with different cost and time features. Then the mobile device transmits this information to the Telehealth pervasive computing platform and cloud platform by wireless network [8, 9].

Consequently, main challenges include finding out the approach of collecting data from users by using sensors and scheduling sensors for achieving energy-aware purposes [10, 11]. The process of transmitting data is a part of real-time system. Different to normal real-time systems, the data transmitting in telehealth is under a wireless condition. Similar to the first step, there are various network paths with different cost and time requirements, which results in a great challenge to security and data integrity [12].

Furthermore, context-aware medical reasoning and decision is another important issue in telehealth system. Context can refer to real world characteristics, such as temperature, time or location. Combining with users' personal information, the medical reasoning and decision focus on data analytic, mining, and profiling issues. In conclusion, all the challenges mentioned above can be summarized as a general problem: how to minimize the total cost of heterogeneous telehealth while finishing the whole diagnosis within certain time constraints [13, 14].

1.2.1 Optimizations in Mobile Systems

All current mobile devices are battery-powered devices. The high usage of mobile devices makes them hard to keep on charging like desktops, so the improvement of battery life on mobile devices is gaining increasing attention. Besides some energy-saving operations by users, there are some researches focusing on the optimization in mobile system [15, 16]. The optimization problem, to some extent, is a tradeoff among multiple constraints [17, 18]. Before talking about the optimization, let us discuss some constraints in mobile systems.

The first and the most important constraint is the energy. The second one is the performance. The third one is the networking speed to the Internet. The fourth one is the resources of the mobile device [19]. These constraints are interrelated and mutually restrict to each other. Suppose in an extreme situation, someone keeps his/her mobile device off. In this situation, the battery life can last an almost unlimited time without considering the self-discharge of the battery. However, the mobile device in that situation is useless, and no one buys a mobile device just for decoration. It is obvious that the more functions users use, the more energy devices consume. Similarly, the performance is related to the networking speed while constrained by the energy and resource. To solve this problem, many researchers proposed various optimization algorithms and frameworks [20, 21, 22].

1.2.2 Mobile Embedded System

An embedded system is a computer system with a dedicated function, which is embedded as a part of a complete devices including hardware and mechanical parts. Embedded systems are driving an information revolution with their pervasion. These tiny systems can be found everywhere, ranging from commercial electronics, such as cell phones, cameras, portable health monitoring systems, automobile controllers, robots, and smart security devices, to critical infrastructure, such as telecommunication networks, electrical power grids, financial institutions, and nuclear plants [23, 24]. The increasingly complicated embedded systems require extensive design automation and optimization tools. Architectural-level synthesis with code generation is an essential stage toward generating an embedded system satisfying stringent requirements, such as time, area, reliability, and power consumption, while keeping the product cost low and development cycle short.

A mobile device is a typical embedded system, which includes mobile processors, storage, memory, graphics, sensors, camera, battery, and other chips for various functions. The mobile device is a high-level synthesis for real-time embedded systems using heterogeneous functional units (FUs) [20, 22]. A functional unit is a part of an embedded system, and it performs the operations and calculations for tasks. As a result, it is critical to select the best FU type for various tasks.

1.3 MOBILE CLOUD

Limited resources is another critical characteristic of mobile devices [25, 26]. With the development of cloud computing, mobile cloud computing has been introduced to the public [27]. Mobile cloud computing, as shown in Fig. 1.5, is the combination of cloud computing, mobile computing, and wireless networks to bring rich computational resources to the mobile system. In general, a mobile device with limited resources can utilize computational resources of various cloud resources to enhance the computational ability of itself. There are several challenges in mobile cloud computing, such as moving computational processes from mobile devices to the cloud, networking latency [28], context processing, energy management [29, 30], security [31], and privacy [32].

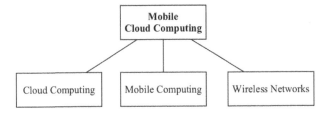

Figure 1.5 Main structure of mobile cloud computing.

Currently, some research and development addresses execution code offloading, seamless connectivity and networking latency; however, efforts still lack in other domains.

Architecture. The architecture for a heterogeneous mobile cloud computing environment is crucial for unleashing the power of mobile computing toward unrestricted ubiquitous computing.

Energy-aware transmission. Offloading executive codes into the cloud can greatly reduce the burden and the time of local mobile devices, but increase the transmission between mobile devices and the cloud. The transmission protocol should be carefully designed for saving energy.

Context-aware computing. Context-aware and socially aware computing are inseparable traits of mobile devices. How to achieve the vision of mobile computing among heterogeneous converged networks among mobile devices is an essential need [33].

Live Virtual Machine (VM) migration. A virtual machine is an emulation of a particular computer system. Executive resource offloading involves encapsulation of a mobile app in a VM instance, and migrating in the cloud is a challenging task.

Security and privacy. Due to lack of confidence in the cloud, many users are concerned with the security and privacy of their information. It is extremely important to improve the security and the privacy of mobile cloud computing.

1.3.1 Big Data Application in Mobile Systems

Big data is an all-encompassing term for any collection of data sets so large or complex that it becomes difficult to process them using traditional data processing applications. Data sets grow in size in part because they are increasingly being gathered by mobile devices. There are 4.6 billion mobile phone subscriptions worldwide and between 1 billion and 2 billion people accessing the Internet [34].

With billions of mobile devices in the world today, mobile computing is becoming the universal computational platform of the world [35]. These mobile devices generate huge amounts of data every day. The rise of big data demands that we be able to access data resources anytime and anywhere about every daily thing. Furthermore, these kinds of data are invaluable and profitable if used well.

However, a few challenges must be addressed to make big data analytics possible. More specifically, instead of being restricted to single computers, ubiquitous applications must be able to execute on an ecosystem of networked devices, each of which may join or leave the shared ubiquitous space at any time. Moreover, there exist analytics tasks that are too computationally expensive to be performed on a mobile device ecosystem. Also, how can we harness the specific capabilities of each device, including varying display size, input modality, and computational resources?

1.3.2   Data Security and Privacy Protection in Mobile Systems

Due to the universality and the particularity of mobile systems to desktop system, the security in mobile systems is much more complicated and important than that in desktop systems [36, 37]. The security in mobile systems can be separated into a few parts [38].

The first threat is the malware (virus). Mobile malware is a malicious software that targets mobile devices and results in the collapse of the system and loss or leakage of information [39]. According to the June 2014 McAfee Labs Threat Report, new mobile malware has increased for five straight quarters, with a total mobile malware growth of 167 percent in the recent past years. Security threats are also growing with 200 new threats every minute [40, 41, 42]. In addition to 2.4 million new samples of mobile malware, 2013 also brought 1 million new unique samples of ransomware, 5.7 million new malicious signed binaries, and 2.2 million new Master Boot Record (MBR)-attack-related samples. The most frequent two incentives are exfiltrating user information and premium calls or SMS. Furthermore, there are some other incentives, such as sending advertisement spam, novelty and amusement, and exfiltrating user credentials [43, 44].

Another research issue is the security frameworks or approaches for detecting mobile malware [45]. There are several approaches for monitoring mobile devices and detecting mobile malware. The signature-based solution is an approach used for detecting attacks, but it fails miserably in detecting the sophisticated cyber-criminal who targets specific organizations with exploits tailored to those victims. From a process perspective, when it comes to validating a threat and subsequent root cause analysis, first-level responders have to send all data that looks like malicious code to the reverse engineers. This process often causes delays, because these malware teams are typically inundated.

Meanwhile, with the development of technology, an efficient representation of malware behaviors using a key observation often reveals the malicious intent even when each action alone may appear harmless [46]. The logical ordering of an application's actions are often over time. Based on this idea, researchers present various approaches to monitor and detect malicious behavior using static analysis on data flow [47, 48, 49, 50].

Next security problem is the data over-collection behaviors in mobile apps. Current mobile phone operating systems only provide coarse-grained permissions that determine whether an app can access private information, while providing few insights into the scope of private information being used. Meanwhile, only a few users are aware of permissions information during the installations. Furthermore, some users choose to stop installing or to uninstall an app when the system warns them and asks for permission, even though they know it may bring some hidden security troubles. For example, we take location data and analyze the current status and discuss the risks caused by over collecting it.

Location data are the most frequently used data in smartphones. It can be used in apps whose main functions include maps, photo organization, shopping and restaurant recommendations, and weather. From the report of Appthority [51], 50% of the top iOS free apps and 24% of the top iOS paid apps track a user's location. Although users are warned whenever an app intends to capture their locations, they usually choose to allow the permission for the function offered by the app. Apps that over collect location data can be separated into two main types: location service as main function and location service as the auxiliary function. The first type of apps normally ask users for permissions to their location information, while the other app type can collect users' location information without noticing users. The first and the most direct risk is a physical security concern. Users' tracks are easily exposed to those who have users' real-time and accurate location data. Users' habits and customs are easy to be inferred by using simple data mining methods.

Furthermore, solving the data over collection problem is also a research issue in mobile apps. PiOS [47], presented by M. Egele et al., to detect privacy leaks in iOS applications, used static analysis to detect sensitive data flow to achieve the aim of detecting privacy leaks in applications in iOS. Sharing a similar goal with PiOS, TaintDroid [48], is a system wide dynamic taint tracking multiple sources of sensitive data. The main strategy of TaintDroid is real-time analysis by leveraging Android's virtualized execution environment [52]. Another secure model via automated validation uses commodity cloud infrastructure to emulate smartphones to dynamically track information flows and actions. This model automatically detects malicious behaviors and sensitive data misuse via further analysis of dependency graphs based on the tracked information flows and actions.

These approaches or techniques mentioned above only focus on monitoring and detecting apps. The prerequisites are that apps already gain permissions from users. However, these solutions only provide methods of monitoring and detecting behaviors of data over-collections. This approach leaves remedying operations to users, such as disabling the permissions of apps or uninstalling those apps. Users have to manually disable permissions of these apps that over collect users' data or uninstall them. Furthermore, running these approaches or tools adds the consumption of energy, which is particularly valuable for smartphones with limited resources. As a result, the active method of avoiding data over collection behaviors in mobile apps is a crucial challenge that needs to be solved.

1.3.3   Concept of Mobile Apps

Mobile apps were originally developed to offer general productivity and information retrieval, including email, calendar, contacts, and weather information. However, with the rapid increment of public requirement, mobile apps expand into lots of other categories, such as games, music, finance, and news.

A lot of people distinguish apps from applications in a perspective of device forms. They think that applications are used on a desktop or laptop, while apps are used on a phone or tablet. Nevertheless, this simplistic view is too narrow and no longer the consensus, because apps can be used on desktops, and, conversely, applications can run on phones. At Gartner Portals, Content and Collaboration Summit 2013, many experts and developers participated a roundtable discussion titled "Why an App is not an Application" [53, 54]. They proposed that the difference between app and application is not about the delivery mechanism and landed on a consensus that:

App = software designed for a single purpose and performs a single function.

Application = software designed to perform a variety of functions.

From the view of users, they don not care whether it is an app or an application by definition, and they just want to accomplish their tasks easily. Meanwhile, from the view of developers, the question they should answer is not whether they should be building an app or an application, but how they can combine the best of both into something users love.

1.3.4   Brief Introduction of Android and Its Framework

1.3.4.1   A Brief History of Android

Android was founded in Palo Alto, California, in October 2003 by Andy Rubin, Rich Miner, Nick Sears, and Chris White in an effort to develop a smarter mobile device that is more aware of its owner's location and preferences. Then to Google acquired Android Inc. and key employees, including Rubin, Miner, and White, on August 17, 2005. At Google, the team, led by Rubin, developed a mobile device platform powered by the Linux kernel. Google had lined up a series of hardware components and software partners and signaled to carriers that it was open to various degrees of cooperation on their part. On November 5, 2007, the Open Handset Alliance unveiled itself with a goal to develop open standards for mobile devices. This alliance includes technology companies, like Google, device manufacturers such as HTC, wireless carriers such as T-Mobile, and chipset makers such as Qualcomm. Then, on October 22, 2008, the first commercially available smartphone running Android came out with a fantasy name: HTC Dream. Since 2008, Android has seen numerous updates that have incrementally improved the operating system, adding new features and fixing bugs in previous releases. There are some milestones of Android SDK, such as Android SDK 2.0 (Eclair) in 2009, Android SDK 3.0 (Honeycomb) for tablets only in 2011, Android SDK 4.0 (Ice Cream Sandwich) in 2011, Android 4.1 to 4.3 (Jelly Bean) in 2012, Android SDK 4.4 (KitKat) in 2013, and Android SDK 5.0 (Lollipop) in 2014.

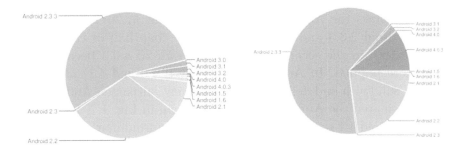

Figure 1.6 Android device distribution in January and July 2012.

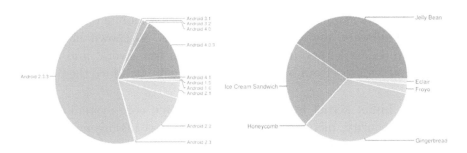

Figure 1.7 Android device distribution in August 2012 and August 2013.

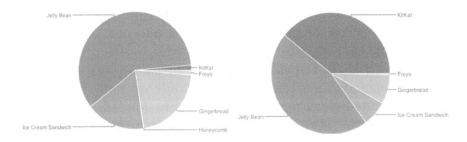

Figure 1.8 Android device distribution in January 2014 and January 2015

1.3.4.2 Android Device Distribution

Fig. 1.6 shows the Android device distributions in 2012. We can see that Android 2.3.3 and 2.2 dominate more than half of the market. Nonetheless, in the second half of 2012, Android 4.0.3 became more and more popular. In August 2013, Android 4.0 and 4.1, named Ice Cream Sandwich and Jelly Bean, respectively, surpassed Android 2.0s and dominated the Android market, as shown in Fig. 1.7. In January 2014, Android 4.1 to 4.3 still dominated the Android market. However, after one year, Android 4.4, named KitKat, rapidly occupied 39.1% of the whole market, as shown in Fig. 1.8.

1.3.4.3 Android SDK

Android SDK is open-source and widely used, which makes it the best choice for teaching and learning mobile development. Android is a software stack for mobile devices, and it includes a mobile operating system, middleware, and some key applications. As shown in Fig. 1.9, there are Linux kernel, libraries, application framework, and applications and widgets, from bottom to top. We will introduce them one by one.

The Linux kernel is used to provide some core system services, such as security, memory management, process management, power management, and hardware drivers. These services cannot be called by Android programs directly and is transparent to users. The next layer above the kernel is the native libraries, which are all written in C or C++. These libraries are compiled for the particular hardware architecture used by the mobile devices. They are responsible for handling structured data storage, graphics, audio, video, and network, which only can be called by higher-level programs. Meanwhile, Android runtime is also on top of the kernel, and it includes the Dalvik virtual machine and the core Java libraries [55].

What is Dalvik? Dalvik is the process virtual machine in Google's Android operating system, which specifically executes applications written for Android. Programs are written in Java and compiled to bytecode for the Java virtual machine, which is then translated to Dalvik bytecode and stored in .dex and .odex files. The compact Dalvik executable format is designed for systems with limited resources.

The application framework layer provides the high-level building blocks used for creating application. It comes preinstalled with An-

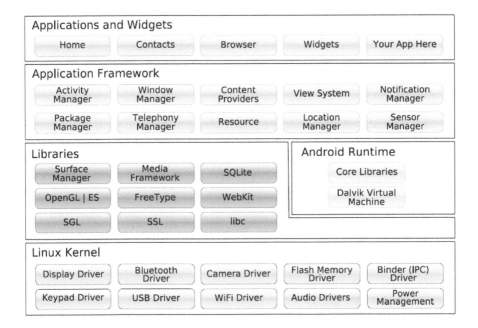

Figure 1.9 Android system architecture.

droid, but can be extended with its own components as needed. We will introduce some basic and important building blocks of Android.

Activity. An activity is a user interface screen. A single activity defines a single screen with a user interface, and it defines simple life cycle methods like onCreat, onResume, and onPause for handling interruptions. Furthermore, applications can define one or more activities to handle different phases of the program.

Intent. An intent is a mechanism for describing a specific action, such as "pick a photo", or "phone home". In Android, everything goes through intents, and developer, have plenty of opportunities to replace or reuse components. Intents can be implicit or explicit. An explicit intent can be to invoke another screen when a button is pressed on the *Activity* in context. An implicit intent is when you create an intent and hand it off to the system to handle it.

Service. A service is a task that runs in the background without the user's direct interaction. In fact, it does the majority of processing for an application. Developers can sub-class the *Service* class to write their own custom service.

Content Provider. A *Content* provider is a set of data wrapped up in a custom Application Programming Interface (API) to read and write it. This is the best way to share global data between applications. The content provider provides a uniform singular interface to the content and data and provides a consistent interface to retrieve/store data via RESTful model supporting create, read, update, and delete (CRUD) operations.

An *Android Emulator*, as shown in Fig. 1.10, called Android Virtual Device (AVD), is essential to testing Android app but is not a substitute for a real device. AVDs have configurable resolutions, RAM, SD cards, skins, and other hardware. If you have installed Android SDKs, the AVD Manager can allow you to create AVDs that target any Android API level.

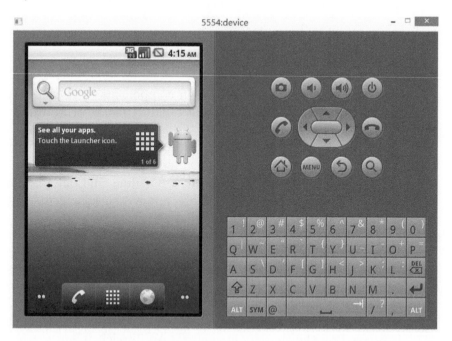

Figure 1.10 Android Emulator.

An Android emulator has the following basic functions:

Host computer's keyboard works as keyboard of device.

Host's mouse acts as finger.

Connecting to the Internet using host's Internet connection.

Buttons: Home, Menu, Back, Search, Volume up and down.

Ctrl-F11 toggle landscape to portrait.

Alt-Enter toggle full-screen mode.

However, emulators have some limitations. They do not support for:

Placing or receiving actual phone calls.

USB and Bluetooth connections.

Camera or video capture as input.

Device-attached headphones.

Determining connected state.

Determining battery charge level and AC charging state.

Determining SD card insert or eject. SD card is a nonvolatile memory card used extensively in portable devices.

Simulating the accelerometer.

Then we will introduce the process of producing an Android app. In Fig. 1.11, an android app is written in Java and generates .java file. Then *javac* compiler .java reads source files and transforms java code into byte code. Then Dalvik takes responsibility for handling these byte codes combining with other byte codes for other .class files, and generates classes.dex. At last, classes.dex, resources, and AndroidManifest.xml cooperate and generate an .apk file, which is a runnable Android app.

Every Android app must have an AndroidManifest.xml file in its root directory. The manifest presents essential information about the application to the Android system, information the system must have

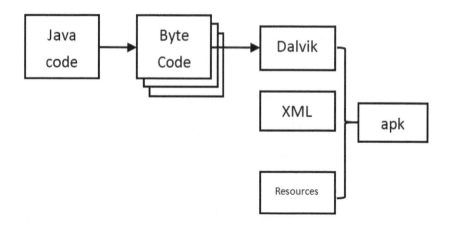

Figure 1.11 Process of producing an Android app.

before it can run any of the application's code. The AndroidMani-fest.xml file names the Java package for the application and describes the components of the application, including the activities, services, broadcast receivers, and content providers that the application is composed of. The file also names the classes that implement each of the components and publishes their capabilities. These declarations let the Android system know what the components are and under what conditions they can be launched.

Furthermore, AndroidManifest.xml file determines, which processes will host application components, and it declares which permissions the application must have in order to access protected parts of the API and interact with other application. The file also declares the permission that others are required to have in order to interact with the application's components and lists the instrumentation classes that provide profiling and other information as the application is running. These declarations are present in the manifest only while the application is published. It declares the minimum level of the Android API that the application requires, and it lists the libraries that the application must be linked to.

In next chapter, we will discuss the mobile embedded system architecture.

1.4 EXERCISES

Basic

1. What components do a mobile systems include?
2. Does the mobile device only mean smartphones?
3. How many mobile operating systems are running on mobile devices? What are they?
4. What is the foundation of the cellular network?
5. How does a mobile device connect to the Internet under the cellular network environment?
6. What is Wi-Fi?
7. How does a mobile device connect to the Internet under the Wi-Fi network environment?
8. What is the relationship between the distance and the signal intensity under the Wi-Fi network environment?
9. Can an Android device run an iOS app?
10. What is the difference between the interface of mobile devices and that of desktops?
11. What is telehealth?
12. What is the greatest challenge in the step of collecting and transmitting data in telehealth systems?
13. What is an optimization problem? (optional question)
14. How many constraints are there in a mobile system? What are they?
15. What is an embedded system?
16. What is a mobile embedded system?
17. What is the biggest benefit of mobile cloud for mobile system?
18. What is big data in mobile system?
19. What is the malware in mobile devices?
20. What is the data over collection behavior in mobile apps?
21. What is Android?
22. What is the Open Handset Alliance?
23. When did Android 2.0 release?
24. What was the name of the first Android device?
25. Which version of Android was the most widely used in January 2014?
26. What are the main functions provided by the Linux Kernel in Android?
27. What is an *Activity* in Android?
28. What is an *Intent*?

29. What is an implicit *Intent*?
30. What is an explicit *Intent*?
31. What is a *Service*?
32. What does a *Content* provider do?
33. What is the process of generating an Android app from Java code to .apk file?

Advanced

34. Why is the energy consumption more important for mobile devices than that of desktops?

35. What is the difference between apps and applications?

36. What is Dalvik? What is the difference between Dalvik and traditional *Java Virtual Machine* (JVM)?

Quick Start on Android

CONTENTS

Before WE JUMP INTO THE ANDROID WORLD, let us have a quick review about Android installations, project creations, and application executions. Introduce the process of installing Android and creating an Android project in this chapter. Main contents include:

Installing Java

Installing integrate development environment

Installing Android SDK

Creating an Android application project

Creating an Android Virtual Device

Running an Android application on the emulator

Running an Android application on a real phone

2.1   INSTALLING JAVA

The Android Software Development Kit (SDK) can work on any operating system, such as Windows, Linux, and Mac OS X. Before starting our installing Android and coding programs, we need to install Java. All the Android development tools require Java, and programs will be using the Java language. From the latest version of the Android Developer website, we suggest that Java 7 or 8 is the best choice.

We recommend getting the Java runtime environment (JRE) 8 from http://java.com/en/download/manual.jsp. For Windows users, there are two kinds of versions offered, which are 32-bit and 64-bit. You can choose the 32-bit download to use with a 32-bit browser, and choose the 64-bit download to use with a 64-bit browser. For Mac OS users, there is only one choice, which needs Mac OS X 10.7.3 version and above. For Linux users, there are four choices, and users can download one of them based on users' operating system.

It is not enough to just have a JRE, and you need the full development kit. We recommend downloading *Java Development Kit* (JDK) 8 from http://www.oracle.com/technetwork/java/javase/downloads/jdk8-downloads-2133151.html. To verify you have the right version, go to your shell window or terminal and type in "java ?version". The result should be something similar to what is shown in Fig. 2.1.

```
C:\>java -version
java version "1.8.0_25"
Java(TM) SE Runtime Environment (build 1.8.0_25-b18)
Java HotSpot(TM) 64-Bit Server VM (build 25.25-b02, mixed mode)
```

Figure 2.1   Verify the version of Java.

2.2   INSTALLING INTEGRATE DEVELOPMENT ENVIRONMENT

A Java development environment is recommended to make Android programming easier. There are many optional *Integrate Development Environments* (IDE), but we only introduce the most widely used one, which is Google's Android Studio.

Android Studio is the official IDE for Android application development. You can download it from http://developer.android.com/sdk/index.html. After downloading and installing Android Studio, you can see a similar screen figure, as shown in 2.2, when you open it.

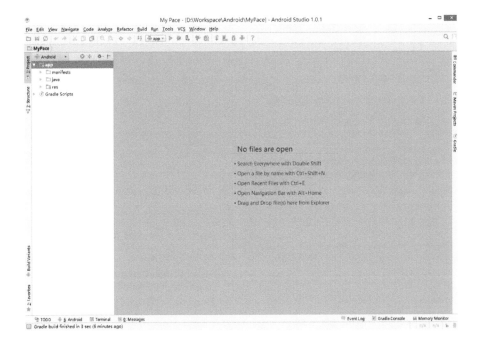

Figure 2.2 Blank interface of Android Studio.

2.3 INSTALLING ANDROID SDK

The Android SDK includes a comprehensive set of development tools. These tools include a debugger, libraries, a handset emulator, documentation, sample code, and tutorials. Using the installed IDE, Android SDK can be downloaded and installed conveniently.

In Android Studio, on the top of the screen, select the Tools menu, then Android, and then SDK Manager (Tools → Android → SDK Manager), as shown in Fig. 2.3. Then we can see the interface of Android SDK Manager, similar to Figure 2.4.

Install Android SDK Tools, Android SDK Platform-tools, at least one Android SDK Build-tools, and at least one Android API, as shown in Fig. 2.5. API is a set of routines, protocols, and tools for building software applications. The Android 5.0.1 (API 21) is the newest version of Android SDK. We suggest installing Documentation for Android SDK, SDK Platform, ARM EABI v7a System Image, and Google APIs. The documentation for Android SDK can help solve program-

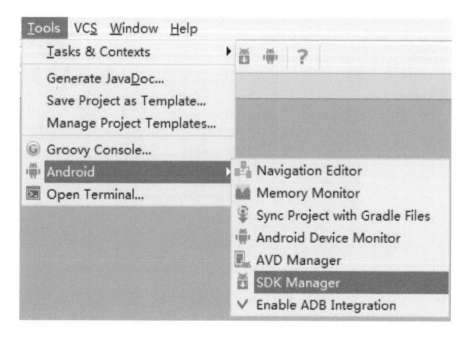

Figure 2.3 Android SDK Manager in Android Studio.

ming problems. The ARM EABI v7a system image is a virtual mobile operating system image running on virtual devices.

2.4 CREATING AN ANDROID APPLICATION

After installing the Android SDK, we can create our first Android Application.

On the top left corner of the Android Studio, select File, and then New Project (File → New Project). You will see the "Create New Project" dialog. In the first step of creating a new Android application, type in the application name, such as "My Application," as shown in Fig. 2.5. You can type in company domain, such as "my.android.example.com". Furthermore, you can choose a directory to store your Android project.

In the second step of creating a new Android application, you can choose which kind of device your application runs on. You can choose more than one device, such as phone and tablet, TV, and Wear. In this Android application, only select "Phone and Tablet", as shown in Fig. 2.6.

Figure 2.4   Details of Android SDK Manager in Android Studio.

In the third step of creating a new Android application, you can add an activity to your Android application, and you have many choices, such as blank activity, blank activity with fragment, fullscreen activity, Google maps activity, login activity, navigation drawer activity, setting activity, and tabbed activity, as shown in Fig. 2.7. In the latest version of Android Studio, fragment was integrated into activity.

In the last step of creating a new Android application, you can change the name of the activity added in the third step, as shown in Fig. 2.8. Then click "finish," the interface of Android Studio will be similar to Fig. 2.9.

2.5   ANDROID VIRTUAL DEVICE

After creating the first Android application, we need to create an *Android Virtual Device* (AVD) to run it. First, on the top of the interface,

Figure 2.5 First Step of creating an Android Application in Android Studio.

select Tools, then Android, and then AVD Manager (Tools → Android → AVD Manager). The AVD Manager is similar to Fig. 2.10.

Click "Create a virtual device"; the interface will be similar to Fig. 2.11. Choose *Phone* in the category list, and Nexus S as the device. Then click "Next."

In the second step of creating an AVD in Android Studio, you can choose the version of Android SDK which you want to use, as shown in Fig. 2.12. Then click "Next."

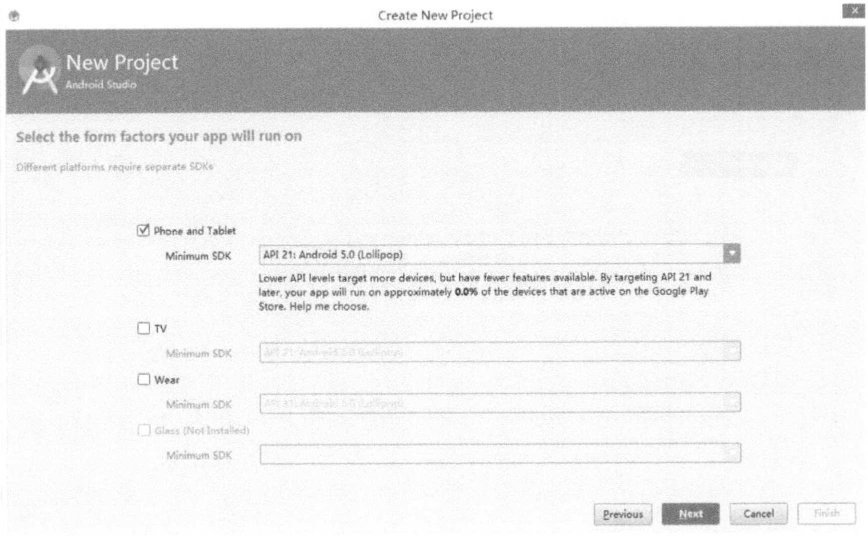

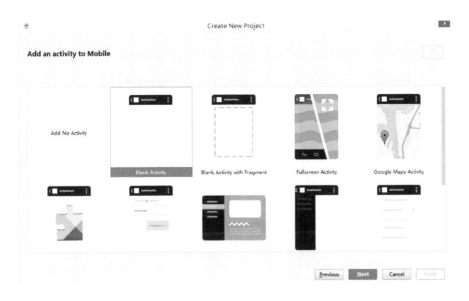

Figure 2.6 First step of creating an Android application in Android Studio.

Figure 2.7 Second step of creating an Android application in Android Studio.

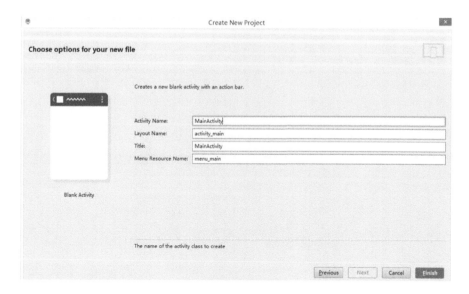

Figure 2.8 Last step of creating an Android application in Android Studio.

Figure 2.9 Interface of Android Studio with a new Android project.

Figure 2.10 Android Virtual Device Manager in Android Studio.

In the last step of creating an AVD in Android Studio, you can change the name of the AVD you want to create, as shown in Fig. 2.13. Then click "Finish".

The AVD is created, as shown in Fig. 2.14. Then click the green arrow on the right side to start this virtual device. After waiting a while, the virtual device is started, as shown in Fig. 2.15.

Then run your Android application on this virtual device. Select the application created before, and then click the green arrow to that was run it. At last, the Android application runs on the virtual device, as shown in Fig. 2.16.

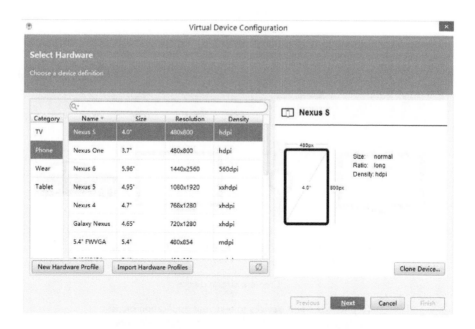

Figure 2.11 First Step of Creating an Android Virtual Device in Android Studio -1.

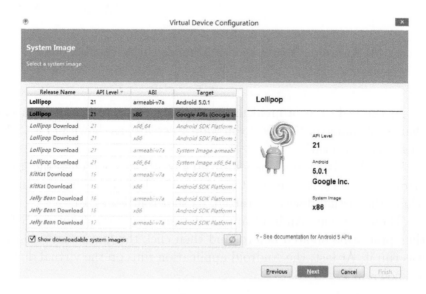

Figure 2.12 Second Step of Creating an Android Virtual Device in Android Studio -2.

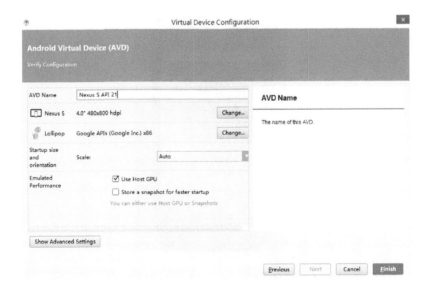

Figure 2.13 Last Step of Creating an Android Virtual Device in Android Studio.

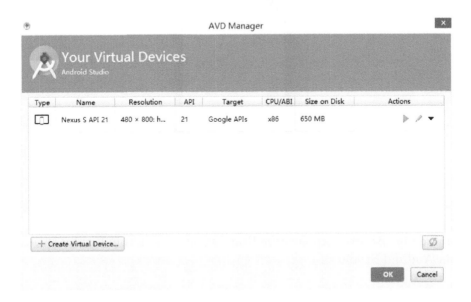

Figure 2.14 New Virtual Device in AVD Manager in Android Studio.

Figure 2.15 Android Virtual Device in Android Studio

Figure 2.16 Android Application Running on the Android Virtual Device in Android Studio

2.6 EXERCISES

1. What operating systems can Android work on?

2. What is the lowest edition of JDK needed for supporting Android?

3. How do you verify the version of Java in your computer?

4. What is Android built on?

5. Why does Android use Linux?

6. Can your programs make Linux calls directly?

7. In which language are the native libraries written?

8. What types of music can Android play?

9. Why does Android use SQLite?

10. What is sitting on top of the kernel of Android?

11. Which type is the file run by Dalvik Virtual Machine?

12. What is the difference between .dex files and standard .class and .jar files?

13. Does Android use the Java Standard Edition or Java Mobile Edition libraries?

14. Which layer is above the native libraries and runtime?

15. What is the main function of Activity Manager?

16. What is the main function of Content Providers?

17. Which layer is the highest one in the Android architecture?

18. What are applications in Android?

19. What is a Widget?

20. Are Widgets operated only in a small rectangle of the Home screen application?

21. Which applications are prepackaged within a new Android phone?

22. Can many applications run and be visible at once in different windows in Android?

23. Which application is the first one when the user turns on his/her phone?

24. Where are programs and screens recorded?

25. Can an application be alive even if its process has been killed?

26. Which states can an Android program be?

27. Which method is called when the activity first starts up?

28. Which method indicates that the activity is about to be displayed to the user?

29. Which method is called when an activity is no longer visible to the user and it will not be needed for a while?

30. Will the onDestroy() function be called if memory is tight?

31. Which method is be called to allow the activity to save per-instance state?

32. What is an activity?

33. What is an intent?

34. What is a service?

35. What is a content provider?

36. What is a resource?

37. What is the main function of class R?

38. How do you access certain critical operations?

CHAPTER 3

Introduction of Key Concepts of Android

CONTENTS

Understanding KEY CONCEPTS OF ANDROID is a basic requirement for designing Android mobile apps. In this chapter, we introduce some basic concepts of Android, including the app components, app resources, and app manifest. Students will able able to answer the following questions after reading this chapter.

1. What is an activity in Android?

2. Can we directly save resource files inside the res/directory?

3. What is an *APP MAINFEST?*

3.1 APP COMPONENTS

App components are the essential building blocks of an Android app. Each component is a different point through which the system can enter your app. Not all components are actual entry points for the user, and some depend on each other, but each one exists as its own entity and plays a specific role. Each one is a unique building block that helps define your app's overall behavior.

The following subsections represent four types of app components, which include activities, services, content providers, and intents.

3.1.1 Activities

An activity represents a single screen with a user interface. For example, an email app might have one activity that shows a list of new emails, another activity to compose an email, and another activity for reading emails. Although the activities work together to form a cohesive user experience in the email app, each one is independent of the others. As such, a different app can start any one of these activities (if the email app allows it). For example, a camera app can start the activity in the email app that composes new mail, in order for the user to share a picture. You can find more information about activities at https://developer.android.com/guide/components/activities.html .

3.1.2 Services

A service is a component that runs in the background to perform long-running operations or to perform work for remote processes. A service does not provide a user interface. For example, a service might play music in the background while the user is in a different app, or it might fetch data over the network without blocking user interaction with an activity. Another component, such as an activity, can start the service and let it run or bind to it in order to interact with it. You can find more information about content providers at https://developer.android.com/reference/android/app/Service.html.

3.1.3 Content Providers

A content provider manages a shared set of app data. You can store the data in the file system, a SQLite database, on the web, or any other persistent storage location your app can access. Through the content provider, other apps can query or even modify the data (if the content provider allows it). For example, the Android system provides a content provider that manages the user's contact information. As such, any app with the proper permissions can query part of the content provider (such as ContactsContract.Data) to read and write information about a particular person.

Content providers are also useful for reading and writing data that is private to your app and not shared. For example, the Note Pad sample app uses a content provider to save notes. You can find more information about content provider at: https://developer.android.com/reference/android/content/ContentProvider.html

3.1.4 Intents

An intent is a mechanism for describing a specific action, such as "pick a photo," "phone home," or "open the pod bay doors." In Android, just about everything goes through intents, so you have plenty of opportunities to replace or reuse components. For example, there is an intent for "send an email." If your application needs to send mail, you can invoke that intent. Or, if you are writing a new email application, you can register an activity to handle that intent and replace the standard mail program. The next time somebody tries to send an email, they'll get the option to use your program instead of the standard one. You can find more information about intents at https://developer.android.com/guide/components/intents-filters.html .

A unique aspect of the Android system design is that any app can start another app's component. For example, if you want the user to capture a photo with the device camera, there's probably another app that does that and your app can use it, instead of developing an activity to capture a photo yourself. You don't need to incorporate or even link to the code from the camera app. Instead, you can simply start the activity in the camera app that captures a photo. When complete, the photo is even returned to your app so you can use it. To the user, it seems as if the camera is actually a part of your app.

When the system starts a component, it starts the process for that app (if it's not already running) and instantiates the classes needed for the component. For example, if your app starts the activity in the camera app that captures a photo, that activity runs in the process that belongs to the camera app, not in your app's process. Therefore, unlike apps on most other systems, Android apps don't have a single entry point (there's no main() function, for example).

Since the system runs each app in a separate process with file permissions that restrict access to other apps, your app cannot directly activate a component from another app. The Android system, however, can. So, to activate a component in another app, you must deliver a message to the system that specifies your intent to start a particular component. The system then activates the component for you.

Intents can be used to activate activities and services, but content providers are activated when targeted by a request from a *ContentResolver*. There are separate methods for activating each type of component:

1. You can start an activity (or give it something new to do) by passing an *Intent to startActivity()* or *startActivityForResult()* (when you want the activity to return a result).

2. You can start a service (or give new instructions to an ongoing service) by passing an *Intent to startService()*. Or you can bind to the service by passing an *Intent to bindService()*.

3. You can perform a query to a content provider by calling *query()* on a *ContentResolver*.

Fig. 3.1 is the default AndroidManifest.xml generated by the Integrated Development Environment (IDE) after we create a blank Android application. The *MainActivity* is the only activity in this project, and it is a subclass of Activity, as "class MainActivity extends Activity" shown. In *MainActivity*, we need to implement callback methods that the system calls when the activity transitions between various states of its life cycle.

The *onCreate()* method is indispensable, and it will be called when the *MainActivity* is created. Within the implementation of the *onCreate()* method, we should initialize the essential components of this activity. We must call *setContentView()* to define the layout for this activity's user interface. Although these processes are implemented by IDE, it is necessary for us to have this knowledge.

```
c  MainActivity.java  ×    content_main.xml  ×

  import ...

  public class MainActivity extends AppCompatActivity {

      @Override
      protected void onCreate(Bundle savedInstanceState) {
          super.onCreate(savedInstanceState);
          setContentView(R.layout.activity_main);
          Toolbar toolbar = (Toolbar) findViewById(R.id.toolbar);
          setSupportActionBar(toolbar);

          FloatingActionButton fab = (FloatingActionButton) findViewById(R.id.fab);
          fab.setOnClickListener((view) -> {
                  Snackbar.make(view, "Replace with your own action", Snackbar.LENGTH_LONG)
                          .setAction("Action", null).show();
          });
      }

      @Override
      public boolean onCreateOptionsMenu(Menu menu) {
          // Inflate the menu; this adds items to the action bar if it is present.
          getMenuInflater().inflate(R.menu.menu_main, menu);
          return true;
      }
      @Override
      public boolean onOptionsItemSelected(MenuItem item) {
          // Handle action bar item clicks here. The action bar will
          // automatically handle clicks on the Home/Up button, so long
          // as you specify a parent activity in AndroidManifest.xml.
          int id = item.getItemId();

          //noinspection SimplifiableIfStatement
          if (id == R.id.action_settings) {
              return true;
          }

          return super.onOptionsItemSelected(item);
      }
  }
```

Figure 3.1 Default MainActivity.java.

3.2 APP RESOURCES

You should always externalize resources, such as images and strings, from your application code, so that you can maintain them independently. You should place each type of resource in a specific subdirectory of your project's *res/* directory, as shown in Fig. 3.2.

drawable/ file contains bitmap files, such as *png*, *jpg* and *gif*.

layout/ contains XML files that define a user interface layout.

menu/ contains XML files that define application menus.

vaules/ contains XML files that contain simple values, such as strings, integers, and colors.

Besides the ones shown in Fig. 3.1, we can add some other resource files into *res/* directory, such as *animator/*, *raw/*, and *xml/* files.

The animator file contains Android property animations. The property animation system is a robust framework that allows you to ani-

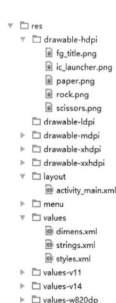

Figure 3.2 File hierarchy for a simple project.

mate almost anything. You can define an animation to change any object property over time, regardless of whether it draws to the screen or not. You can find more information about property animation at http://developer.android.com/guide/topics/graphics/prop-animation.html.

The raw file stores any files in their raw form. You must call *Resource.openRawResource()* to open these resources with a raw *Input-Stream*.

The XML file contains arbitrary XML files that can be read at runtime by calling *Resource.getXML()*. Various XML configuration files must be saved here, such as a searchable configuration.

HINT: Never save resource files directly inside the res/ directory, because it will cause a compiler error.

3.3 APP MAINFEST

The manifest file is indispensable in every Android application. The manifest file presents essential information about your app to the Android system, information the system must have before it can run any of the app's code. Among other things, the manifest does the following:

1. It names the Java package for the application. The package name serves as a unique identifier for the application.

2. It describes the components of the application, the activities, services, broadcast receivers, and content providers that the application is composed of. It names the classes that implement each of the components and publishes their capabilities (for example, which Intent messages they can handle). These declarations let the Android system know what the components are and under what conditions they can be launched.

3. It determines which processes will host application components.

4. It declares which permissions the application must have in order to access protected parts of the Application Programming Interface (API) and interact with other applications.

5. It also declares the permissions that others are required to have in order to interact with the application's components.

6. It lists the Instrumentation classes that provide profiling and other information as the application is running. These declarations are present in the manifest only while the application is being developed and tested; they're removed before the application is published.

7. It declares the minimum level of the Android API that the application requires.

8. It lists the libraries that the application must be linked against.

3.3.1 Elements

Only the <manifest> and <application> elements are required, they each must be present and can occur only once. Most of the others can, occur many times or not at all, although at least some of them must be present for the manifest to accomplish anything meaningful.

If an element contains anything at all, it contains other elements.

All values are set through attributes, not as character data within an element.

Elements at the same level are generally not ordered. For example, <activity>, <provider>, and <service> elements can be intermixed in any sequence. (An <activity-alias> element is the exception to this rule: It must follow the <activity> it is an alias for.)

3.3.2 Attributes

In a formal sense, all attributes are optional. However, there are some that must be specified for an element to accomplish its purpose. Use the documentation as a guide. For truly optional attributes, it mentions a default value or states what happens in the absence of a specification.

Except for some attributes of the root <manifest> element, all attribute names begin with an android: prefix, for example, android:alwaysRetainTaskState. Because the prefix is universal, the documentation generally omits it when referring to attributes by name.

3.3.3 Declaring Class Names

Many elements correspond to Java objects, including elements for the application itself (the <application> element) and its principal components, activities (<activity>), services (<service>), broadcast receivers (<receiver>), and content providers (<provider>).

If you define a subclass, as you almost always would for the component classes (Activity, Service, BroadcastReceiver, and Content-Provider), the subclass is declared through a name attribute. The name must include the full package designation. However, as a shorthand, if the first character of the string is a period, the string is appended to the application's package name (as specified by the <manifest> element's package attribute).

When starting a component, Android creates an instance of the named subclass. If a subclass isn't specified, it creates an instance of the base class.

3.3.4 Multiple Values

If more than one value can be specified, the element is almost always repeated, rather than listing multiple values within a single element.

3.3.5 Resource Values

Some attributes have values that can be displayed to users, for example, a label and an icon for an activity. The values of these attributes should be localized and therefore set from a resource or theme.

The package name can be omitted if the resource is in the same package as the application, type is a type of resource, such as "string" or "drawable," and name is the name that identifies the specific resource.

3.3.6 Sting Values

Where an attribute value is a string, double backslashes ('\\') must be used to escape characters, for example, '\\n' for a newline or '\\uxxxx' for a Unicode character.

```
MainActivity.java ×   AndroidManifest.xml ×
<?xml version="1.0" encoding="utf-8"?>
<manifest xmlns:android="http://schemas.android.com/apk/res/android"
    package="com.example.csis.pace.edu.mypace" >

    <application
        android:allowBackup="true"
        android:icon="@drawable/ic_launcher"
        android:label="My Pace "
        android:theme="@style/AppTheme" >
        <activity
            android:name=".MainActivity"
            android:label="My Pace " >
            <intent-filter>
                <action android:name="android.intent.action.MAIN" />

                <category android:name="android.intent.category.LAUNCHER" />
            </intent-filter>
        </activity>
    </application>

</manifest>
```

Figure 3.3 Default AndroidManifest.xml

Fig. 3.3 is the default AndroidManifest.xml file generated by IDE after a blank Android application. In the third creating line, "com.example.csis.pace.edu.mypace," is the package name of the project, and it exactly as the same as the first line of *MainActivity.java*.

Many elements inside the <application> and </application> correspond to Java objects, including activities (<activity>), services

(<service>), broadcast receivers (<receiver>), and content providers (<provider>). In our project, we only create an activity, thus, there is only one <activity> in *AnroidManifest.xml* file. In this <activity>, the android:name=".MainActivity" shows the name of the activity.

The <intent-filter> specifies the type of intents that an activity, service, or broadcast receiver can respond to. An intent filter declares the capabilities of its parent component, what an activity or service can do and what types of broadcasts a receiver can handle. It opens the component to receiving intents of the advertised type, while filtering out those that are not meaningful for the component.

When adding an action to an intent filter. An <intent-filter> element must contain one or more <action> elements. If it doesn't contain any, no Intent objects will get through the filter. Some standard actions are defined in the Intent class as `ACTION_string` constants. To assign one of these actions to this attribute, prepend "android.intent.action." to the string that follows `ACTION_`. In our project, use "android.intent.action.MAIN" for `ACTION_MAIN`.

The <category> is used to add a category name to an intent filter. Standard categories are defined in the Intent class as `CATEGORY_name` constants. The name assigned here can be derived from those constants by prefixing "android.intent.category." to the name that follows `CATEGORY_`. In our project, the string value is "android.intent.category.LAUNCHER" for `CATEGORY_LAUNCHER`.

3.4 EXERCISES

3.4.1 Basic Exercises

1. What does procedural mean?

2. What is declarative design?

3. What does Android do to straddle the gap between the procedural and declarative?

4. What does the onCreate() method do?

5. What does setContentView() method do?

6. What is R.layout.main?

7. What does main.xml do?

8. How does the R class work?

9. How does Android handle XML?

10. What is layout?

11. What does FrameLayout do?

12. What does LinearLayout do?

13. What does RelativeLayout do?

14. What does TableLayout do?

15. How do you switch the emulator to landscape mode?

16. What is the first thing to start an activity in Android?

17. What does public intents mean?

18. What does private intents mean?

19. What is a theme?

20. What kinds of menus does Android support?

21. What does the Log class do?

3.4.2 Advanced Exercises

1. After reading the textbook about the user interface, please talk about your understanding of theuser interface.

2. Give some examples to explain what is use-friendlyin your opinion.

CHAPTER 4

2-D Graphics and Multimedia in Android

CONTENTS

2-D GRAPHICS AND UI DESIGN are two important aspects in User Interface (UI) design. In this chapter, we will introduce 2-D graphics and some advanced UI design techniques. Main techniques of 2-D graphics include `Color`, `Paint`, `Path`, `Canvas`, `Drawable`, and `Button Selector`. Students will also learn how to create multiple screens, action bars, and custom views on the UI. Moreover, multimedia on Android systems is a functionality increasing your mobile apps' adoptability. In this chapter, we will introduce multimedia in Android and how to add multimedia to our Android app. Three main aspects in multimedia include *Media*, *Audio*, and *Video*.

4.1 INTRODUCTION OF 2-D GRAPHICS TECHNIQUES

Android implements complete 2-D functions in one package, named android.graphics. This package provides various kinds of graphics tools, such as canvas, color filter, point, line, and rectangles. We can use these graphics tools to draw the screen directly. We will introduce some basic knowledge in detail. First of all, we create a new Android application project named ColorTester.

4.1.1 Color

Colors are represented as packed integers, made up of 4 bytes: Alpha, Red, Green, and Blue. Alpha is a measure of transparency, from value 0 to value 255. The value 0 indicates the color is completely transparent. The value 255 indicates the color is completely opaque. Besides alpha, each component ranges between 0 and 255, with 0 meaning no contribution for that component, and 255 meaning 100% contribution.

We can create a half-opaque purple color like:
int color1 = Color.argb(127, 255, 0, 255);

Or in XML resource file, like:
<color name="half_op_purple">#7fff00ff</color>

The colors in Android XML resource files must be formulated as "#" + 6 or 8 bit Hexadecimal number.

Furthermore, Android offers some basic colors as constants, as shown in Fig. 4.1. We can use them directly, like:
int color2 = Color.Black;

In Android Studio, we can preview the color we created in XML file, as shown in Fig. 4.2. There are some small squares with the color created in the same line. We can see that the *#ffffffff* is opaque-white, and the *#ff000000* is opaque-black.

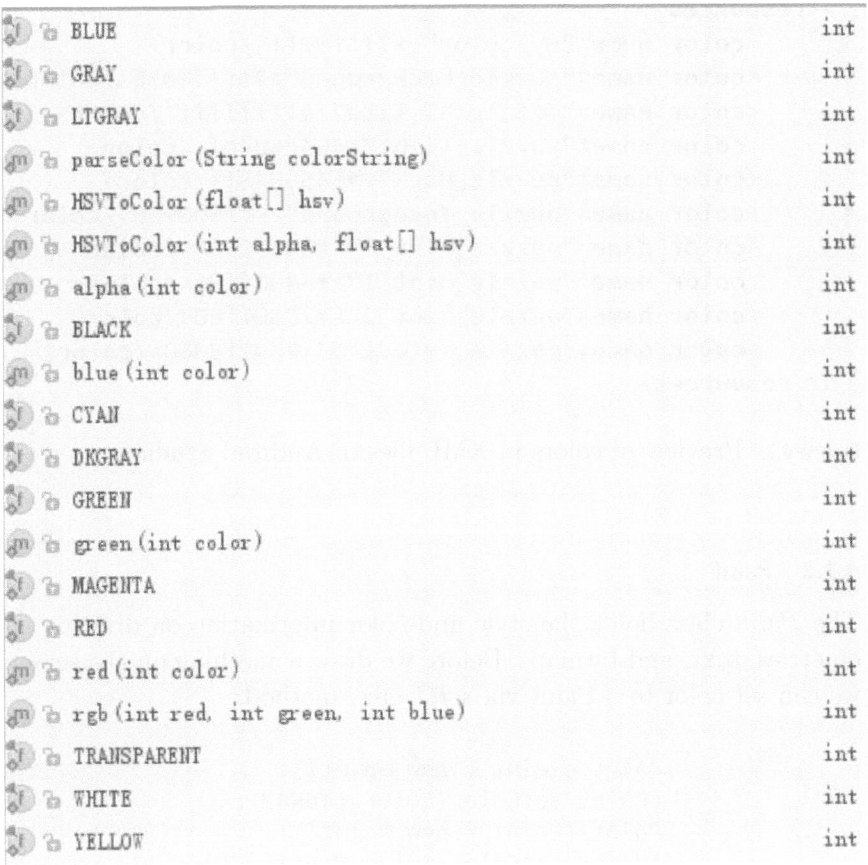

BLUE		int
GRAY		int
LTGRAY		int
parseColor (String colorString)		int
HSVToColor (float[] hsv)		int
HSVToColor (int alpha, float[] hsv)		int
alpha (int color)		int
BLACK		int
blue (int color)		int
CYAN		int
DKGRAY		int
GREEN		int
green (int color)		int
MAGENTA		int
RED		int
red (int color)		int
rgb (int red, int green, int blue)		int
TRANSPARENT		int
WHITE		int
YELLOW		int

Figure 4.1 Colors as constants provided by Android.

We can use these color, created in colors.xml by "color/color_name". For example, android:background="color/my_color".

After we define some colors in the XML file, we can reference them by their names, as we did for strings, or we can use them in Java code like:

int color3 = getResource().getColor(R.color.my_color); or
int color3 = R.color.text_color

The *getResources()* method returns the *ResourceManager* class for the current activity, and get *getColor()* asks the manager look up a color given a resource ID.

```
<resources>
    <color name="my_color">#7fff00ff</color>
    <color name="puzzle_background">#ffff0000</color>
    <color name="puzzle_hi_lite">#ffffffff</color>
    <color name="puzzle_light">#64c6d4ef</color>
    <color name="puzzle_dark">#6456648f</color>
    <color name="puzzle_foreground">#ff000000</color>
    <color name="puzzle_hint_0">#64ff0000</color>
    <color name="puzzle_hint_1">#6400ff80</color>
    <color name="puzzle_hint_2">#2000ff80</color>
    <color name="puzzle_selected">#64ff8000</color>
</resources>
```

Figure 4.2 Preview of colors in XML files in Android Studio.

4.1.2 Paint

The *Paint* class holds the style and color information on drawing geometries, text, and bitmaps. Before we draw something on the screen, we can set color to a Paint via *setColor()* method.

```
Paint cPaint = new Paint();
cPaint.setColor(Color.LTGRAY);
Paint tPaint = new Paint();
tPaint.setColor(Color.BLUE);
tPaint.setTextSize((float) 20.0);
```

Figure 4.3 Paint class in Android.

As shown in Fig. 4.3, we create two *Paint*s, which are *cPaint* to draw a circle and *tPaint* to draw text. We set the color of the circle as light gray and the color of text as blue. Beside colors, we also can set other attributes to Paint class, such as the *TextSize*.

4.1.3 Path

The *Path* class encapsulates multiple contour geometric paths, such as lines, rectangles, circles, and curves. Fig. 4.4 is an example that defines a circular path and a rectangle path.

The second line defines a circle, whose center is at position x=300,

```
Path path = new Path();
path.addCircle(300, 200, 150, Path.Direction.CW);

Path path2 = new Path();
path2.addRect(150, 400, 400, 650, Path.Direction.CW);
```

Figure 4.4 Create two *Path* object and add details to them.

y=200, with a radius of 150 pixels. The fourth line defines a rectangle whose left top point is at position x=150, y=400, and right bottom point is at position x=400, y=650. The *Path.Direction.CW* indicates that the shape will be drawn clockwise. The other direction is CCW, which indicates counter-clockwise.

4.1.4 Canvas

To draw something, we need to prepare four basic components, including a *Bitmap* to hold the pixels, a *Canvas* to host the draw call, a drawing primitive, and a *Paint*. The *Bitmap* is the place where to draw something, and the Canvas is used to hold the "draw" calls. A drawing primitive can be a Rect, a Circle, a Path, a Text, and a Bitmap.

In Android, a display screen is taken up by an Activity, which hosts a *View*, which in turn hosts a Canvas. We can draw on the canvas by overriding the *View.onDraw()* method. A Canvas object is the only parameter to *onDraw()* method. We create a new activity, which contains a view called *GraphicsView*, but not the layout.xml, as shown in Fig. 4.8.

In Fig. 4.5, we comment the original code and set the content view of this activity to some layout.xml, and set it to some new view we created, which is *GraphicsView*.

Let's review the two methods of designing Android apps. There are two methods to design Android apps, which are procedural and declarative. The "setContentView(R.layout.activity_main)" is a typical example of declarative, which is described all objects in the activity using XML files. The "setContentView(new GraphicsView(this))" is a typical example of a procedural, which means writing Java code to create and manipulate all the user interface objects [56].

This new class, *GraphicsView*, extends the class *View*. The *on-Draw()* method is over-rider and used to implement the function of

```
        @Override
ϡ       protected void onCreate(Bundle savedInstanceState) {
            super.onCreate(savedInstanceState);
//          setContentView(R.layout.activity_main);
            setContentView(new GraphicsView(this));

ϡ       }

ϡ       static public class GraphicsView extends View {
ϡ           public GraphicsView(Context context){
                super(context);
ϡ           }

            @Override
ϡ           protected void onDraw(Canvas canvas){...}
ϡ       }
```

Figure 4.5 A new activity whose contentView is the view created ourselves but not layout.xml.

drawing. Fig. 4.6 shows the details of the *onDraw()* method. We use Paint with different colors to draw a Path on the View via calling *onDraw(Canvas)* method.

Meanwhile, we have another choice to create a Canvas, as shown in Fig. 4.8. In Fig. 4.8, we create a Bitmap that is a square whose size is 100*100 and will use it as the argument of Canvas. Then we can use this canvas as the same as the one offered in the onDraw() method.

4.1.5 Drawable

Android.graphics.drawable provides classes to manage a variety of visual elements, which are intended for display, such as bitmaps and gradients. We can combine drawables with other graphics, or we can use them in UI widgets, such as the background for a button. Android offers following types of drawables:

Bitmap: A bitmap graphic file (.png, .jpg, or .gif).

Nine-Patch: A PNG file with stretchable regions to allow image resizing based on content (.9.png).

Layer: A *Drawable* that manages an array of other *Drawables*. These are drawn in array order, so the element with the largest index is be drawn on top.

```
@Override
protected void onDraw(Canvas canvas){

    String QUOTE = "PACE UNIVERSITY CSIS DEPT.";

    Paint cPaint = new Paint();
    cPaint.setColor(Color.LTGRAY);
    Paint tPaint = new Paint();
    tPaint.setColor(Color.BLUE);
    tPaint.setTextSize((float) 20.0);

    Path path = new Path();
    path.addCircle(300, 200, 150, Path.Direction.CW);

    Path path2 = new Path();
    path2.addRect(150, 400, 400, 650, Path.Direction.CW);

    canvas.drawPath(path, cPaint);
    canvas.drawTextOnPath(QUOTE, path, 0, 20, tPaint);

    canvas.drawPath(path2, tPaint);
}
```

Figure 4.6 The "onDraw()" method that draws a circle and a rectangle.

Figure 4.7 Running result of GraphicsView.

```
//Creating a new Canvas object
Bitmap bitmap = Bitmap.createBitmap(100,100,Bitmap.Config.ARGB_8888);
Canvas canvas = new Canvas(bitmap);
```

Figure 4.8 Use Bitmap to create a new Canvas.

State: An XML file that references different bitmap graphics for different states (for example, to use a different image when a button is pressed).

Level: An XML file that defines a drawable that manages a number of alternate *Drawables*, each assigned a maximum numerical value. Creates a *LevelListDrawable*.

Transition: An XML file that defines a drawable that can cross-fade between two drawable resources.

Inset Drawable: An XML file that defines a drawable that insets another drawable by a specified distance. This is useful when a View needs a background drawable that is smaller than the View's actual bounds.

Clip: An XML file that defines a drawable that clips another *Drawable* based on this *Drawable's* current level value.

Scale: An XML file that defines a drawable that changes the size of another *Drawable* based on its current level value.

Shape: An XML file that defines a geometric shape, including colors and gradients.

A drawable resource is a general concept for a graphic that can be drawn to the screen and that can be retrieved with *Application Programming Interface* (API). Now we will add a gradient background to our ColorTester. We create a drawable resource file in res\drawable, and then create a *Shape* inside the background.xml file, as shown in Fig. 4.9 and Fig. 4.10.

Figure 4.9 The first step of creating a new Drawable resource file.

As shown in Fig. 4.11, we define a gradient from the start color to the end color. The angle indicates the direction of the gradient, and

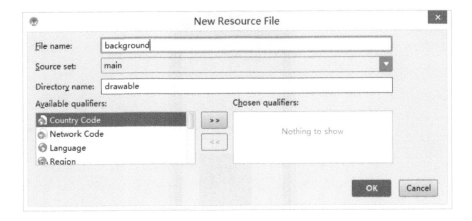

Figure 4.10 The second step of creating a new Drawable resource file.

```xml
<?xml version="1.0" encoding="utf-8"?>
<shape xmlns:android="http://schemas.android.com/apk/res/android">
    <gradient
        android:startColor="#FFFFFF"
        android:endColor="#aed130"
        android:angle="90" />
</shape>
```

Figure 4.11 Shape Drawable.

it must be the extract times 45. When the angle = 0, the sequence is from left to right. When the angle = 90, the sequence is from bottom to top. When the angle = 180, the sequence is from right to left. When the angle = 270, the sequence is from top to bottom.

Then add one attribute into the RelativeLayout in `activity_main` `.xml` as "android:background:@drawable/background". The running result is shown in Fig. 4.12.

Besides gradient, there are some other common attributes that can be added into a shape, including stroke, corners, and padding. We add them into the shape of background.xml, and set the color of the stroke is red, the width of the dash is 10dp, etc. The attributes and the running result are shown in Fig. 4.13. From Fig. 4.13, we can see that the background is stroked by a red dash, and every corner has a round edge.

Figure 4.12 Gradient background.

```
<shape xmlns:android="http://schemas.android.com/apk/res/android">
    <gradient
        android:startColor="#FFFFFF"
        android:endColor="#aed130"
        android:angle="90" />
    <stroke
        android:width="2dp"
        android:color="#ff0000"
        android:dashWidth="5dp"
        android:dashGap="3dp" />
    <corners
        android:radius="2dp" />
    <padding
        android:left="10dp"
        android:top="10dp"
        android:right="10dp"
        android:bottom="10dp" />
</shape>
```

Figure 4.13 Stroke, Corners, and Padding Drawables

4.1.6   Button Selector

We want to set different colors to buttons when they are at different states. We set the default color of a button as light purple, and the color when it is pressed is light orange. As we introduced in the previous section, we need to create a drawable resource file to implement this function. Thus, we create a new drawable resource file named "button_selection", and between the <selector> and < /selector> add two items. The first one is the pressed state, which indicates that the button is pressed, as shown in Fig. 4.14. The second one is the default state, as shown in Fig. 4.15.

```
<item android:state_pressed="true" >
    <shape>
        <gradient
            android:startColor="#ffc2b7"
            android:endColor="#FFFFFF"
            android:type="radial"
            android:gradientRadius="50" />
        <stroke
            android:width="2dp"
            android:color="#dcdcdc"
            android:dashWidth="5dp"
            android:dashGap="3dp" />
        <corners
            android:radius="2dp" />
        <padding
            android:left="10dp"
            android:top="10dp"
            android:right="10dp"
            android:bottom="10dp" />
    </shape>
</item>
```

Figure 4.14   Default state of button.

Then, we add one attribute to all the three buttons as follows: android:background="@drawable/button_selector".

The running result is shown in Fig. 4.16.

4.2   ADVANCED UI DESIGN

Android provides a flexible framework for UI design that allows apps to display different layouts for different devices, create custom UI widgets, and control aspects of the system UI beyond the apps' window.

4.2.1   Multiple Screens

The goal of this part is to build a UI, which is flexible enough to fit perfectly on any screen and to create different interaction patterns that are optimized for different screen sizes.

To ensure that your layout is flexible and adapts to different

```
<item android:state_focused="false">
    <shape>
        <solid android:color="#8f0000f0"/>
        <stroke
            android:width="2dp"
            android:color="#fad3cf" />
        <corners
            android:topRightRadius="5dp"
            android:bottomLeftRadius="5dp"
            android:topLeftRadius="0dp"
            android:bottomRightRadius="0dp"
            />
        <padding
            android:left="10dp"
            android:top="10dp"
            android:right="10dp"
            android:bottom="10dp" />
    </shape>
</item>
```

Figure 4.15 Pressed state of the button.

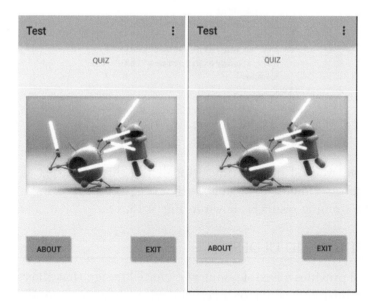

Figure 4.16 Running result of the button selector.

screen sizes, you should use "wrap_content" and "match_parent" for the width and height of some view components. If you use "wrap_content", the width or height of the view is set to the minimum size necessary to fit the content within that view, while "match_parent" (also known as "fill_parent" before API level 8) makes the component expand to match the size of its parent view.

You can construct fairly complex layouts using nested instances of LinearLayout and combinations of "wrap_content" and "match_parent" sizes. However, LinearLayout does not allow you to precisely control the spacial relationships of child views; views in a LinearLayout simply line up side by side. If you need child views to be oriented in variations other than a straight line, a better solution is often to use a RelativeLayout, which allows you to specify your layout in terms of the special relationships between components. For instance, you can align one child view on the left side and another view on the right side of the screen.

Supporting different screen sizes usually means that your image resources must also be capable of adapting to different sizes. For example, a button background must fit whichever button shape it is applied to.

If you use simple images on components that can change size, you will quickly notice that the results are somewhat less than impressive, since the runtime will stretch or shrink your images uniformly. The solution is using nine-patch bitmaps, which are specially formatted PNG files that indicate which areas can and cannot be stretched.

Therefore, when designing bitmaps that will be used on components with variable sizes, always use nine-patches. To convert a bitmap into a nine-patch, you can start with a regular image. Then run it through the draw9patch utility of the Software Development Kit (SDK) (which is located in the tools/ directory), in which you can mark the areas that should be stretched by drawing pixels along the left and top borders. You can also mark the area that should hold the content by drawing pixels along the right and bottom borders. The process is shown from Fig. 4.17 to Fig. 4.18.

Figure 4.17 Original image (.png).

The black pixels are along the borders. The ones on the top and

Figure 4.18   Nine-patch image (.9.png).

left borders indicate the places where the image can be stretched, and the ones on the right and bottom borders indicate where the content should be placed.

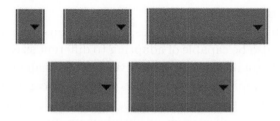

Figure 4.19   A nine-patch image used in various sizes.

4.2.2   Action Bar

The action bar, also called app bar, is one of the most important design elements in activities. It provides a visual structure and interactive elements that are familiar to users. A typical action bar is shown in Fig. 4.20.

Figure 4.20   A typical action bar.

An action bar has some key functions listed as follows:

1. Dedicated space for giving the app an identity and indicating the user's virtual location in the app.

2. Access to important actions in a predictable way, such as search.

3. Support for navigation and view switching (with tabs or drop-down lists).

In its most basic form, the action bar displays the title for the activity on one side and an overflow menu on the other. Beginning with Android 3.0 (API level 11), all activities that use the default theme have an ActionBar as an app bar. However, app bar features have gradually been added to the native ActionBar over various Android releases. As a result, the native ActionBar behaves differently depending on what version of the Android system a device may be using. By contrast, the most recent features are added to the support library's version of Toolbar, and they are available on any device that can use the support library.

For this reason, you should use the support library's Toolbar class to implement your activities' app bars. Using the support library's toolbar helps ensure that your app will have consistent behavior across the widest range of devices. For example, the Toolbar widget provides a material design experience on devices running Android 2.1 (API level 7) or later, but the native action bar doesn't support material design unless the device is running Android 5.0 (API level 21) or later.

4.2.3 Custom Views

Android has a large set of view classes for interacting with users and displaying various types of data. However sometimes we have some unique requirements that are not covered by the built-in views. To be a well-designed class, a custom view should:

1. conform to Android standards;

2. provide custom styleable attributes that work with Android XML layouts;

3. send accessibility events;

4. be compatible with multiple Android platforms.

All of the view classes defined in the Android framework extend the *View*. The custom view can also extend View directly, or we can extend some existing view subclasses, such as Button. Then we need to define some attributes for the custom view. To define custom attributes, add <declare-styleable> resources to our project. It's customary to put these resources into a res/values/attrs.xml file.

After a view is created from an XML layout, all of the attributes in the XML tags are read from the resource bundle and passed into the view's constructor as an AttributeSet. Then we will pass the Attribute-Set to obtainStyledAttributes(). This method passes back a TypedArray array of values that has already been dereferenced and styled.

Then we need to add properties and events to the custom view. To provide dynamic behavior, we need to expose a property getter and setter pair for each custom attribute, for example, showing text and image. After creating and initiating the custom view, we move to the most important part of a custom view, which is its appearance. Furthermore, the most important step in drawing a custom view is to override the onDraw() method. The parameter to onDraw() is a Canvas object that the view can use to draw itself. The Canvas class defines methods for drawing text, lines, bitmaps, and many other graphics primitives. You can use these methods in onDraw() to create your custom UI.

Drawing a UI is only one part of creating a custom view. You also need to make your view respond to user input in a way that closely resembles the real-world action you're mimicking. We need to make the view interactive, including input gestures, physically plausible motion, and making transactions smooth.

4.3 OVERVIEW OF MULTIMEDIA IN ANDROID

4.3.1 Understanding the MediaPlayer Class

Android support audio and video output through the MediaPlayer class in the android.media package. The android.media is used to manage various media interfaces. The Media APIs are used to play and record media files, including audio and video [57, 58]. The MediaPlayer class can be used to control playback of audio/video files and streams [59]. The control of audio/video files and streams is managed as a state machine, as shown in Fig. 4.21.

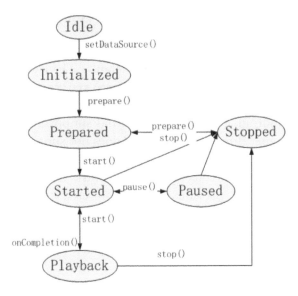

Figure 4.21 State diagram of the MediaPlayer.

4.3.2 Life Cycle of the MediaPlayer State

The life cycle and the state of a *MediaPlayer* object are driven by the supported playback control operations. The *setDataSource()* method is called to transfer a *MediaPlayer* object from the idle state to the initialized state. A *MediaPlayer* object must enter the prepared state first before it is started and played back. A *MediaPlayer* can enter the prepared state by call the *prepare()* or *prepareAsync()* method. The *prepare()* method transfers the object to the prepared state once the method call is returned. The *prepareAsync()* method first transfers the object to the preparing state after the call returns while the internal player engine continues working to complete the rest of the preparation work.

The *start()* method must be called to start the playback. The *MediaPlayer* object is in the started state, after *start()* returns. Calling *start()* has no effect on a *MediaPlayer* object that is already in the started state.

4.4   AUDIO IMPLEMENTATIONS IN ANDROID

To learn how to play audio, we create a new project named "MediaT-ester" and keep other configuration default. Then we copy one song from local directory to "MediaTester\app\src\main\res\raw" directory. Notice that we need to ensure that the file format can be recognized by Android. Fortunately, Android supports most all kinds of audio file formats. However, if Android does not support the file format of your audio, try to transform it to a common format.

First, create two buttons to show the "start" and "pause" functions. As introduced in the previous chapter, we create two buttons in the `activity_main.xml`, as shown in Fig. 4.22. Meanwhile, we need to add two strings in the strings.xml file as:

$< stringname = $ "start_button" $> Start < /string >$

$< stringname = $ "pause_button" $> Pause < /string >$

```
<Button
    android:layout_width="wrap_content"
    android:layout_height="wrap_content"
    android:text="@string/start_button"
    android:id="@+id/button_start"
    android:layout_below="@+id/textView"
    android:layout_alignParentStart="true" />

<Button
    android:layout_width="wrap_content"
    android:layout_height="wrap_content"
    android:text="@string/pause_button"
    android:id="@+id/button_pause"
    android:layout_below="@+id/button_start"
    android:layout_alignParentStart="true" />
```

Figure 4.22   Creating two buttons in `activity_main.xml`.

Then jump into the MainActivity.java file and add a new MediaPlayer object into the MainActivity class as:

private MediaPlayer mp

Then we modify the MainActivity to implement OnClickListener, as introduced in previous chapter, and create onClick(View v) method to implement the functions of these two buttons. Then set OnClickListener to these two buttons, and now the MainActivity.java is shown as Fig. 4.23.

```
public class MainActivity extends Activity implements View.OnClickListener {

    private MediaPlayer mp;

    @Override
    protected void onCreate(Bundle savedInstanceState) {
        super.onCreate(savedInstanceState);
        setContentView(R.layout.activity_main);

        findViewById(R.id.button_1).setOnClickListener(this);
        findViewById(R.id.button_2).setOnClickListener(this);
    }

    public void onClick(View v)
    {...}
```

Figure 4.23 MediaPlayer object and the OnClickListener.

Then in the *onClick()* method, we implement functions to these two buttons, which are start a song, pause, and resume it. Before starting a song, we need to create a resource to the *MediaPlayer* object. Then we need to tell the computer which audio we want to play. We can use an integer ID of audio resource to identify the audio resource. In our example, we use resId = R.raw.test, then we call the *start()* method to play music. Before use pause a song, we need to judge whether it is playing. If it is playing, we call *pause()* method to pause it; if not, we call *start()* method to resume it. The code is shown in Fig. 4.24.

The running result is shown in Fig. 4.25. When we click the "START" button, Android plays the song that we previously put in the raw file. When we click the "PAUSE" button, Android will pause the song if it is playing or resume it if it is paused.

4.5 EXECUTING VIDEO IN ANDROID

The MediaPlayer class works with video the same way it does with audio. However, we need to create a surface to play video, and the surface is VideoView class. The VideoView class can load images from various sources and takes charge of computing its measurement from the video. Furthermore, it provides various display options, such as scaling.

HINT: VideoView does not retain its full state when going into the background. It does not restore the current play state, position, selected tracks, or any subtitle tracks.

We will add something about video into the MediaTester project.

```
public void onClick(View v) {
    int resId;
    switch (v.getId()) {
        case R.id.button_start:
            resId = R.raw.test;
            if (mp != null) {
                mp.release();
            }
            mp = MediaPlayer.create(this, resId);
            mp.start();
            break;
        case R.id.button_pause:
            if (mp.isPlaying()) {
                mp.pause();
            } else {
                mp.start();
            }
            break;
    }
```

Figure 4.24 Implementing the functions of two buttons in onClick() method.

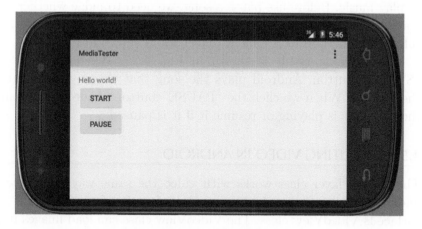

Figure 4.25 Running result of the MediaTester.

First, we create a new VideoView below the pause button in activity_main.xml as follows:
    <VideoView
android:layout_width="wrap_content"

```
android:layout_height="wrap_content"
```
android:id="@+id/video"
```
android:layout_below="@+id/button_pause"
```
```
android:layout_gravity="center" />
```
Then, jumping into Java file, we create a View object named video and connect it to the VideoView as follows:

VideoView video = (VideoView) findViewById(R.id.video);

Then we need to set a path to identify the location of the video. However, the *Android Virtual Device* (AVD) cannot recognize the local path in our computer. Android offers several options to store persistent application data as follows:

> *Shared Preferences* The SharedPreferences class provides a general framework that allows you to save and retrieve persistent key-value pairs of primitive data types.

> *Internal Storage* We can save files directly on the device's internal storage. Files saved to the internal storage are private in default.

> *External Storage* Android devices support a shared external storage to save files. The external storage can be a removable storage media, such as an SD card, or internal storage.

> *SQLite Databases* We can use SQLite in Android to create databases that will be accessible by name to any class in the app.

> *Network Connection* We can use the network to store and retrieve data in our own services.

Before we play a video using VideoView, we need to set a path to locate the video, and this path must be inside the AVD itself.

First of all, run an AVD, and jump into Dalvik Debug Monitor Service (DDMS) after the AVD runs. In Android Studio, select Tools, then Android, then click Android Device Monitor (Tools → Android → Android Device Monitor), as shown in Fig. 4.26. The Android Device Monitor will be similar to Fig. 4.27.

Then select the AVD we just run, and then in the "File Explorer" tab, we can see many folders and files listed. Find the "data" folder and click "Push a file onto the device" on the right top of the interface, as shown in Fig. 4.28. Then select and push a local video file onto the device.

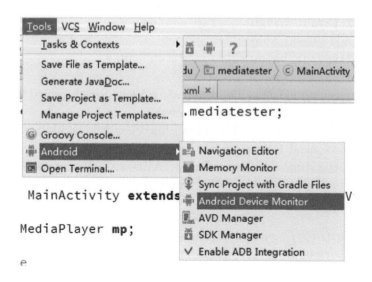

Figure 4.26 Android device monitor.

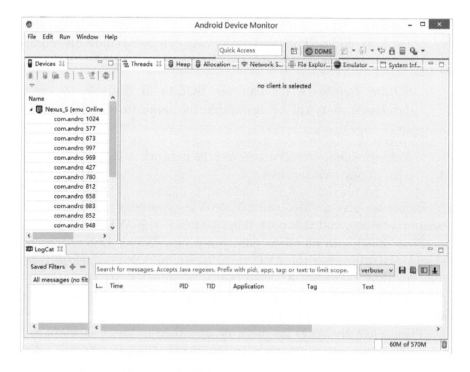

Figure 4.27 Android device Monitor.

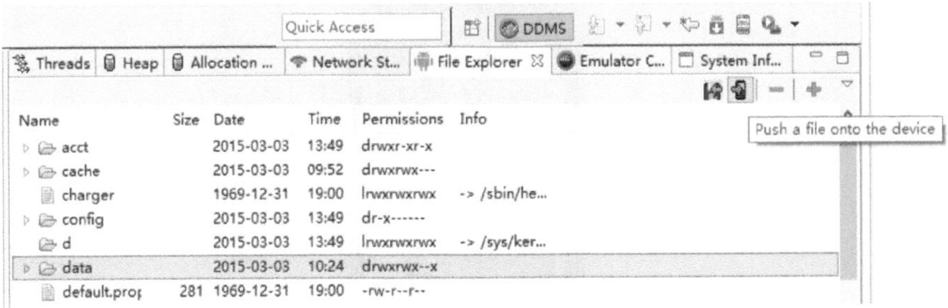

Figure 4.28 Push a file onto the device.

```
@Override
protected void onCreate(Bundle savedInstanceState) {
    super.onCreate(savedInstanceState);
    setContentView(R.layout.activity_main);

    //audio part
    findViewById(R.id.button_start).setOnClickListener(this);
    findViewById(R.id.button_pause).setOnClickListener(this);

    //video part
    //Before we play a video, we need to push the video resource
    //into AVD
    VideoView video = (VideoView) findViewById(R.id.video);
    video.setVideoPath("/data/samplevideo.3gp");
    video.start();
}
```

Figure 4.29 Setting video path and start a video.

The DDMS is used to operate the AVD, not the Android app. If we have pushed some video into a device before, we do not need to push it again in Android Project. Then add two methods to the onCreate() method to set the Video path and play it as follows:

video.setVideoPath("/data/samplevideo.3gp");

video.start();

Then the current onCreate() method can refer to Fig. 4.29.

In the end, the running result is shown in Fig. 4.30.

Figure 4.30 The running result of the MediaTester.

4.6 EXERCISES

Part 1: 2-D Graphics

4.6.1 Basic Exercises

1. Which package does Android provide a complete native 2-D graphics library?

2. How does Android represent colors?

3. Which data type is an instance of the Color class?

4. What does alpha 0 means?

5. What is Paint? What is Canvas?

6. What is the parameter of method onDraw()?

7. What does Path class contain?

8. Which class can offer some fancy effects to path?

9. What is Drawable class used for?

10. Where are Drawables often defined?

11. Where do you register an activity?

12. How do you get the real size of a view?

13. What method will be called by Android when any part of the view needs to be updated?

14. What is the main difference between Android and iOS when handling input?

15. Which method contains operations about the trackball?

16. How do you use drawing functions in the onDraw() method?

17. Which method handles keyboard input?

18. What will happen if call to invalidate() with no parameters?

19. What is the keypad?

Part 2: Multimedia

1. How does Android support sound and music output?

2. Which directory stores sound files?

3. What does the setVolumeControlStream() method do?

4. What do we call the release() method inside the onKeyDown() method?

5. What will happen if we forget to release resources associated with the old MediaPlayer?

6. How does Android's MediaPlayer work?

7. What is the difference between Android's MediaPlayer playing on video and audio?

8. What does setVideoPath() method do?

9. How do you make a video to take over the whole screen including the title bar and status bar?

10. Why does it restart the video when rotating the display?

11. What can onRetainNonConfigurationInstance() method do in an activity?

12. What will happen if you are using a service for a music application when it ends?

13. What is the relation between onPause() method and onResume() method?

4.6.2 Advanced Exercises

Part 1: 2-D Graphics

1. Use eclipse to choose a color you like most and post the ARGB (*Red Green Blue Alpha*) value of it.

2. Describe the process of coloring in Android.

Part 2: Multimedia

1. Please explain the difference between using some music as an activityand using it as a*service*.

II

Advanced Mobile App Optimizations

CHAPTER 5

Mobile Embedded System Architecture

CONTENTS

Mobile DEVICE is the indispensable part of a mobile system, and all the chips used in a mobile device are embedded systems. These embedded systems with various functions are controlled by the mobile operating system and collaborate with each other to complete every task mobile apps request.

In this chapter, we introduce the mobile embedded system architecture, including:

Overview of embedded systems

Applications of embedded system.

The processor technology in embedded systems

Basic concepts in processor technology in embedded systems

The scheduling algorithms in processor technology in embedded systems

Memory technology in embedded systems

Embedded systems in mobile devices

Embedded systems in Android

5.1 EMBEDDED SYSTEMS

5.1.1 Embedded Systems Overview

Embedded systems are anything that uses a micoprocessor but is not a general-purpose computer. An embedded system is a computer system with a dedicated function, which is embedded as a part of a complete device, including hardware and mechanical parts [60]. These tiny systems can be found everywhere, ranging from commercial electronics, such as cell phones, cameras, portable health monitoring systems, automobile controllers, robots, and smart security devices, to critical infrastructure, such as telecommunication networks, electrical power grids, financial institutions, and nuclear plants [61, 62, 63]. The increasingly complicated embedded systems require extensive design automation and optimization tools.

Modern embedded systems are often based on microcontrollers [64, 65], such as Central Processing Unit (CPU)s with integrated memory or peripheral interfaces, but ordinary microprocessors, which use external chips for memory, and peripheral interface circuits are still common. Embedded systems are commonly used in telecommunication systems, consumer electronics, transportation systems, and medical equipment [66].

Telecommunication Systems

Telecommunication systems employ numerous embedded systems, from telephone switches to cell phones.

Consumer Electronics

Consumer electronics include personal digital assistants (PDAs), such as audio players, mobile phones, videogame consoles, digital cameras, video players, and printers. Embedded systems are used to provide flexibility, efficiency, and features.

Home Automation

Embedded devices are used for sensing and controlling in-home automation using wired and wireless networks. Embedded devices can be used to control lights, climate, security, audio/visual, and surveillance.

Transportation Systems

Embedded systems are increasingly used from flight to automobiles in transportation systems. New airplanes contain advanced avionics, such as Inertial Guidance Systems (IGS) and Global Positioning System (GPS) receivers that also have considerable safety requirements. Various electric motors use electric motor controllers. Automobiles, electric vehicles, and hybrid vehicles increasingly use embedded systems to maximize efficiency and reduce pollution.

Medical Equipment

Medical equipment uses embedded systems for vital signs monitoring, electronic stethoscopes for amplifying sounds, and various medical imaging for non invasive internal inspections. Embedded systems within medical equipment are often powered by industrial computers.

Besides the usages mentioned above, embedded systems are also widely used in a new kind of technology, which is *wireless sensor networking* (WSN). The WSN consists of spatially distributed autonomous sensors to monitor physical or environmental conditions. Commonly monitored parameters are temperature, humidity, pressure, wind direction and speed, illumination intensity, vibration intensity, sound intensity, power-line voltage, chemical concentrations, pollutant levels, and vital body functions [67]. WSN enables people and companies to measure myriad things in the physical world and acts on this information under the help of embedded Wi-Fi systems. Furthermore, the network wireless sensors, using optimization technologies of embedded systems, are completely self-contained and will typically run off a battery source for years before the batteries need to be changed or charged.

Embedded systems also can be defined as computers purchased as part of some other piece of equipment. They always have a dedicated software in them, and the software may be customizable to users. There are often no "keyboard" and limited display or no general purpose display in an embedded system.

Embedded systems are important for three kinds of reasons:

Engineering reasons. Any device that needs to be controlled can be controlled by a microprocessor. In many situations, it is impossible or unnecessary for the devices to being a complete computer. McDonald's POS (Point of Sale) terminal is only in charge of recording purchases, calculating and showing price, collecting money, giving change, and printing receipts. This kind of functions is simple, so the POS terminals have little calculating resources. It is unnecessary for the POS terminal to be complete as a general computer, because it is really a waste.

Market reasons. The general-purpose computer market worths billions of dollars; meanwhile the embedded systems market is also worths billions of dollars. Although the price of an embedded system may be much lower than that of a general-purpose computer, the amount of embedded systems are much larger than that of general-purpose computers. In 2009, about 200 embedded systems were used in every new car. There are more than 80 million personal computers were sold every year. While over 3 billion embedded CPUs were sold annually. Furthermore, the personal computer market is mostly saturated, but the embedded market is still growing.

Pedagogical reasons. Embedded system designers often need to know hardware, software, and some combination of networking, control theory, and signal processing. This makes the teaching methods of designing embedded systems different from that for designing general-purpose systems.

In this section, we introduce the overview of embedded systems, analyze their usages, explain their importance, list some real applications of embedded systems, and give a high-level of the design of embedded system. We introduce deeper knowledge after introducing the design of embedded system. The first and the most important thing is scheduling.

5.2 SCHEDULING ALGORITHMS

5.2.1 Basic Concepts

First of all, some basic concepts must be introduced and explained. Scheduling is central to operating system design. The success of CPU scheduling depends on two executions. The first one is the process execution consisting of a cycle of CPU execution and Input/Output (I/O) wait. The second one is the process execution, which begins with a CPU processing, followed by I/O processing, then followed by another CPU processing, then another I/O processing, and so on. The CPU I/O Processing Cycle is the basic concept of processor technology. The processing time is the actual time that is required to complete some job.

The CPU scheduler selects from among the processes in memory that are ready to execute, and allocates the CPU to one of them. CPU scheduling decisions take place when a process is switching from running to waiting state; switching from running to ready state; switching from waiting to ready and terminating.

Beside the CPU scheduler, dispatcher is also a basic and important concept in processor technology. The dispatcher module gives control of the CPU to the process selected by the short-term scheduler, and this involves: switching context, switching to user mode, and jumping to the proper location in the user program to restart that program. Most dispatchers have dispatch latency, which is the time they take for the dispatcher to stop one process and start another running.

Then we discuss some criteria of scheduling.

CPU Utilization. The CPU utilization refers to a computer's usage of processing resources, or the amount of work handled by a CPU, and it is used to gauge system performance. Actual CPU utilization varies depending on the amount and type of managed computing tasks. The first aim of processor technology is increasing the CPU utilization by keeping the CPU as busy as possible.

Throughput. The throughput means the amount of processes that complete their execution per time unit.

Turnaround Time. The turnaround time means the amount of time to execute a particular process, and it can be calculated as the sum of the time waiting to get into memory, waiting in the ready queue, and executing on the CPU and the I/O.

Waiting Time. The waiting time means the amount of time a process has been waiting in the ready queue.

Response Time. The response time means the amount of time it takes from when a request was submitted until the first response is produced.

Completion Time. The completion time of one job means the amount of time needed to complete it, if it is never preempted, interrupted, or terminated.

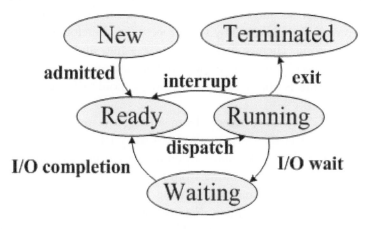

Figure 5.1 The diagram of the process states.

As shown in Fig. 5.1, processes have five types of states. At the *new* state, the process is in the stage of being created. At the *ready* state, the process has all the resources available that it needs to run, but the CPU is not currently working on this process's instructions. At the *running* state, the CPU is working on this process's instructions. At the *waiting* state, the process cannot run at the moment, because it is waiting for some resource to become available or for some event to occur. At the *terminate* state, the process was completed.

5.2.2 First-Come, First-Served Scheduling Algorithm

An important measurable indicator of processor is the average completion time of jobs. Fig. 5.2 represents an example of the schedule for k jobs. As shown in the figure, there are k jobs, marked as j_k, to be completed in the processor. The first job j_1 requires t_1 time units so that the job j_1 can be finished by time t_1. The second job j_2 starts after the fist job j_1 is finished, and the required length of time is t_2. Therefore, the second job j_2 can be accomplished by the time $t_1 + t_2$. Repeat this procedure until the last job j_k is done.

The total completion time:

$$A = t_1 + (t_1 + t_2) + (t_1 + t_2 + t_3) + \dots + (t_1 + t_2 + t_3 + \dots + t_k)$$
$$= k * t_1 + (k - 1) * t_2 + (k - 2) * t_3 + \dots + t_k$$
$$(5.1)$$

Figure 5.2   A schedule for k jobs.

One of the simplest scheduling algorithm is First Come, First Served (FCFS). The FCFS policy is widely used in daily life. For example, it is the standard policy for the processing of most queues, in which people wait for a service that was not prearranged or preplanned. In the processor technology field, it means the *jobs* are handled in the orders.

For instance, there are four jobs, j_1, j_2, j_3, and j_4, with different processing times, which are 7, 4, 3, and 6 respectively. These jobs arrive in the order: j_1, j_2, j_3, j_4. In FCFS policy, they are handled by the order of j_1, j_2, j_3, j_4, as shown in Fig. 5.3. The waiting time for j1 is 0, for j_2 is 7, for j_3 is 11, and for j_4 is 14. The average waiting time is $(0+7+11+14)/4 = 8$. The average completion time is $[7 + (7+4) + (7+4+3) + (7+4+3+6)] / 4 = 13$.

Suppose that the jobs arrive in the order j_2, j_3, j_4, j_1; the result produced by using FCFS is shown in Fig. 5.4. The waiting time for j_1 is 13, for j_2 is 0, for j_3 is 4, and for j_4 is 7. The average waiting time is $(13+0+4+7)/4 = 6$. The average completion time is $[4 + (4+3) + (4+3+6) + (4+3+6+7)] / 4 = 11$. Both the average waiting time and the average completion time of this scheduling is less than the previous one.

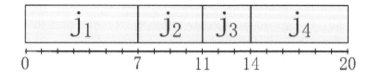

Figure 5.3 An example of FCFS scheduling.

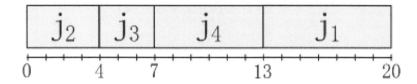

Figure 5.4 Another FCFS result if changing arrival sequence.

5.2.3 Shorted-Job-First Scheduling Algorithm

Then we will introduce another scheduling policy, which is Shortest Job First (SJF). SJF is a scheduling policy that selects the waiting process with the smallest execution time to execute first. SJF is advantageous because of its simplicity, and it minimizes the average completion time. Each process has to wait until its execution is complete.

Using the example mentioned in Section 2.2, while ignoring their arrival time, we first sort these jobs by their processing time, as j_3, j_2, j_4, j_1. The SJF scheduling result is shown in Fig. 5.5. The waiting time for j_1 is 13, j_2 is 3, j_3 is 0, and j_4 is 7. The average waiting time is $(13+3+0+7) = 5.75$. The completion time for j_1 is $(13+7)$, j_2 is $(3+4)$, j_3 is $(0+3)$, j_4 is $(7+6)$. The average completion time is $(20+7+3+13)/4 = 10.75$. This scheduling has lower average waiting time and average completion time than the previous two schedules.

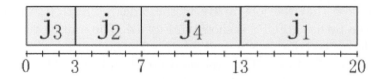

Figure 5.5 An example of SJF scheduling.

Theorem: *SJF scheduling has the lowest total completion time with a single processor.*

Proof by contradiction: Assuming that there are a series of jobs that were sorted by their completion time from short to long, as $j_1, j_2, j_3, \ldots, j_i, j_{i+1}, \ldots, j_k$, which also means the completion time of them can be ordered as $t_1 < t_2 < t_3 < \cdots < t_i < t_{i+1} < \cdots < t_k$. Using the SJF scheduling algorithm, the result is exactly the same as the order $j_1, j_2, j_3, \ldots, j_i, j_{i+1}, \ldots, j_k$. Then we suppose that there is another order A that has lower total completion time than the one produced by SJF, $j_1, j_2, j_3, \ldots, j_{i+1}, j_i, \ldots, j_k$. Based on Equation 5.1, the total completions time is $T = k * t_1 + (k - 1) * t_2 + (k - 2) * t_3 + \cdots + (k - i + 1) * t_i + (k - i) * t_{i+1} + \cdots + t_k$. So, we can get the total completion time of both orders. The SJF one is $T_s = k * t_1 + (k - 1) * t_2 + (k - 2) * t_3 + \cdots + (k - i + 1) * t_i + (k - i) * t_{i+1} + \cdots + t_k$. The A one is $T_a = k*t_1 + (k-1)*t_2 + (k-2)*t_3 + \cdots + (k-i+1)*t_{i+1} + (k-i)*t_i + \cdots + t_k$. From the supposing condition, $T_s < T_a$.

$T_s > T_a$;
$k*t_1 + (k-1)*t_2 + (k-2)*t_3 + \cdots + (k-i+1)*t_i + (k-i)*t_{i+1} + \cdots + t_k$
$> k*t_1 + (k-1)*t_2 + (k-2)*t_3 + \cdots + (k-i+1)*t_{i+1} + (k-i)*t_i + \cdots + t_k$;
$(k - i + 1) * t_i + (k - i) * t_{i+1} > (k - i + 1) * t_{i+1} + (k - i) * t_i$;
$t_i > t_{i+1}$.

However, $t_i > t_{i+1}$ is contradictory to $t_i < t_{i+1}$, in the assuming condition. As a result, A does not exist, which means there is no solution that has lower total completion time than the SJF scheduling.

In the end, we can conclude that SJF scheduling has the lowest average waiting time with a single processor. However, is SJF still optimal with multiple processors?

5.2.4 Multiprocessors

After discussing the single processor, we will expand the topic into multiprocessors. There are nine jobs with different completion times in three processors, as shown in Fig. 5.6, and we first give an optimal schedule using SJF. The average completion time is $\{(3+5+6) + [(6+10)+(5+11)+(3+14)] + [(3+14+15)+(5+11+18)+(6+10+20)] \} / 9 = 18.33$. There is another optimal schedule, as shown in Fig. 5.7. The average completion time is $\{(3+5+6) + [(5+10)+(3+11)+(6+14)] + [(5+10+15)+(6+14+18)+(3+11+20)] \} / 9 = 18.33$.

In multiprocessors, there are three theorems:

Job	Time
j1	3
j2	5
j3	6
j4	10
j5	11
j6	14
j7	15
j8	18
j9	20

(a) Jobs and time

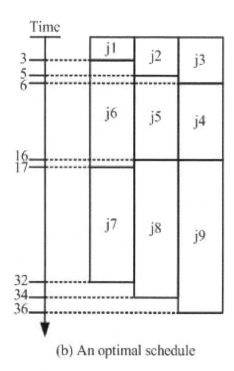

(b) An optimal schedule

Figure 5.6 An SJF schedule to complete nine jobs in three processors.

Theorem 5.1 *SJF scheduling has the optimal average waiting time and completion time in the multiprocessor.*

Theorem 5.2 *With the same average waiting time, there is more than one schedule with various final completion time.*

Theorem 5.3 *The algorithm to find the optimal final completion time is NP-Hard.*

Assuming that the processing time of j_1 to j_{3k} is t_1 to t_{3k}, respectively, the average completion time in three processors calculates as Equation 5.2: The average completion time is

$$\{(t_1 + t_2 + t_3) + (t_1 + t_2 + t_3 + t_4 + t_5 + t_6) + \cdots + (t_1 + t_2 + \cdots + t_{3k})\}/3k$$
$$= \{k(t_1 + t_2 + t_3) + (k - 1)(t_4 + t_5 + t_6) + \cdots + (t_{3k-2} + t_{3k-1} + t_{3k})\}/3k.$$
$$(5.2)$$

Then we assign that $T_1 = t_1 + t_2 + t_3$, $T_2 = t_4 + t_5 + t_6$, ...,

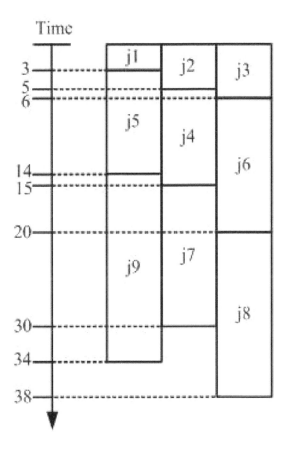

Figure 5.7 Another schedule to complete nine jobs in three processors.

$T_k = t_{3k-2} + t_{3k-1} + t_{3k}$. The total completion time in three processors can be formulated as $kT_1 + (k-1)T_2 + \cdots + T_k$. At last, we can formulate this problem into the one in a single processor. In the end, we can use the same method as the one in Section 2.3 to prove that the SJF schedule has the optimal average completion time in multiprocessors.

From Equation 5.2, we can see that the detailed sequence of j_1, j_2, j_3 does not impact the average waiting time of the whole schedule. As a result, the two schedules in Fig. 5.6 and Fig. 5.7 have the same average waiting time. However the time when the last job is completed these two schedules are different, which are 36 and 38. If there is a time constraint that is less than 38, the second schedule is not suitable, while the first schedule can be chosen. Furthermore, there are many other schedules having the same average waiting time with these two schedules, because changing the sequence of $j_{3i+1}, j_{3i+2}, j_{3i}$ does not change the average waiting time. Nevertheless, the time when the last job is completed is various, and how to find the optimal schedule that has the least time when the last job is completed is too hard to be solved by normal algorithms. This problem is a typical NP-Hard problem, and we will discuss this problem and how to solve it in later chapters.

5.2.5   Priority Scheduling Algorithm

The next scheduling algorithm is Priority Scheduling algorithm. In priority scheduling, a priority number, which can be an integer, is associated with each process. The CPU is allocated to the job with the highest priority, and the smallest integer represents the highest priority. The priority scheduling can be used in the preemptive and nonpreemptive schemes. The SJF scheduling is a priority scheduling, where priority is the predicted next CPU processing time. The following is a given example about the implementation of the priority scheduling in preemptive schemes, as shown in Fig. 5.8. The priority of each job is inverse with its processing time. As a result, the result using the priority scheduling algorithm is the same as the result from SJF scheduling.

The priority scheduling has the potential restrictions deriving from process starvations. The *Process Starvation* is the processes that require a long completion time, while processes requiring shorter completion times are continuously added. A scheme of *"Aging"* is used to solve this problem. As time progresses, the priority of the process increases. Another disadvantage is that the total execution time of a job must be known before the execution. While it is not possible to exactly predict the execution time, a few methods can be used to estimate the execution time for a job, such as a weighted average of previous execution times.

At last, we will introduce the Round Robin (RR) scheduling. In RR scheduling, each job gets a small unit of CPU time, called *imequantum*, usually 10 - 100 milliseconds. After this time has elapsed, the job is preempted and added to the end of the ready queue. If there are n jobs in the ready queue and the *timequantum* is q, then each job gets $1/n$ of the CPU time in chunks of at most q time units at once. No job waits more than $(n-1)$ time units. If the q is large, the RR scheduling will be the FCFS scheduling. Nevertheless, if the q is small, the overhead may be too high because of the too-often context switch.

Jobs	BurstTime	Priority	Arrival Time
j_1	7	4	0.0
j_2	4	2	2.0
j_3	3	1	4.0
j_4	6	3	5.0

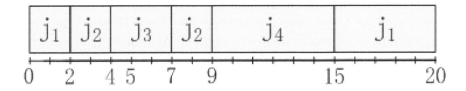

Figure 5.8 An example of the priority scheduling.

Actually, there are two kinds of scheduling schemes that are non-preemptive and preemptive.

Nonpreemptive.

The nonpreemptive scheduling means that once the CPU has been allocated to a process, the process keeps the CPU resource until it releases the CPU either by terminating or switching to a waiting state.

Preemptive.

In the preemptive schemes, a new job can preempt CPU resources, if its CPU processing length is less than the remaining time of the current executing job. This scheme is known as the Shortest-Remaining-Time-First (SRTF).

In computer science, preemption is the act of temporarily interrupting a job being carried out by a computer. It is normally carried out by a privileged job on the system that allows interruptions. Fig. 5.5 shows

SJF scheduling in the situation when all the jobs arrive at the same time, but situation will be complicated when considering their different arrival times, especially in preemptive scheme.

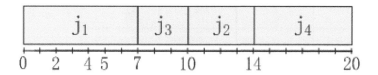

Figure 5.9 An example of the nonpreemptive SJF solution.

Still taking the example mentioned in Section 5.2.2, add arrival times to them, j_1 arriving at time 0.0; j_2 arriving at time 2.0; j_3 arriving at time 4.0; j_4 arriving at time 5.0. The SJF scheduling in a nonpreemptive scheme is shown in Fig. 5.9. At time 0, j_1 arrives, and there are no other jobs competing with it, so j_1 is in the running list. At time 2, 4, and 5, j_2, j_3, and j_4 arrive, respectively.

However, they cannot interrupt j_1 and grab the resource j_1 is using, so they are all in the waiting list. At time 7, j_1 is finished, and now there are three jobs in the waiting list. Among these three jobs, j_3 needs the shortest processing time, so it gets the resource and turns into the running list. At time 10, j_3 is finished, and now there are two jobs in the waiting list, which are j_2 and j_4. Since j_2 needs a shorter processing time than j_4 does, j_2 gets the resource and turns into the running list. At time 14, j_2 is finished, and now there is only one job in the waiting list, which is j_4. So j_4 gets the resource and turns into the running list. Finally, j_4 is finished at time 20. In this scheduling, the waiting time for j_1 is 0, j_2 is (10-2), j_3 is (7-4), and j_4 is (14-5). The average waiting time is (0+8+3+9)/4 = 5. The completion time for j_1 is 7, j_2 is (14-2), j_3 is (10-4), and j_4 is (20-5). The average completion time is (7+12+6+15)/4 = 10.

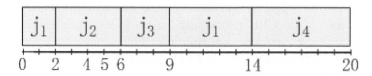

Figure 5.10 Example of the preemptive SJF solution.

The SJF scheduling in a preemptive scheme is shown in Fig. 5.10. At time 0, j_1 arrives, and there are no other jobs competing with it, so j_1 is in the running list. At time 2, j_2 arrives, and j_2 has shorter processing time than j_1, so it preempts j_1. j_1 goes to the waiting list, while j_2 in the running list. At time 4, j_3 arrives. j_3 needs 3 time to be completed, while j_2 needs 2 time. So j_3 cannot preempt j_2 and stays in the waiting list. At current stage, j_1 and j_3 are both in the waiting list.

Next, at time 5, j_4 arrives, but it has longer processing time than j_2, so it cannot preempts j_2. j_4 joins in the waiting list. At time 6, j_2 is finished, and now there are three jobs in the waiting list. Among them, j_3 needs the shortest processing time, so j_3 get the resource, while others are still waiting. At time 9, j_3 is finished, and now there are two jobs in the waiting list. Since j_1 needs a shorter processing time, which is 5, than j_4 does, which is 6. j_1 gets the resource and turns into the running list. At time 14, j_1 is finished, and now there is only one job in the waiting list, which is j_4. As a result, j_4 get the resource and is finally finished at time 20. In this scheduling, the waiting time for j_1 is 9-2, j_2 is (0), j_3 is (6-4), and j_4 is (14-5). he average waiting time is $(7+0+2+9)/4 = 4.5$. The completion time for j_1 is 14, j_2 is (6-2), j_3 is (9-6), and j_4 is (20-5). The average completion time is $(14+4+3+15)/4 = 9$.

5.2.6 ASAP and ALAP Scheduling Algorithm

First, we will introduce the Directed Acyclic Graphs (DAG) to model the scheduling problem about the delay in processors. A DAG is a directed graph with no directed cycles. It is formed by a collection of vertices and directed edges, each edge connecting one vertex to another. There is no way to start at some vertex and follow a sequence of edges that eventually loop back to this vertex. We create a DAG with a source node and a sink node, as shown in Fig. 5.11. The source node is V_0, and the sink node is V_n. The solid lines refer to the execution delay between nodes. Broken lines mean there is no execution delay between nodes. For example, neither source node nor sink node has the execution time.

Moreover, students need to understand two concepts before introducing the algorithm, including *Predecessor* and *Successor*. A *Predecessor* refers to the node that needs to be finished before the current node. For example, in Fig. 5.11, v_2 and v_3 are the predecessors of v_5.

A *Successor* refers to the node that succeeds the current node. In Fig. 5.11, v_4 is v_1's successor.

As exhibited in Fig. 5.11, we define $V = \{v_0, v_1, \ldots v_n\}$ in which v_0 and v_n are pseudo nodes denoting the source node and sink node, respectively. $D = \{d_0, d_1, \ldots, d_n\}$ where d_i denotes the execution delay of v_i;

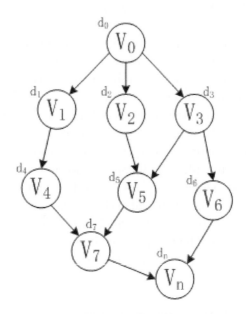

Figure 5.11 A sample of the directed acyclic graph.

Then we use a topological sorting algorithm to produce a legal sequence, which is scheduling for uniprocessor. A topological sorting of a directed acyclic graph is a linear ordering of its vertices, such that for every directed edge $\{u, v\}$ from vertex u to vertex v, u comes before v in the ordering. First, finding a list of nodes whose indegree = 0, which means they have no incoming edges, inserting them into a set S, and removing them from V. Then starting the loop that keeps removing the nodes without incoming edges until V is empty. The output is the result of topological sorting and the scheduling for the uniprocessor. Referring to Fig. 5.11, we can get three results: $\{v_0, v_1, v_4, v_7, v_n\}$, $\{v_0, v_2, v_5, v_7, v_n\}$, and $\{v_0, v_3, v_6, v_n\}$.

To eliminate the latency, we assign values to d_i and simplify the problem. We set d_1, d_2, d_3, d_4, and d_5 as 1. We use two scheduling algorithms, which are As-Soon-As-Possible (ASAP) and As-Late-As-Possible (ALAP) Scheduling Algorithms.

5.2.6.1 ASAP

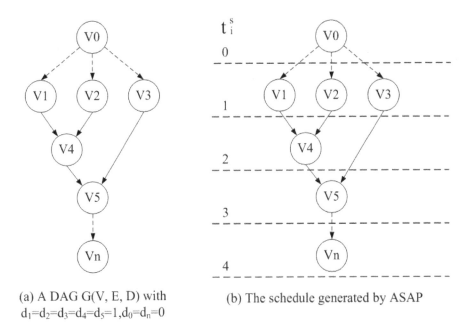

(a) A DAG G(V, E, D) with
$d_1=d_2=d_3=d_4=d_5=1, d_0=d_n=0$

(b) The schedule generated by ASAP

Figure 5.12 A simple ASAP for minimum latency scheduling.

As shown in Fig. 5.12, first, set $t_0^s = 1$, and v_0 has no predecessors, and d_0 is 0. Thus, v_0 has the same latency as its successors, v_1, v_2, and v_3. In this step, v_0 is scheduled. Then because v_1's predecessor v_0 is scheduled, it can be selected at the 1 latency time. The same operations can be implemented with v_2 and v_3 at the first latency time unit. In this step, v_1, v_2, and v_3 are scheduled. Then v_4 can be selected at the 2 latency, because its predecessors, v_1 and v_2, are scheduled. However, v_5 cannot be selected at the 2 latency, because one of its predecessors, v_4, is not scheduled before the 2 latency. Then after v_4 is scheduled, v_5 can be selected at the 3 latency, because its predecessors, v_3 and v_4, are scheduled. At last, v_n is selected at 4 latency, because its predecessor, v_5 is scheduled.

In ASAP for minimum latency scheduling algorithm:

Step 1: schedule v_0 by setting $t_0^s = 1$. This step is for launching the calculation of the algorithm.

Step 2: select a node v_i whose predecessors are all scheduled. This process will be repeated until the sink node V_n is selected.

Step 3: schedule v_i by setting $t_i^s = \max\limits_{j:v_j \rightarrow v_i \in E} t_j^s + d_j$. The equation represents the current node status at the exact timing unit. It represents the latency time at the current node is summing up the maximum latency time of the predecessors' nodes.

Step 4: repeat Step 2 until v_n is scheduled.

5.2.6.2 ALAP

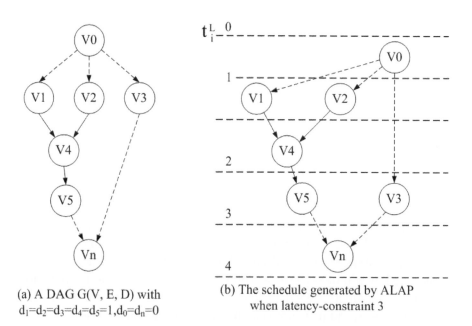

(a) A DAG G(V, E, D) with $d_1=d_2=d_3=d_4=d_5=1,d_0=d_n=0$

(b) The schedule generated by ALAP when latency-constraint 3

Figure 5.13 ALAP scheduling for latency-constraint scheduling.

As shown in Fig. 5.13, first, schedule the button node v_n at the time latency 3+1, and set $t_n^L = 4$. In this step, v_n is scheduled. Then v_3 and v_5 can be selected at the 3 time latency, because their successor, v_n, is scheduled. In this step, v_3 and v_5 are scheduled. Then v_4 can be selected at the 2 time latency, because its successor, v_5, is scheduled. In this step, v_4 is scheduled. In this time latency, although v_0 is the predecessor of v_3, it cannot be selected at the 2 time latency, because v_0's other successors, v_1 and v_2, are not scheduled. Then v_1 and v_2 can be selected at the 1 time latency, because their successor, v_4, is scheduled. In this step, v_1 and v_2 are scheduled. At last, v_0 can be selected at 1 time latency, because its successor, v_1, v_2, and v_3, are scheduled, and d_0 is 0.

In ALAP for latency-constraint (λ) scheduling algorithm:

Step 1: schedule v_n by setting $t_n^L = \lambda + 1$. This step means the first scheduled node is v_n.

Step 2: select a node v_i whose successors are all scheduled. It means the selected node must be a node whose successors must be scheduled. This process will be repeated until the source node v_0 is selected.

Step 3: schedule v_i by setting $t_i^L = \min\limits_{j:v_j \to v_i \in E} t_j^L + d_j$. The equation represents the current node status at the exact timing unit. It represents that the latency time at the current node is subtracting the sum of minimum latency times from the sink node's latency-constraint.

Step 4: repeat Step 2 until v_0 is scheduled. Fig. 5.13 exhibits an ALAP scheduling for latency-constraint scheduling.

Comparing ASAP and ALAP scheduling as shown in Fig. 5.12 and Fig. 5.13, we can find that v_3 can be completed at several time latencies. It can be completed at 1 time latency as soon as possible, and 3 time latency as late as possible.

In this section, we introduce some basic concepts, such as CPU utilization, waiting time, response time, and completion time. Then we introduce some scheduling algorithms, including *First-Come, First Server, Shortest-Job-First, priority scheduling, Round Robin, As-Soon-As-Possible*, and *As-Late-As-Possible*. In the next section, we introduce the processor technology about scheduling algorithm in single processor and multi-processor.

5.3 MEMORY TECHNOLOGY

Memory is one of the fastest evolving technologies in embedded systems over the recent decade. No matter how fast processors can run, there is one unchanged fact so that every embedded system needs memory to store data. Furthermore, with the rapid development of the processor, more and more data pass back and forth between the processor and the memory. The bandwidth of a memory, which is the speed of the memory, becomes the major constraint impacting the system's performance.

When building an embedded system, the designers should consider the overall performance of the memory in the system. There are two key metrics for memory performance: *write ability* and *storage permanence*. Writing in memory can be various in different memory technologies. Some kinds of memories, such as *Random-Access Memory* (RAM), require special devices or techniques for writing. A RAM device allows data items to be read and written in roughly the same amount of time regardless of the order in which data items are accessed. The two main forms of modern RAM are *Static RAM* (SRAM) and *Dynamic RAM* (DRAM). In SRAM, a bit of data is stored using the state of a six transistor memory cells. This form of RAM is more expensive to produce, but it is generally faster and requires less power than DRAM and, in modern computers, is often used as cache memory for the CPU. DRAM stores a bit of data using a transistor and capacitor pair, which together comprise a DRAM memory cell. The capacitor holds a high or low charge (1 or 0, respectively), and the transistor acts as a switch that lets the control circuitry on the chip read the capacitor's state of charge or change it. As this form of memory is less expensive to produce than static RAM, it is the predominant form of computer memory used in modern computers.

At the high end of the memory technology, we can select the memory that the processor can write to simply in a short time. There are some kinds of memories that can be accessed by setting address lines, or data bits, or control lines appropriately. At the middle of the range of memory technology, some slow written memory can be chosen. At the low end are the types of memory that require special equipment for writing.

Besides the write ability, we also need to take storage permanence into consideration. How long the memory can hold the written bits in themselves can have a key impact on the reliability of the system.

In the aspect of storage permanence, there are two kinds of memory technologies: *nonvolatile* and *volatile*. The major difference is that the nonvolatile memory can hold the written bits after power is no longer supplied, but volatile cannot. The nonvolatile memory is typically used for the task of secondary storage, or long-term persistent storage. Meanwhile, the most widely used form of primary storage today is volatile memory. When the computer is shut down, anything contained in the volatile memory is lost. The advanced memory technology needs to attach to the operating system. Dynamic programming is an option for heterogeneous memories' optimizations, which will be discussed in Chapter 7.

5.4   MOBILE EMBEDDED SYSTEMS

5.4.1   Embedded Systems in Mobile Devices

A mobile device is a typical embedded system, which is formed by a group of electronic components, such as mobile processors, storage, memory, graphics, sensors, camera, battery, and other chips. Integrating these electronic parts is to achieve a variety of desired functions for different purposes. In this section, we will use the smartphone to represent an example of a mobile embedded system. A smart phone is one of the most adopted mobile devices in contemporary people's lives.

Currently, the hardware structures of most smartphones are two-processor frameworks. The two processors are the application processor and the baseband processor, which are shown in Fig. 5.14. The *Application Processor* is in charge of running a mobile operating system and various kinds of mobile apps. It is the one that controls the whole system. Most functions provided by chips, such as the keyboard, screen, camera, and sensors, are controlled by the application processor.

Meanwhile, the *Baseband Processor* is responsible for wireless communication. This wireless communication is not the cellular or Wi-Fi network, and it is the telephone network with *Radio Frequency* (RF). The radio frequency is a rate of oscillation, which corresponds to the frequency of radio waves, and the alternating currents that carry radio signals. The radio frequency module is used to send signals to the telephone network. There are two other basic modules in the *baseband processor*, which are the *Digital Baseband* (DBB) and the *Analog Baseband* (ABB). They modulate and demodulate the voice signal and the digital signal, encode and decode the communication channel,

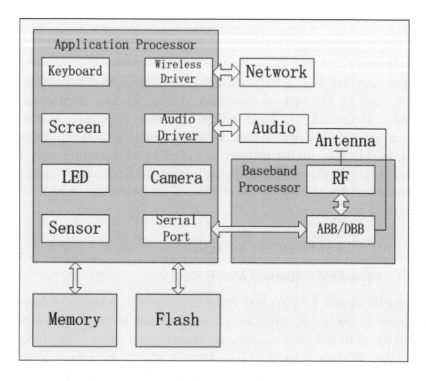

Figure 5.14 Hardware structure of a smartphone.

and control the wireless modem (modulator-demodulator). The application processor communicates with the baseband processor via the serial port, USB, and others.

5.4.2 Embedded Systems in Android

After introducing the hardware structure of the smartphone, we will take Android as an example to explain the Kernel inside Android and show how the Kernel works. As discussed in Chapter 1, Android is based on the Linux Kernel, and the Linux Kernel is an abstract layer between the hardware and the software. The basic functions of Android are provided by the Linux Kernel core system service, such as file management, memory management, process management, network stack, and drivers. The Linux Kernel also provides drivers to support all the hardware related to the mobile embedded system. As shown in Fig. 5.15, there are display driver, keyboard driver, audio driver, power management, Wi-Fi driver, camera driver, and other sensor drivers. We will list some of them and explain what they do.

Display Driver. It is based on the framebuffer driver in Linux. The framebuffer offers a mechanism that allows the application to directly control the change of the screen.

Keyboard Driver. It is the driver for buttons on the mobile device, such as the Home button, the Menu button, the Return button, and the Power button.

Wi-Fi Driver. It is the driver for Wi-Fi connection based on IEEE 802.11.

Sensor Driver. Most Android-powered devices have built-in sensors that measure motion, orientation, and various environmental conditions. These sensors are capable of providing raw data with high precision and accuracy, and are useful if you want to monitor three-dimensional device movement or positioning, or you want to monitor changes in the ambient environment near a device.

For example, a game might track readings from a device's gravity sensor to infer complex user gestures and motions, such as tilt, shake, rotation, or swing. Likewise, a weather application might use a device's temperature sensor and humidity sensor to calculate and report the dewpoint, or a travel application might use the geomagnetic field sensor and accelerometer to report a compass bearing.

Above the Linux Kernel is the hardware abstraction layer, which provides an easy way for applications to discover the hardware on the system. The "abstract" of the hardware abstraction layer does not mean the real operations of the hardware, and the operations of the hardware are still achieved by drivers. However, the interfaces offered by the hardware abstraction layer make it simple for developers to "use" the hardware.

Hardware Abstraction Layer *Hardware abstraction layer is a software subsystem for UNIX-based operating systems providing hardware abstraction. The purpose of the hardware abstraction layer is to allow application to discover and use the hardware of the host system through a simple, portable, and abstract Application Programming Interface (API), regardless of the type of the underlying hardware.*

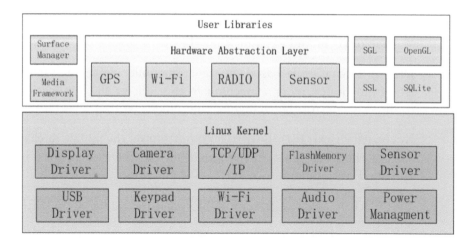

Figure 5.15 Linux Kernel of Android.

5.4.3 Power Management of Android

Android supports its own power management (on top of the standard Linux power management) designed with the premise that the CPU should not consume power if no applications or services require power. As shown in Fig. 5.16, Android requires that applications and services request CPU resources with *wake locks* through the Android application framework and native Linux libraries. If there are no active *wake locks*, Android will shut down the CPU. The *wake locks* are used by applications and services to request CPU resources. The power management uses *wake locks* and time-out mechanism to switch the state of system power, so that system power consumption decreases.

Currently, Android only supports screen, keyboard, buttons backlight, and the brightness of the screen. As shown in Fig. 5.17, when a user application acquires full wake lock or a screen/keyboard touch activity event occurs, the machine will enter "awake" state. If timeout happens or the power key is pressed, the machine will enters the "notification" state. If partial wake locks are acquired, it will remain in "notification". If all partial locks are released, the machine will go into "sleep."

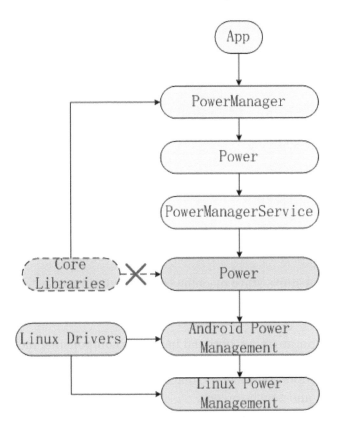

Figure 5.16 Power management of Android.

5.4.4 Embedded Systems in Mobile Apps

The mobile embedded systems are under the layer of mobile operating systems. The mobile embedded systems cannot directly used by mobile apps, and they only can be used through mobile operating systems, such as iOS and Android. We will take Android as an example.

Android is already an embedded operating system, and its roots are derived from embedded Linux. The main hardware platform for Android is the Acorn RISC Machine (ARM) architecture. ARM is a family of instruction set architectures for computer processors based on a reduced instruction set computing architecture. An approach that is based on reduced instruction set reduces costs, heat, and power consumption. Such reductions are desirable traits for light, portable, battery-powered devices, and other embedded systems. Android de-

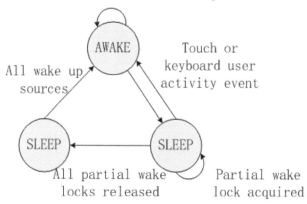

Figure 5.17 A finite-state machine of the Android power management.

vices incorporate many optional hardware components, including cameras, GPS, orientation sensors, dedicated gaming controls, accelerometers, gyroscopes, barometers, magnetometers, proximity sensors, thermometers, and touch-screens.

We can use Android *Software Development Kit* (SDK) to develop our own mobile apps, and via the methods that are already implemented to use the embedded systems inside a mobile device. For example, developers only can use the camera of a mobile device through calling methods encapsulated in the Android SDK. This design method makes the process of developing mobile apps much simper than old methods. The developers do not need to spend time designing the interaction with embedded systems inside an Android device, and they only need to know what functions Android SDK can provide. We will introduce more knowledge about Android SDK and developing technologies in the next chapter.

5.5   MESSAGING AND COMMUNICATION MECHANISMS

In this section, we will introduce two mechanisms used in Android, including message and communication mechanisms.

5.5.1 Message Mechanisms

Android provides message mechanisms in three core classes: Looper, Handler, and Message. Similar to some other operating system, there is a Message Queue in Android. However, this Message Queue is packaged in Looper class. This class is mainly used to run a message loop for a thread. Threads by default do not have a message loop associated with them. We can call the *prepare()* method in the thread that is to run the loop, and then call *loop()* to process the message queue. The main function of *prepare()* method is defining the Looper object as a ThreadLocal object. After calling the *loop()* method, the Looper thread begins to work, and it continually processes the first message in the message queue. The working mechanism of the *prepare()* and *loop()* method, are shown in Fig. 5.18.

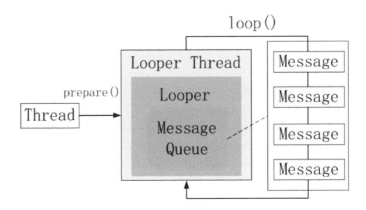

Figure 5.18 prepare() and loop() methods.

Furthermore, we will introduce how to add a message into the message queue. In Android, a Handler allows us to send and process Message and Runnable objects associated with the thread's Message-Queue. Each Handler instance is associated with a single thread and that thread's message queue. A Handler has two main functions: (1) to schedule messages and runnable to be executed as some point in the future, and (2) to enqueue an action to be performed on a different thread than our own.

Fig. 5.19 shows the process of adding a message into the message queue using Handler. First, Handler creates a message. Then, find the

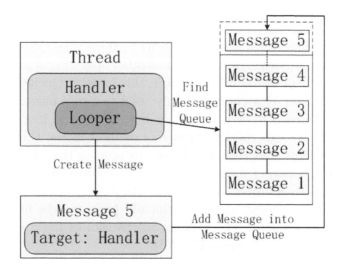

Figure 5.19 Use handler to add message into Message Queue.

related message queue based on the looper. Then add the new message to the end of the message queue.

Message class in Android defines a message containing a description and arbitrary data object that can be sent to a Handler. Although the constructor of Message is public, the best way to get one of these is to call *obtain()* method or *obtainMessage()* method of Handler to save resource costs.

5.5.2   Communication Mechanisms

Android provides the process-unit component model. All Android operations are expressed as Linux processes eventually. Android runs based on the Linux Kernel, and the memory, process, and file management are controlled by the Linux Kernel. The system service is isolated by Linux processes for protection. To support mobile devices, all the default system functions of Android are provided as the server processes. Meanwhile, the functions realized by apps belong to application processes.

In Android, the server process and the application process are implemented by the class *Binder*. Binder is the most important part in Android, and it is the core part of a lightweight Remote Procedure Call (RPC) mechanism. We can derive directly from Binder to implement our own custom RPC protocol or simply instantiate a raw Binder object directly to use a token that can be shared across processes. RPC is a form of Inter Process Communication (IPC), which is a set of techniques for the exchange of data among multiple threads in one or more processes.

Android Interface Definition Language (AIDL) allows us to define the programming interface that both the client and service agree upon in order to communicate with each other using IPC. Normally, one process cannot access the memory of other processes. Processes need to decompose their objects into primitives that the operating system can understand and configure the objects across that boundary.

All system functions of Android are provided as a server process, which makes the optimized communication method between processes extremely important. *Binder* refers to Kernel memory that is shared between all processes to minimize the overhead caused by memory copy. Furthermore, the RPC framework provided by Binder is written in C++, which is more efficient than Java.

In the RPC framework, the kernel space is a place where all processes can share and let each process refer to the memory address. In the Kernel space, a *Binder Driver* is implemented to use the kernel space to convert the memory address that each process has mapped with the memory address of the kernel space for reference. The Binder Driver supports the system call Input/Output Control (ioctl) and the file operations, including open, map, release, and poll. In computer science, ioctl is a system call for device-specific input/output operation and other operations which cannot be expressed by regular system calls.

Fig. 5.20 shows an example of the process of transmitting data from process A to process B. The first thing process A must do is to open the Binder kernel module, and this module uses the descriptor to identify the initiators and recipients of Binder IPCs. After defining the transmission (process A) and the reception (process B) of this operation, process A transmits the data to the Binder Driver first. Then, the Binder Driver converts the memory address of the data to allow process B to access it.

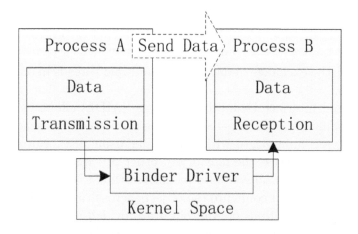

Figure 5.20 Transmit data via Binder Driver in RPC framework.

5.6 EXERCISES

1. What is an embedded system?

2. How are embedded systems used in medical equipment?

3. What is the CPU utilization?

4. What is the average waiting time of some processor jobs?

5. What is First-Come, First-Served scheduling?

6. What is Shortest-Job-First?

7. What is the difference between nonpreemptive and preemptive schemes?

8. What is the key metric for memory performance?

9. What is RAM?

10. What are the constraints for the optimization in embedded systems?

11. Why is a mobile device a embedded system?

12. What is the application processor in mobile devices?

13. What is the baseband processor in mobile devices?

14. What is the hardware abstraction layer in Android?

15. What is the name of the CPU of the iPhone 6?

16. What is the name of the CPU of the HTC One?

17. How does a developer use the function provided by an embedded system inside a mobile device in his/her own apps?

Advanced

1. How do you prove that SJF scheduling has the lowest average waiting time of nonpreemptive schemes with single processors?

2. Is SJF optimal in multiple processors? Considering the average time and the total completion time.

3. Consider that there are six jobs with different completion times and arrival times, as shown in Table 5.1. Please use the FCFS scheduling algorithm to schedule these jobs. You can draw a chart to answer this question.

4. Following the above problem, please use the SJF scheduling algorithm to scheduling these jobs. Calculate the waiting time of each job, the average waiting time, and the total completion time.

5. Following the above problem, consider that we have 3 processors, then use the SJF scheduling algorithm to schedule these jobs. Calculate the waiting time of each job, the average waiting time, and the total completion time.

Table 5.1 Scheduling table for the Question One

Jobs	Arrival Time	Processing Time
j1	0.0	7
j2	2.0	4
j3	3.0	1
j4	5.0	4
j5	6.0	5
j6	8.0	3

6. As shown in Fig. 5.21, use the ASPA and ALAP algorithms to analyze them, and draw charts to explain them.

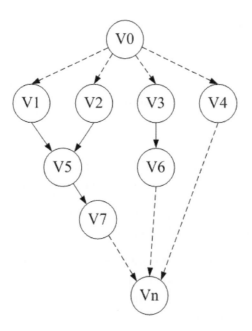

A DAG G-(V, E, D) and
d1=d2=d3=d4=d5=d6=d7=1; d0=dn=0

Figure 5.21 Scheduling DAG for the Question Two

Data Storage and SQLite Operations

CONTENTS

Data STORAGE ON MOBILE DEVICES is a great issue throughout the executions of mobile apps. In the last chapter, we introduced the multimedia in Android, and applied 2-D graphics to improve our Android mini-game. However, if a user is interrupted by some other app when he or she is playing the game, all the data will be lost. We need to consider how to store the data from apps on mobile devices for later use.

In this chapter, we introduce the techniques about storing data in Android. We can store data using several different techniques depending on the size, structure, and lifetime of the data, and whether it will be shared with other apps. We will introduce three methods to store local data, including the preferences Application Programming Interface (API), instance state bundles, and flash memory files. Then we introduce SQLite on Android.

6.1 LOCAL DATA

We can store data using several different techniques depending on the size, structure, and lifetime of the data, and whether it will be shared with other apps. We introduce three methods to store local data, including the preferences API, instance state bundles, and flash memory files.

6.1.1 Internal and External Storage

Android uses a file system that is similar to file systems based on hard drive. In the previous chapter, we briefly introduced several options to store data in Android. Now we introduce the Internal Storage and External Storage in detail.

All Android devices have two file storage areas: "internal" and "external" storage. In the early days of Android, most devices offered built-in, nonvolatile memory, called internal storage, and a removable storage medium, such as SD cards, as the external storage. There are always two storage spaces. The Table 6.1 lists the difference in these two kinds of storage space.

Table 6.1 Differences between Internal and External Storage.

Internal Storage	External Storage
Always available	Not always available
Files are only accessible by the app by default	Files can be read outside, they are world-readable
Files will be removed when uninstalling the app	When uninstalling the app, the system removes the app's files from here only if they are saved in the directory from getExternalFilesDir().

1

As shown in Table 6.1, there are three main difference between the internal storage and the external storage. First, the internal storage is a built-in the mobile device; thus, the data and files stored in the internal storage are always available. Meanwhile, the external storages are removable, such as the SD card and USB storage. The files and data stored in the external storages are not available if the external storages are removed from the device.

Second, the files and data are only accessible by the app that generates these files or data before by default. However, the files and data stored in external storages are world-readable, which means these files and data can be used by all apps [68].

Third, the files and data will be removed when the user uninstalls the app, but the files and data will not be removed unless they are saved in the directory from the *getExternalFilesDir()* method.

In conclusion, internal storage is better when we want to keep the files and data not accessible to the user or other apps. External storage is a better place for files and data that do not require access restrictions and for files and data that are intended to be shared with other apps.

6.1.2   Save a File on Internal Storage

Android runs Linux Kernel at the "low-level," and there is a real file system mounted in there with a root directory and everything. In fact, the main thing an app can access is a package private directory created at install time, (/data/data/packagename), as shown in Fig. 6.1.

When saving a file to internal storage, we can get the directory as a *File* by calling the *getFilesDir()* or *getCacheDir()* methods. The *getFilesDir()* method returns a *File* representing an internal directory for the app. The *getCacheDir()* method returns a *File* representing an internal directory for the app's temporary cache files.

HINT: Remember to delete a cache file once it is no longer needed and implement a reasonable size limit for the amount of memory used every time. The cache files will be deleted without warning if the system needs more capacity on storage.

We can use the *File()* constructor to create a new file in one of these directories, via the *File* provided by one of the above methods. For example:

File file = new File(context.getFilesDir(), filename);

The *Context* class offers some helper methods to let us read and write data there. We list some of the most widely used methods:

openFileInput(), to open a private file for reading.

openFileOutput(), to open a private file for writing.

fileList(), to get a list of all files in the app's private area.

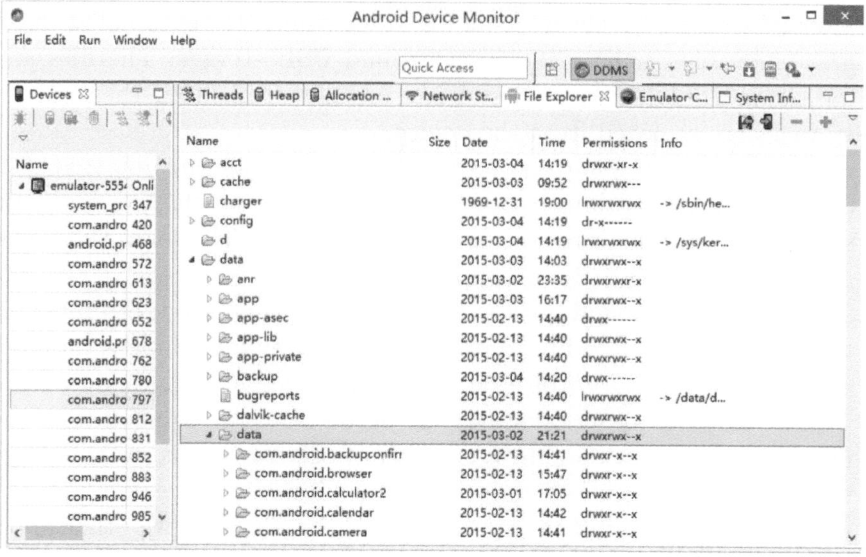

Figure 6.1 "/data/data/" directory in Android device monitor.

deleteFile(), to delete a private file.

For example, we can call *openFileOutput()* to get a *FileOutput-Stream* that writes into a file in the internal directory. The *openFile-Output()* method opens a private file associated with this *Context's* app package for writing, and creates the file if it doesn't exist.

FileOutputStream outputStream;
```
try {
outputStream = openFileOutput("test.txt", Context.MODE_PRIVATE);
outputStream.write("something new".getBytes());
outputStream.close();
} catch (Exception e) {
e.printStackTrace();
}
```

After running the above Android code, we can find that the system writes "something new" into "test.txt" on the directory of "/data/data/(package name)/files", similar to Fig. 6.2. When we create a new Android app project and use an Android Virtual Devices (AVD) to run it, this AVD automatically creates a folder with the same name of the package name of the app in "/data/data" directory.

Furthermore, the "Context.MODE_PRIVATE" indicates that this folder is never accessible to other apps. We can use other flags to let these data be shared with other apps. Using MODE_WORLD_READABLE and MODE_WORLD_WRITEABLE can make data readable and writeable to other apps.

The internal memory is limited, so we suggest keeping the size of any data low, and carefully handle Input/Output (I/O) errors and exceptions when writing in case the space runs out. Then we introduce the other places to store data.

Name	Size	Date	Time	Permissions	Info
▷ 🗀 com.android.smoketest.tests		2015-02-13	14:41	drwxr-x--x	
▷ 🗀 com.android.soundrecorder		2015-02-13	14:41	drwxr-x--x	
▷ 🗀 com.android.speechrecorder		2015-02-13	14:41	drwxr-x--x	
▷ 🗀 com.android.systemui		2015-02-13	14:41	drwxr-x--x	
▷ 🗀 com.android.vpndialogs		2015-02-13	14:41	drwxr-x--x	
▷ 🗀 com.android.wallpaper.livepicker		2015-02-13	14:41	drwxr-x--x	
▷ 🗀 com.android.webview		2015-02-13	14:41	drwxr-x--x	
▷ 🗀 com.android.widgetpreview		2015-02-13	14:41	drwxr-x--x	
▷ 🗀 com.example.android.apis		2015-02-13	14:41	drwxr-x--x	
▷ 🗀 com.example.android.livecubes		2015-02-13	14:41	drwxr-x--x	
▷ 🗀 com.example.android.softkeyboard		2015-02-13	14:41	drwxr-x--x	
▷ 🗀 com.example.csis.pace.edu.colortester		2015-02-28	11:57	drwxr-x--x	
▷ 🗀 com.example.csis.pace.edu.mediatester		2015-03-02	16:44	drwxr-x--x	
▷ 🗀 com.example.csis.pace.edu.mypace		2015-02-17	17:36	drwxr-x--x	
▲ 🗀 com.example.csis.pace.edu.project		2015-03-04	15:33	drwxr-x--x	
▷ 🗀 cache		2015-02-25	21:25	drwxrwx--x	
▲ 🗀 files		2015-03-04	16:55	drwxrwx--x	
📄 test.txt	13	2015-03-04	16:55	-rw-rw----	
📄 lib		2015-02-25	21:25	lrwxrwxrwx	-> /data/a...
▷ 🗀 com.example.csis.pace.edu.sudoku		2015-02-13	17:52	drwxr-x--x	

Figure 6.2 Example of the directory of the new file.

6.1.3   Save a File on External Storage

Currently, all apps have the ability to read the external storage without special permission, but from the official document of Android, it says this will change in a future release. To ensure that our apps continue to work, we should declare the "read" permission now.

<manifest>
<user-permission android:name="android.permission.READ_EXTERNAL_STORAGE"/>
</manifest>

To write to the external storage, we must get the permission first.

<manifest>

<user-permission android:name="android.permission.WRITE_EXTERNAL_STORAGE" />

</manifest>

Different from the internal storage, the external storage may be unavailable some time, such as the files and data in the external storage maybe transferred to a computer, or the SD card is removed from the smartphone. As a result, we must verify whether the external storage is available before accessing it.

The *getExternalStorageState()* method is called to query the external storage state. If the returned state is equal to MEDIA_MOUNTED, then we can read and write the files and data in external storage. Fig. 6.3 is the example for checking the external storage state for reading. There are two conditions that need to be satisfied, which are whether the external storage is available and whether it can be read.

```
//Check the external storage state for read
public boolean isExternalStorageReadable(){
    String state = Environment.getExternalStorageState();
    if(Environment.MEDIA_MOUNTED.equals(state) ||
            Environment.MEDIA_MOUNTED_READ_ONLY.equals(state)){
        return true;
    }
    return false;
}
```

Figure 6.3 Checking the external storage state for reading.

Fig. 6.4 is the example for checking the external storage state for reading and writing files in external storage.

In Android, the external storage can be modified by users and apps, and there are two categories of files:

Public files. The public files should be available to other apps and to the user. When the user uninstalls apps, these files should remain available to the user.

Private files. The private files that rightfully belong to some specific app and should be deleted when the app is uninstalled. Although these files are technically accessible by the user and other apps because they are on the external storage, these files realistically do not provide value to the user outside the app.

```
//Check external storage state for reading and writing
public boolean isExternalStorageWritable(){
    String state = Environment.getExternalStorageState();
    if (Environment.MEDIA_MOUNTED.equals(state)){
        return true;
    }
    return false;
}
```

Figure 6.4 Checking the external storage state for reading and writing

We can use the *getExternalStoragePublicDirectory()* method to save public files on the external storage. This method gets a *File* representing the appropriate directory on the external storage, and it takes an argument specifying the type of file to be saved. For example, we want to get the directory that stores user's public pictures.

```
//get the directory for the public directory
public File getAlbumStorageDir(String name){
    File file = new File(Environment.getExternalStoragePublicDirectory(
            Environment.DIRECTORY_PICTURES), name);
    return file;
}
```

Figure 6.5 Getting the directory of public files.

Then we can call the *getExternalFilesDir()* method to save files and data in private folder. Similar to the *getExternalStoragePublicDirectory()* method, this method also gets a *File* representing the directory on the external storage. However, all directories created this way are added to a parent directory that encapsulates all the app's external storage files, which will be deleted when the app is uninstalled.

The *getExternalFilesDir()* method automatically creates a specific directory that will be deleted when the app is uninstalled. If the files and data should remain available after the app is uninstalled, we should use the *getExternalStoragePublicDirectory()* method.

Both of these two method must use directory names provided by API constants, such as the **DIRECTORY_PICTURES** in the above two examples. These directory names ensure that the files and data are treated properly by the Android system. Besides the

```
//get the directory for the private directory
public File getAlbumStorageDir(Context context, String name){
    File file = new File(context.getExternalFilesDir(
            Environment.DIRECTORY_PICTURES), name);
    return file;
}
```

Figure 6.6 Getting the directory of private files.

DIRECTORY_PICTURES, there are some other API constants, as shown in Fig. 6.7.

DIRECTORY_PICTURES	String
DIRECTORY_ALARMS	String
DIRECTORY_DCIM	String
DIRECTORY_DOCUMENTS	String
DIRECTORY_DOWNLOADS	String
DIRECTORY_MOVIES	String
DIRECTORY_MUSIC	String
DIRECTORY_NOTIFICATIONS	String
DIRECTORY_PODCASTS	String
DIRECTORY_RINGTONES	String

Figure 6.7 Directory names provided by API constants.

6.1.4 Delete a File

As mentioned in the first chapter, mobile devices have limited resources; thus, it is extremely important to delete files that are no longer needed. The most straightforward and widely used way to delete a file is to have the opened file reference call *delete()* on itself. The *delete()* method returns true if the file is deleted, and returns false otherwise.

If we want to delete a file on internal storage, we can get the directory using the *getFilesDir()* method, and then create a new *File* that is the file to be deleted. Fig. 6.8 shows the process of deleting a *File* on internal storage and the result of logcat, which shows the result that the file is deleted successfully.

If we want to delete a file on external storage, we can use the *getEx-*

```
public void deleteTest(){
    //delete a File on internal storage via its name
    File dir = getFilesDir();
    File file = new File(dir, "test.txt");
    Boolean bool = file.delete();
    Log.i("DELETE A FILE", bool.toString());
}
```

logcat

03-05 16:03:39.449   4951-4951/com.example.csis.pace.edu.project I/DELETE A FILE: true

Figure 6.8 Deleting a File from Internal Storage

ternalFilesDir() and *getExternalStoragePublicDirectory()* methods to get the directory of the file, and then create a new *File* that is the file to be deleted. However, before we delete some files, we need to make sure that we have the permission to delete them. Jump into AndroidManifest.xml and check whether we have the `WRITE_EXTERNAL_STORAGE` permission. If not, add the permission as introduced in Section 6.1.3

The first step of deleting files in public and private directories is similar to the processes of getting the directory of public and private directories. Fig. 6.9 is an example of deleting an album file in public directory.

```
public void deleteAlbumStorage(String name){
    File file = new File(Environment.getExternalStoragePublicDirectory(
            Environment.DIRECTORY_PICTURES), name);
    file.delete();
}
```

Figure 6.9 Deleting Album File in Public Directory with Name.

6.1.5 Query the Space

Before we store some files or data into a device, we can check whether sufficient space is available to avoid causing IOException. We can use *getFreeSpace()* to get the amount of space available and *getTotalSpace()* to get the amount of total space in the storage volume. Both of these two methods return numbers in bytes and return 0 if the path does not exist. For example, Fig. 6.10 shows the function of getting the current available and total space in the internal storage. The result is shown in Fig. 6.11.

```
public void getSpace(){
    File dir = getFilesDir();
    String free = ""+ dir.getFreeSpace();
    String total = "" + dir.getTotalSpace();
    Log.i("Free Space", free);
    Log.i("Total Space", total);
}
```

Figure 6.10 Getting the current available and total space in the internal storage.

```
logcat                                                                                    ⟶
  03-05 20:32:57.547    901-901/com.example.csis.pace.edu.project I/Free Space:  390037504
  03-05 20:32:57.548    901-901/com.example.csis.pace.edu.project I/Total Space: 567640064
```

Figure 6.11 Result of getSpace().

In fact, the Android system does not guarantee that we can store as many bytes as the number gotten by the *getFreeSpace()* method, because the system needs some space to deal with other operations. If the number gotten by the *getFreeSpace()* method is a few more than the space we need, or if there is more than 10% available space, it is safe to store the file. Otherwise, the process of storing may not be successful.

If we do not know exactly how much space we need to store a file, we can try to write the file, and then catch an *IOException* if one occurs. In many situations, we cannot know the exact size of a file beforehand, such as extracting a file from a compressed format.

6.2 SQLITE DATABASE

SQLite is an open-source SQL database that stores data to a text file on devices. It supports all the relational database, so we do not need to establish any kind of connections for using it, such as Java Database Connectivity (JDBC) and Open Database Connectivity (ODBC). The SQLite database is embedded in Android, and the APIs to use a

Table 6.2 Contacts Table Structure

Field	Type	Key
ID	Int	Primary
Name	Text	
Phone_number	Text	

database on Android are available in the *android.database.sqlite* package.

6.2.1 Table Structure

One of the main principles of SQL databases is the schema, a formal declaration of how the database is organized. The schema is reflected in the SQL statements that you use to create your database. We will build a simple table, called contacts, to illustrate the SQLite techniques on Android. The table structure is shown in Table 6.2.

The ID is the primary key, and its type is int, while name and **phone_number** are regular attributes whose types are Text. Before we use SQLite techniques to implement create, update, delete, and read functions, we need to create an individual class, named Contact, with getters and setters, as follows.

6.2.2 CRUD Operations

Then we need to create our own class to handle all database CRUD (create, read, update, and delete) operations. Similar to the process of Contact class, we create a new class, named DatabaseHandler, and make it extend SQLiteOpenHelper.

public class DatabaseHandler extends SQLiteOpenHelper

After extending DatabaseHandler class from SQLiteOpenHelper, we need to override two methods, which are *onCreate()* and *onUpgrade()*. The *onCreate()* method is where we need to write table statements. It is called when a database is created. The *onUpgrade()* method is called when a database is upgraded, like modifying the table structure, adding constraints to database etc.

Before overriding these two methods, we need to create and define some private attributes, as shown in Fig. 6.13. We define the database name, table name, and column names. The DatabaseHandler(Context context) is the constructor.

```java
public class Contact {
  int _id;
  String _name;
  String _phone_number;

  public Contact(){}

  public Contact(int id, String name, String _phone_number){
    this._id = id;
    this._name = name;
    this._phone_number = _phone_number;
  }

  public Contact(String name, String _phone_number){
    this._name = name;
    this._phone_number = _phone_number;
  }

  // getting ID
  public int getID(){
    return this._id;
  }

  // setting id
  public void setID(int id){
    this._id = id;
  }

  // getting name
  public String getName(){
    return this._name;
  }

  // setting name
  public void setName(String name){
    this._name = name;
  }

  // getting phone number
  public String getPhoneNumber(){
    return this._phone_number;
  }

  // setting phone number
  public void setPhoneNumber(String phone_number){
    this._phone_number = phone_number;
  }
}
```

Figure 6.12 Example of contact.

```
// All Static variables
// Database Version
private static final int DATABASE_VERSION = 1;

// Database Name
private static final String DATABASE_NAME = "contactsManager";

// Contacts table name
private static final String TABLE_CONTACTS = "contacts";

// Contacts Table Columns names
private static final String KEY_ID = "id";
private static final String KEY_NAME = "name";
private static final String KEY_PH_NO = "phone_number";

public DatabaseHandler(Context context) {
    super(context, DATABASE_NAME, null, DATABASE_VERSION);
}
```

Figure 6.13 Some private attributes in DatabaseHandler Class.

Then we override the *onCreate()* and *onUpgrade()* methods. In the *onCreate()* method, we create and define a sql sentence to create a table, and use the execSQL() method to implement it. In the *onUpgrade()* method, we delete the Contacts table and recreate it. The code of these two methods are shown in Fig. 6.14. The SQL sentence of creating a table is: *CREATE TABLE table_name (attribute1 TYPE PRIMARY KEY, attribute2 TYPE, ...)*.

```
@Override
public void onCreate(SQLiteDatabase db) {
    String CREATE_CONTACTS_TABLE = "CREATE TABLE " + TABLE_CONTACTS + "("
            + KEY_ID + " INTEGER PRIMARY KEY," + KEY_NAME + " TEXT,"
            + KEY_PH_NO + " TEXT" + ")";
    db.execSQL(CREATE_CONTACTS_TABLE);
}

@Override
public void onUpgrade(SQLiteDatabase db, int oldVersion, int newVersion) {
    // Drop older table if existed
    db.execSQL("DROP TABLE IF EXISTS " + TABLE_CONTACTS);

    // Create tables again
    onCreate(db);
}
```

Figure 6.14 onCreate() and onUpgrade() methods.

Now we need to implement CRUD operations of the database. Fig. 6.15 is an overview of the methods we used. We implement the following functions: adding a new contact, getting a single contact, getting all contacts, updating a single contact, and deleting a single contact.

```
//CRUD
//Add new contact
public void addContact(Contact contact){...}

//Get single contact
public Contact getContact(int id){...}

//Get all contacts
public List<Contact> getAllContacts(){...}

//Update single contact
public int updateContact(Contact contact){...}

//Delete single contact
public void deleteContact(Contact contact){...}
```

Figure 6.15 Overview of CRUD operations.

Create Operation: addContact()

The parameter of the addContact() method is Contact object, which will be created and added into the database. We need to build Content-Values parameters using Contact object. ContentValues class is similar to Hashtable class, and it is in charge of storing key-value pairs. The detailed implementation of the addContact() method is shown in Fig. 6.16. Once we insert data in the database, we need to close the database connection.

```
public void addContact(Contact contact){
    SQLiteDatabase db = this.getWritableDatabase();

    ContentValues values = new ContentValues();
    values.put(KEY_NAME, contact.getName());
    values.put(KEY_PH_NO, contact.getPhoneNumber());

    db.insert(TABLE_CONTACTS, null, values);
    db.close();
}
```

Figure 6.16 addContact() Method.

Read Operations: getContact() and getAllContacts()

We use the getContact() method to read a single contact and the getAllContacts() method to read all contacts from database. The parameter of the getContact() method is ID, and we do not need any parameter. The implementation of getContact() is shown in Fig. 6.17, and the implementation of getAllContacts() is shown in Fig. 6.18. In these two methods, we use a cursor to point a single row of the result fetched by the query.

```java
public Contact getContact(int id){
    SQLiteDatabase db = this.getReadableDatabase();

    Cursor cursor = db.query(TABLE_CONTACTS, new String[]{KEY_ID,KEY_ID,KEY_PH_NO},
            KEY_ID + "=?", new String[] { String.valueOf(id) }, null, null, null, null);
    if(cursor != null){
        cursor.moveToFirst();
    }
    Contact contact = new Contact(Integer.parseInt(cursor.getString(0)),
            cursor.getString(1), cursor.getString(2));

    return contact;
}
```

Figure 6.17 getContact() Method.

```java
public List<Contact> getAllContacts(){
    List<Contact> contactList = new ArrayList<Contact>();

    String sql_select = "SELECT * FROM "+ TABLE_CONTACTS;

    SQLiteDatabase db = this.getWritableDatabase();
    Cursor cursor = db.rawQuery(sql_select, null);

    if(cursor.moveToFirst()){
        while(cursor.moveToNext()){
            Contact contact = new Contact();
            contact.setID(Integer.parseInt(cursor.getString(0)));
            contact.setName(cursor.getString(1));
            contact.setPhoneNumber(cursor.getString(2));
            // Adding contact to list
            contactList.add(contact);
        }
    }
    return contactList;
}
```

Figure 6.18 getAllContacts() Method.

Update Operation: updataContact()

We use updateContact() to update single contacts in the database.

The parameter of this method is Contact object. Similar to addContact(), we use a ContentValues to encapsulate as a contact object, and then replace the old contact with the new encapsulated one via ID. The implementation of the updateContact() method is shown in Fig. 6.19.

```java
public int updateContact(Contact contact){
    SQLiteDatabase db = this.getWritableDatabase();

    ContentValues values = new ContentValues();
    values.put(KEY_NAME, contact.getName());
    values.put(KEY_PH_NO, contact.getPhoneNumber());

    return db.update(TABLE_CONTACTS, values, KEY_ID + " =?",
            new String[] {String.valueOf(contact.getID())});
}
```

Figure 6.19 updateContact() Method.

Delete Operation: deleteContact()

We use deleteContact() method to delete single contact from database using the parameter of a Contact object. The implementation of the deleteContact() method is shown in Fig. 6.20.

```java
public void deleteContact(Contact contact){
    SQLiteDatabase db = this.getWritableDatabase();
    db.delete(TABLE_CONTACTS, KEY_ID + " =?",
            new String[]{String.valueOf(contact.getID())});
    db.close();
}
```

Figure 6.20 deleteContact() Method.

6.2.3   Usage of SQLite Techniques

After we create a Contact class and a DatabaseHandler class, we will introduce how to use them in an Android app. In the onCreate() method of an activity, we create an object of DatabaseHandler as follows: *DatabaseHandler db = new DatabaseHandler(this).*
Then we test the usage of the addContact() method as follows. To make it simple to trace the result, we use Log.d() to print some note information. The running results are shown in Fig. 6.21.

Then we test the usage of getAllContacts() as follows. We use a

```
Log.d("Insert", "Inserting ...");
db.addContact(new Contact("AAA", "1233211232"));
Log.d("Insert AAA", "Success!");
db.addContact(new Contact("BBB", "9143493981"));
Log.d("Insert BBB", "Success!");
```

```
10-27 17:23:32.200    2287-2287/? D/Insert : Inserting ...
10-27 17:23:32.230    2287-2287/? D/Insert AAA : Success!
10-27 17:23:32.240    2287-2287/? D/Insert BBB : Success!
```

Figure 6.21 Running result about addContact() and getAllContacts().

```
Log.d("Reading: ", "Reading all contacts..");
contacts = db.getAllContacts();
for (Contact cn : contacts) {
    String log = "Id: " + cn.getID() + " ,Name: " + cn.getName() + " ,Phone: " +
cn.getPhoneNumber();
    // Writing Contacts to log
    Log.d("Name: ", log);
}
```

```
Reading:    Reading all contacts..
Name:       Id: 2 ,Name: AAA ,Phone: 1233211232
Name:       Id: 3 ,Name: BBB ,Phone: 9143493981
```

Figure 6.22 Running result about getAllContacts().

foreach loop in our implementation and print every record of contacts fetched from the database. The running result is shown in Fig. 6.22.

For deleting one contact from database, the implementation is similar to the previous ones. We use a loop to delete all contacts in the database and print them before they are deleted. Furthermore, we use getAllContacts() to double-check the function of the delectContact() method, and the result is shown in Fig. 6.23. After "Reading all contacts..", there are no records printed, which indicates that we have deleted all the contacts in database.

Last, we test the updateContact() method. From the printed log before, we know that the ID of AAA contact is 2. We plan to update this contact from ("AAA", "1233211232") to ("CCC", "3213213121"). Before updating this contact, we print some information to help us to locate useful information in logcat. The running result is shown in Fig. 6.24.

```
Log.d("deleting:", "Deleting all contacts..");
for (Contact c : contacts){
    String log = "Id: " + c.getID() + " ,Name: " + c.getName() + " ,Phone: " +
c.getPhoneNumber();
    Log.d("Delete:", log);
    db.deleteContact(c);
}
```

```
deleting:   Deleting all contacts..
Delete:     Id: 2 ,Name: AAA ,Phone: 1233211232
Delete:     Id: 3 ,Name: BBB ,Phone: 9143493981
Reading:    Reading all contacts..
            HostConnection::get() New Host Connection established 0
            0, tid 3546
```

Figure 6.23 Running Result of deleteContact()

```
Log.d("Update", "AAA->CCC");
Contact contact1 = db.getContact(2);
Log.d("Old Contact", contact1.getName());
contact1.setName("CCC");
contact1.setPhoneNumber("3213213121");
Log.d("New Contact", contact1.getName());
db.updateContact(contact1);
```

```
Update          AAA->CCC
Old Contact     AAA
New Contact     CCC
Reading:        Reading all contacts..
Name:           Id: 2 ,Name: CCC ,Phone: 3213213121
Name:           Id: 3 ,Name: BBB ,Phone: 9143493981
```

Figure 6.24 Running result of updateContact().

6.3   CONTENT PROVIDER

If we need to share data among multiple applications, we can use content providers to achieve this purpose. Content providers are one of the primary building blocks of Android applications, providing content to applications. They encapsulate data and provide it to applications through the single *ContentResolver* interface.

When a request is made via a *ContentResolver*, the system inspects the authority of the given *Uniform Resource Identifier* (URI) and passes the request to the content provider registered with the authority. The content provider can interpret the rest of the URI however it wants. The *UriMatcher* class is helpful for parsing URIs.

The primary methods that need to be implemented are:

1. onCreate(), which is called to initialize the provider

2. query(Uri, String[], String, String[], String), which returns data to the caller

3. insert(Uri, ContentValues), which inserts new data into the content provider

4. update(Uri, ContentValues, String, String[]), which updates existing data in the content provider

5. delete(Uri, String, String[]), which deletes data from the content provider

6. getType(Uri), which returns the MIME type of data in the content provider

We will use a simple example to show how to use content providers. After creating a regular blank Android app, create a normal Java class, named BirthProvider, extends *ContentProvider*. First thing we need to do is to override onCreate(), query(), insert(), update(), delete(), and getType() methods. All content providers have to implement the same interface for further use.

Then we will use *Urimatcher* class to map the content URIs with particular patterns, which will help us to choose the desired action for an incoming content URI. Data in content providers are similar to a single database. Every column has a unique numerical type value, **named_ID**, which is used to locate specific record. The return result of content provider query is Cursor. Every content provider must have a unique public URI, which is used to determine the data set pointing to it. One content provider can have multiple data sets (like multiple tables), and in this kind of situation, multiple URIs are needed to be corresponding to each data set. These URIs must be started with "content: //".

BirthProvider.java codes are provided in the Appendices.

From the beginning to here, we finished the implementation part of our content provider Android app. The next thing we need to do is the user interface. We add two EditTexts into the layout to let users fill in the name and the birthday, and three buttons to add, show, and delete records corresponding to the three methods in activity respectively. Fig. 6.25 shows the user interface. The running result is shown in Fig. 6.26.

Figure 6.25   The user interface of CPTester.

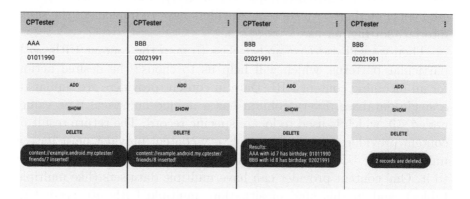

Figure 6.26   The running result of CPTester.

6.4   EXERCISES

6.4.1   Basic Exercises

1. What aspects of data are considered for storing?

2. What does PreferenceActivity do?

3. What can preferences API do for more than just options?

4. Which method will be overriden when restoring from saved game?

5. What do normal Android views do aiming at the screen orientation?

6. Is instance state permanent?

7. Where is instance state stored?

8. What is instance state used for?

9. Is there a real file system in Android?

10. Where are the usual Java file I/O routines methods in Android?

11. What are common methods for reading and writing data provided by the Context class?

12. What does deleteFile() method do?

13. What does fileList() method do?

14. What does openFileInput() do?

15. What does operFileOutput() do?

16. What is an SD card? Can an SD card be used for code?

17. How do you get the directory on the external file system?

6.4.2 Advanced Exercises

1. How many kinds of techniques can be used to store data in Android? What are they?

2. What is the difference between storing data in a device and on an SD card?

CHAPTER 7

Mobile Optimization by Dynamic Programming

CONTENTS

Optimization BY USING HETEROGENEOUS COM-PUTINGS is one of the crucial methods for increasing performances. Embedded systems have many constraints, such as time, reliability, and energy consumption. Balancing these constraints is an efficient mechanism to increase the performance of an embedded system. Therefore, leveraging heterogeneous computing in mobile embedded systems is an optimization problem. Dynamic programming is an important approach for optimizing embedded systems, and this has been broadly used in multiple industries and mobile domains. This chapter focuses on introducing the updated mechanism of adopting dynamic programming in embedded systems. The represented schema is named Heterogeneous Embedded Systems (HES) that can be used to enable embedded systems to accomplish works with the least resource costs under a specific timing constraint. Two models of heterogeneous embedded systems are introduced in this chapter. The main contents of this chapter include:

1. Dynamic programming

2. Heterogenous embedded systems

3. Fixed time model of heterogenous embedded systems

4. Probabilistic time model of heterogenous embedded systems

This chapter intends to instruct students to learn an important mechanism being used in the current mobile optimization domains, which is HES. This is an important mechanism for increasing the performance of the heterogeneous memory. The system is based on leveraging dynamic programming algorithm and the corresponding implementations will be covered in this chapter. A few examples and case studies will be given in this chapter to aid students to further understand the schemas of dynamic programming. Throughout this chapter, students should be able to answer the following questions:

1. What is the HES?

2. What is dynamic programming?

3. What are main schemas of optimizing HES?

4. How many main phases for optimizing HES? What are they?

5. How can you optimize a Fixed Time Model of HES?

6. How can you optimize a Probabilistic Time Model of HES?

7. Why can the optimization problems of HES be considered a pseudo polynomial problem?

8. What is a non-deterministic polynomial-time problem?

7.1 INTRODUCTION OF HETEROGENEOUS EMBEDDED SYSTEMS AND DYNAMIC PROGRAMMING

Modern embedded systems have a variety of features, such as specific-purpose design, dependability to other devices, and readable only memory [69, 70, 30, 71]. An embedded system may have all or some of these features, which depend on the practical demands. A Heterogeneous Embedded System (HES) is a method of deploying multiple functional units in an embedded system for achieving a higher-level performance [72, 35, 73]. In a real-time perspective, heterogeneity is one of the significant characteristics [74]. The term *Heterogeneity* refers to multiple basic operating units, such as memories, processors, and graphic processing units. Addressing the executive timing issues, there are two types of HESs. The first type is Fixed Time Model (FTM), which represents a model that has a fixed value for each task's execution time. The other type is Probabilistic Time Model (PTM) that has a non-fixed value for each task's execution time. The non-fixed value is defined as a random variable in PTM.

Moreover, the process costs can be reduced when heterogeneous functional units can efficiently collaborate with each other [75]. In computer science, a *Functional Unit* is a low-level component or a group of components that are used for a specific purpose, such as arithmetic functions, assignments [76], logic operations, or to compare operations. Multiple hardware can be a carrier of a functional unit, such as memories, registers, or storage units. The benefit of functional units is associated with multiple aspects, such as energy, system reliability, or infrastructure usage. Discerning this model can assist students to further understand the concept of an embedded system and its heterogeneity-based solutions. An efficient solution usually consists of two phases, including *Heterogeneous Assignment* phase and *Minimizing Costs by Scheduling* phase. The following sections represent the details of these two phases.

The crucial mechanism of heterogeneous embedded systems optimizations is applying dynamic programming [77]. *Dynamic Programming* is an approach of solving complicated problem by dividing the problem into smaller-sized sub-problems [78]. Dynamic programming approaches are usually used for optimizing systems or processes via minimizing the resourcing costs under a or a number of desired constraints [79, 80]. In HES, dynamic programming mainly offers the timing constraints under which the computing resources are minimized, such as energy costs and reliability risks [19, 81]. The following content covers *FTM of HES* in Section 7.2 and *PTM of HES* in Section 7.3.

7.2 FIXED TIME MODEL

A Fixed Time Model (FTM) is a model consisting of a number of nodes that all have fixed value with the specific execution times [82]. As mentioned in Section 7.1, optimization of FTM is formed by two steps: the *Heterogeneous Assignment* phase and the *Minimizing Costs by Scheduling* phase. *Heterogeneous Assignment* is a process of creating a table that represents crucial information concerning the optimizations, such as functional units and executive time [83, 84]. The second phase, *Minimizing Costs by Scheduling*, is to use dynamic programming to schedule the working modes for achieving the minimum costs [85, 86]. The following contents will give a detailed introduction about these two phases.

7.2.1 Heterogeneous Assignment

This section focuses on explaining what the *Heterogeneous Assignment* is and what methods can accomplish the work. In the first phase, the task of *Heterogeneous Assignment* is to generate a table with the information of process types and the corresponding costs [87, 88, 89]. The costs can be in multiple types or manners, such as energy, time, or probabilities. Fig. 7.1 represents an example of a data flow graph for functional units being used to minimize the costs. A Data Flow Graph (DFG) is an approach using graphic diagrams to represent data dependencies or functional units between operations [69, 90]. In the given example, the DFG workflow has a variety of nodes that demand distinct executive time and energy consumptions when using various types of functional units.

As displayed in Fig. 7.1, circles with coded numbers represent nodes. For completing each node, there might be a variety of functional types with different consumption demands. Each functional type can accomplish the task but the performances can be various. For instance, a node can run slower but with less energy on one type of functional unit than it does on another [91].

Fig. 7.2 gives an example of DFG with two types of functional units, which is associated with Fig. 7.1. The figure illustrates a scenario assuming that two functional units are selected from functional

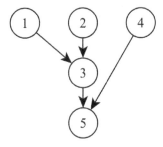

Figure 7.1 An example of a data flow graph with functional units.

units libraries, which are P1 and P2. The trade-off options are time and energy costs, which are shown in the figure. Five tables in the figure represent functional types and the corresponding accomplishment times and energy consumptions. *P* refers to a path by using one type of functional unit. The number attached to *P* represents the exact functional type, and the relevant parameters are given in the following columns. For example, *P1* at node 1 needs 9-unit energy cost to finish the task in 2-unit time.

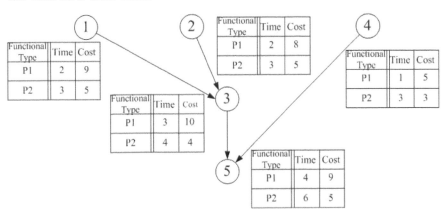

Figure 7.2 An example of a data flow graph with two types of functional units.

Deploying different functional units at nodes can result in different performances under distinct timing constraints. An optimization can be made if a combination of functional units selections can cause less energy consumption within a specific timing constraint. This aim

Table 7.1 Nodes with Different Functional Units.

Nodes	P1		P2	
	T_1	C_1	T_2	C_2
1	2	9	3	5
2	2	8	3	5
3	3	10	4	4
4	1	5	3	3
5	4	9	6	5

means that an output concerning the minimized costs for each node aligning with the corresponding functional unit will be generated. Constraints are variables that will determine the types of functional units. Considering the configuration of timing constraints, a functional unit can be selected to achieve the lowest costs.

Aligning with Fig. 7.1, all selections can be synthesized into a table, which is shown in Table 7.1. In the table, "T_i" represents the executive time and "C_i" means the executive costs for each functional units type P_i. Among T and C, "i" can be either 1 or 2. Once finishing the *Heterogeneous Assignment*, using the approach introduced in Section 7.2.2 can achieve an optimal solution. Fig. 7.3 represents two ways of scheduling by different assignments under a timing constraint 11. Fig. 7.3 (a) gives an optimal solution with a total cost 26. Fig. 7.3 (b) also can finish the work within timing constraint 11, but the total cost is 35.

7.2.2 Minimizing Costs by Scheduling

For reaching the goal mentioned in Section 7.2.1, the second phase is required to find out the approach by selecting a proper functional unit at each node and obtain a minimum summation of costs. Therefore, this phase is to create a schedule aiming to use minimum resources by using the outcomes obtained from the prior phase. The method of reaching this goal is leveraging a Minimum Resource Scheduling Algorithm (MRSA). The outcome of this phase configures the amount and the types of functional units that will be used for minimizing the total costs.

A form-based calculation is represented in Fig. 7.4 in order to assist students to understand MRSA. According to the structure displayed in the figure, operations that occurred at each node are aligned by the

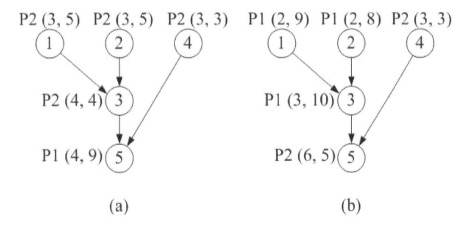

Figure 7.3 (a) Assignment 1 with a cost of 26. (b) Assignment 2 with a cost of 35.

timing constraints. The first row represents the timing constraints that can determine the optimal path for the final outcome. The black spot at the first row provides an example of timing constraint, which means the first time unit ends by the broken line attached to the black spot. The following rows are grouped by nodes that consist of the corresponding costs and working modes. The working mode refers to the selection of functional unit. The cost rows display the exact amounts of the cost at the specific times with the specific functional unit executions. The following part explains the approach of using the form given in Fig. 7.4.

An example of leveraging the MRSA form is given, which is connected to the example provided in Section 7.2.1. For the purpose of explanations, the example represents a scenario that has a simple path with four nodes, namely A, B, C, and D. Each node has two working modes that need different executive times and energy costs. In the provided assumption, the working mode needs longer executive time when cutting the costs. For example, node A has two working modes, A1 and A2. A1 can accomplish the work in 2 time units, which is shorter than A2. However, A1 demands more energy than A2 does. Table 7.2 represents the detailed information about the four nodes.

Node A

According to Table 7.2, the maximum amount of time of the path A → B → C → D is max(A, B, C, D) = 19. First of all, we need to find

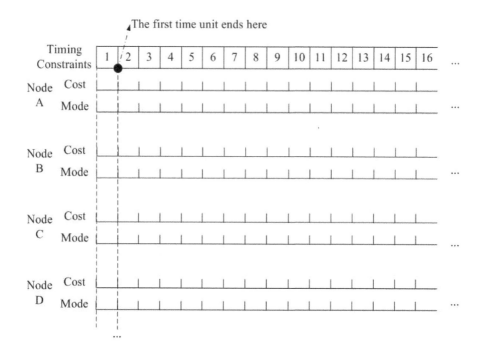

Figure 7.4 The calculation form for a minimum resource scheduling algorithm.

Table 7.2 Nodes with Two Different Working Modes (Different Executive Times and Costs)

Nodes	Time	Cost
A1	2	9
A2	3	5
B1	3	10
B2	4	4
C1	4	9
C2	6	5
D1	2	6
D2	6	2

the minimum cost node for Node A for any given timing constraint J. Starting with the timing constraint, no node can perform the instruction at the first time unit. Switching to the second time unit, we can find a node, Node A1, can accomplish the job by 9 units of energy consumption. The form in Fig. 7.4 can be updated for Fig. 7.5.

Timing Constraints	1	2	3	4	5	6	7	8	9	10	11	12	13	14	15	16	17	18	19
Node A Cost	-	9																	
Node A Mode	-	A1																	

Figure 7.5 The first update of the MRSA form.

Next, at the third timing constraint, working mode A2 can finish the job with 5 units of cost, which is less than the cost by using A1, 9 units of cost. Consistently, A2 has the lowest cost at all other timing constraints. Fig. 7.6 represents an updated table that uses A2 working mode when timing constraint is longer than 2.

Timing Constraints	1	2	3	4	5	6	7	8	9	10	11	12	13	14	15	16	17	18	19
Node A Cost	-	9	5	5	5	5	5	5	5	5	5	5	5	5	5	5	5	5	5
Node A Mode	-	A1	A2	A2	A2	A2	A2	A2	A2	A2	A2	A2	A2	A2	A2	A2	A2	A2	A2

Figure 7.6 The second update of the MRSA form.

Path A → B

The next step is to find out the minimum cost of path A → B within the timing constraint J. The shortest executive time for Node B is 3 time units offered by the working mode B1, and B1 can only start after Node A is finished. The earliest path A → B is A1 → B1, and B1 starts at the fifth time unit. This also means that there is no path for timing constraints less than 5 time units. Fig. 7.7 represents the first path from A to B.

When the timing constraint becomes 6, the path A → B can be A1 → B2. The cost of A1 → B2 is 13 derived from (9+4), which is less than path A1 → B1 that costs 19. Fig. 7.8 shows two paths A → B under two timing constraints, 5 and 6.

When the timing constraint becomes 7, the path A → B can be A2 → B2 with the cost 9 deriving from (5+4). This selection uses two working modes A2 and B2 that require less energy but need more

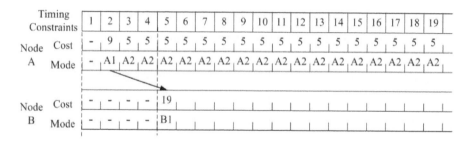

Figure 7.7 The first possible path from A to B under timing constraint 5.

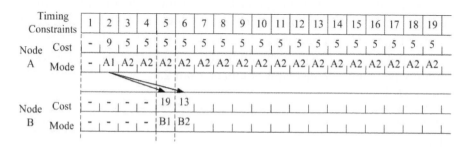

Figure 7.8 The paths from A to B under timing constraint 6.

executive time. Therefore, the best path A → B will be A2 → B2 from timing constraint 7. Fig. 7.9 shows all optimal selections from timing constraint 5.

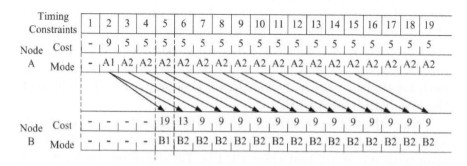

Figure 7.9 Optimal paths for A → B under different timing constraints.

Path A → B → C

The following step is to calculate the minimum cost of path A → B → C under timing constraints. Similar to path A → B, there is no path for timing constraints shorter than 9 time units because the minimum timing constraint is 4. Fig. 7.10 illustrates an updated MRSA table with potential optimal paths B → C.

Under timing constraint 9, path B1 → C1 is the optimal path, with a cost of 28 from (19+9).

Under timing constraint 10, path B2 → C1 is the optimal path, with a cost of 22 from (13+9).

Under timing constraint 11, path B2 → C1 is the optimal path, with a cost of 18 from (9+9).

Under timing constraint 12, both path B2 → C1 and path B2 → C2 cost 18.

Under timing constraint 13, path B2 → C2 is the optimal path, with a cost of 14 from (9+5). Moreover, path B2 → C2 is the optimal path for B → C if the timing constraint is longer than 13 timing units.

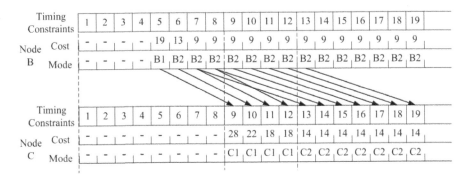

Figure 7.10 Optimal paths for B → C under different timing constraints.

Path A → B → C → D

The final step is to calculate the minimum cost of path A → B → C → D under the timing constraints. The earliest starting time for D is at the 11 timing constraint. Fig. 7.10 represents the path C → D.

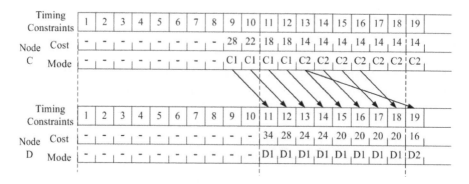

Figure 7.11 Optimal paths for C → D under different timing constraints

Under timing constraint 11, path C1 → D1 is the optimal path, with a cost of 34 from (28+6).

Under timing constraint 12, path C1 → D1 is the optimal path, with a cost of 28 from (22+6).

Under timing constraint 13, path C1 → D1 is the optimal path, with a cost of 24 from (18+6). The same optimal path C1 → D1 is under timing constraint 14 as well.

Under timing constraints 15 and 16, path C2 → D1 is the optimal path, with a cost of 20 from (14+6).

Under timing constraints 17 and 18, path C1 → D2 is the optimal path, with a cost of 20 from (18+2). The same cost can be also achieved by path C2 → D1, which is 20 from (14+6).

Finally, the path C1 → D2 is the optimal path, costing 16 from (14+2).

As discussed before, 19 timing units is the longest timing constraint in this case.

Fig. 7.12 represents all optimal paths for A → B → C → D under different timing constraints. According to the figure, the earliest accomplishment time is 11 time units. The range of timing constraints for all working modes is between 11 and 19 time units.

In summary, MRSA is an efficient approach for solving the *Heterogeneous Assignment Problem* if the DFG is a simple path or a tree.

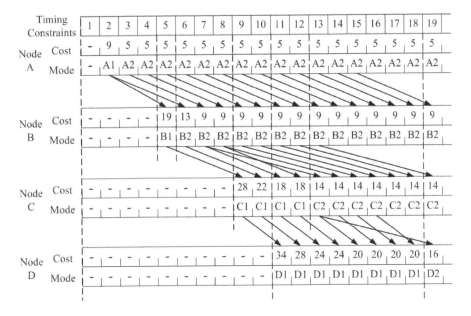

Figure 7.12 Optimal paths for A → B → C → D under different timing constraints

The complexity of the problem is related to the values of the nodes' maximum executive times so that the problem can be considered a pseudo-polynomial problem. The method is efficient when the value is small or can be normalized to a small one. In the next section, we introduce *Probabilistic Time Model of Heterogeneous Embedded Systems*.

7.3   PROBABILISTIC TIME MODEL

7.3.1   Introduction of Probabilistic Time Model

Based on the algorithm given in Section 7.2, an advanced model is introduced in this section, which is *Probabilistic Time Model*. This section introduces an optimization algorithm that operates in a probabilistic environment to solve the Heterogeneous Assignment with Probability (HAP) problems. The *Probabilistic Time Model* is a model consisting of a number of nodes that are restricted by the conditional executive times that are associated with the multiple inputs or hardware usages. In a HAP program, the executive time of a task is modeled as a random variable [74]. Functional units in the *Heterogeneous Systems* have different costs in various manners, such as size and reliability. Each functional unit is associated with a type of cost, such as timing consumption and energy cost, in the heterogeneous system. In general, the performance of the functional units has a positive relationship with a typical cost. The performance of each functional unit is associated with one or a few types of costs. With confidence probability P , we can guarantee that the total execution time of the DFG is less than or equal to the timing constraint with a probability that is greater than or equal to P .

In a practical scenario, many tasks processed at embedded applications are restricted by the fixed executive time. The tasks usually consist of conditional instructions, as well as operations with various execution times for different inputs. The existing approaches are not efficient for solving the problems with uncertainties. The current solution is making assumptions for either worst-case or average-case timing consumptions required by tasks. However, this method results in an inefficient implementation of embedded systems in designing a soft real-time system.

For example, a higher-performance unit may cost more in energy usage but can execute faster. The method of assigning an appropriate functional unit type into a DFG node is a crucial step for minimizing total costs. It needs the timing constraint satisfied by a Guaranteed Confidence Probability (GCP). A GCP is a possibility statement that can guarantee the targeted task can be completed by the given timing constraint. With defining a confidence probability P, it is guaranteed that the total executive time of the DFG is equal to or less than the timing constraints with a greater value.

An example is given in this section in order to assist students to fully discern the solution to HAP problems. An assumption is made to picture the scenario addressing the problem, which selects functional units from a functional units library that provides two types of functional units. R_1 and R_2 represents these two functional units types. Fig. 7.13 exhibits an exemplary Probabilistic Data Flow Graph (PDFG) showing a tree with four nodes.

Table 7.4 represents the time cumulative distribution functions and the cost at each node by using different functional unit types. T refers to the execution times, C means the costs, and P represents probabilities. Each node can select one of two functional units types and executes each functional unit type with probabilistic executive times. This implies that the execution time (T) of each functional unit should

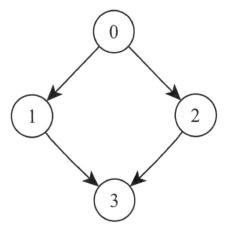

Figure 7.13 A given probabilistic data flow graph.

be a random variable. For example, node 1 can be executed in 1 time unit with a probability 0.9 (90%) or be executed in 3 time units with a probability of 0.1 (10%) when implementing R_1. It also means that the execution of node 1 can be accomplished in 3 time units with a 100% probability.

Table 7.3 Nodes with Times, Probabilities, and Costs by Using Different Functional Units.

Nodes	R1			R2		
	T_1	P_1	C_1	T_2	P_2	C_2
0	1	0.8	9	2	0.8	5
	2	0.2	9	3	0.2	5
1	1	0.9	10	2	0.7	4
	3	0.1	10	4	0.3	4
2	1	0.9	9	2	0.8	5
	4	0.1	9	6	0.2	5
3	1	0.2	8	3	0.4	2
	2	0.8	8	6	0.6	2

Table 7.4 represents the time cumulative distribution functions and the cost at each node by using different functional unit types. The table uses similar notations to Table 7.3, such as T and C. P represents the cumulative probabilities. Each node can select one of two functional

units types and executes each functional unit type with probabilistic executive times. This implies that the execution time (T) of each functional unit should be a random variable. For example, node 1 can be executed in 1 time unit, with a probability 0.9, or be executed in 3 time units, with a cumulative probability of 1.0 when implementing R_1. Based on the value given in the table, the shortest completion time is 4 time units, and the longest completion time is 19 time units.

Table 7.4 The Time Cumulative Distribution Functions and the Cost at Each Node by Using Different Functional Unit Types

Nodes	R1			R2		
	T_1	P_1	C_1	T_2	P_2	C_2
0	1	0.8	9	2	0.8	5
	2	1.0	9	3	1.0	5
1	1	0.9	10	2	0.7	4
	3	1.0	10	4	1.0	4
2	1	0.9	9	2	0.8	5
	4	1.0	9	6	1.0	5
3	1	0.2	8	3	0.4	2
	2	1.0	8	6	1.0	2

The efficiency of the solution introduced in this section has been proved in the previous research [92][72][35]. The algorithm can solve the hard Heterogeneous Assignment (HA) problems for both hard and soft real-time situations. Moreover, the algorithm is able to provide more choices with *Guaranteed Confidence Probabilities* and lower total costs, and some choices are efficient solutions to some certain timing constraints.

The development of the probabilistic heterogeneous scheduling and assignment framework can be simply applied to solving the dynamic voltage scaling problems by using *Probabilistic Graph Models*. One of the existing approaches is finding the proper voltage levels for each node that can be associated with different execution time and energy consumption with probabilities. Our solution is using loop scheduling with multicore architecture that offers an advanced performance. The solution considers each voltage level a functional unit type, with defining the expected energy consumption as the cost. Using the HAP framework can convert this problem into a special case of the HAP problem. The following is an example of explaining the implementation of the HAP framework.

7.3.2 Solutions to Heterogeneous Assignment Problems

This section aims to solve the HAP problem with the data provided by Table 7.4. There are two phases for solving the HAP problem, including *Generating B Table* and *Minimizing Costs by Scheduling D Table*. The *B Table* is a tabulation that can represent the costs and probabilities of the node completions under different timing constraints. Table 7.5 displays a B table that is aligned with Table 7.4.

Table 7.5 An Example of B Table (Associated with Table 7.4). TC: Timing Constraints.

TC	1	2	3	4	5	6
Node 0	(0.8, 9)	(0.8, 5)	(1.0, 5)			
		(1.0, 9)				
Node 1	(0.9, 10)	(0.9, 10)	(1.0, 10)	(1.0, 4)		
		(0.7, 4)				
Node 2	(0.9, 9)	(0.8, 5)	(0.8, 5)	(0.8, 5)	(0.8, 5)	(1.0, 5)
		(0.9, 9)	(0.9, 9)	(1.0, 9)	(1.0, 9)	
Node 3	(0.2, 8)	(1.0, 8)	(0.4, 2)	(0.4, 2)	(0.4, 2)	(1.0, 2)
			(1.0, 8)	(1.0, 8)	(1.0, 8)	

In a B table, the functional unit types are represented in a manner of (P_i, C_i). "P_i" refers to the probabilities, and "C_i" is the cost at a node under one specific timing constraint. As shown in Table 7.5, the first row shows the timing constraints. In this case, the longest timing constraint for each node is 6 timing units. Under each timing constraint, a node can have one or two working modes by using different functional units. For example, under timing constraint 2, Node 0 has two modes, which are (0.8, 5) and (1.0, 9). This means both working modes can accomplish the node under timing constraint 2 but the performances are vary. The first mode, (0.8, 5), has a probability rate at 80% and costs 5 units of resources. The other mode, (1.0, 9), has a higher-level probability that is 100%, but the cost is higher than the first mode. Moreover, under timing constraint 1, Node 2 only has one mode, (0.9, 9), which means there is only one mode option under this timing constraint for Node 2.

7.3.3 Generating a D Table

The *D Table* is a tabulation that represents optimal solutions with probabilities and costs under different timing constraints, which are generated by using dynamic programming. The method of creating the D table is using data from the B table and selecting paths depending on the demanded criterion. Table 7.6 gives an example of the D table, with values derived from Table 7.5. In the table, Vk represents the nodes, $X(k-1)$, which is aligned with Table 7.5. For instance, V1 represents Node 0 and V2 represents Node 1. Under each timing constraint shown in the columns, all potential combinations of probabilities and costs need to be listed, which correlates with Vk rows.

Table 7.6 An Example of D Table (Associated with Table 7.4 and 7.5). TC (Timing Constraints)

TC	1	2	3	4	5	6	...
V1	(0.8, 9)	(1.0, 9)	(1.0, 5)				...
		(0.8, 5)					...
V2		(0.72, 19)	(0.56, 13)	(0.7, 13)	(0.8, 13)	(1.0, 13)	...
			(0.9, 19)	(0.56, 9)	(1.0, 19)	(0.8, 9)	...
			(0.72, 15)	(0.9, 15)			...
...	...	...	...	...	...	...	...

The method of calculating values for each cell in D table is given in Definition 1. In the definition, $(P_{(i,j)}^k, C_{(i,j)}^k)$ refers to the pair (Probability, Cost). i represents the working mode paths. j represents *executive time*. k represents the nodes involved in the operations. Symbol $\odot$ stands for an *Operator* that combines two pairs of (Probability, Cost).

Definition 1 $(P_{(i,j)}^k, C_{(i,j)}^k) \odot (P_{(i,j)}^{k+1}, C_{(i,j)}^{k+1}) = (P_{(i,j)}^k \times P_{(i,j)}^{k+1}, C_{(i,j)}^k + C_{(i,j)}^{k+1})$

Using the operator $\odot$ can generate a new pair (P', C') followed by Algorithm 1. For example, assuming two pairs H_1 and H_2, $(P_{(i,j)}^1, C_{(i,j)}^1)$ and $(P_{(i,j)}^2, C_{(i,j)}^2)$, the new pair (P', C') can be generated from P' $= P_{(i,j)}^1 \times P_{(i,j)}^2$ and C' $= C_{(i,j)}^1 + C_{(i,j)}^2$. This process of the operation is denoted by $H_1 \odot H_2$. The operating principle follows the rules:

1. The total cost is gained by summing up all the nodes' costs.

2. The probability attached to the total cost derives from multiplying the probabilities of all nodes.

The algorithm representing these rules is given in Algorithm 1. Operations occurred in the operator follow the process and method given by the algorithm.

Algorithm 1 Algorithm of the operator for combining pairs

Require: A list of paris $(P_{(i,j)}^k, C_{(i,j)}^k)$

Ensure: Generate a redundant-pair-free list (P, C)

1: Sorting the given list by comparing $P_{(i,j)}$ in an ascending order and gain $P_{(i,j)}^k \leq P_{(i,j)}^{(k+1)}$

2: FOR each two neighboring pairs $(P_{(i,j)}^k, C_{(i,j)}^k)$ and $(P_{(i,j)}^{(k+1)}, C_{(i,j)}^{(k+1)})$

3:     IF the probabilities of the neighboring pairs are the same, $P_{(i,j)}^k = P_{(i,j)}^{(k+1)}$

4:         IF the total cost with a lower probability, $C_{(i,j)}^k$, is no less than the total cost of the neighboring pair with higher probability, $C_{(i,j)}^{(k+1)}$, $C_{(i,j)}^k \geq C_{(i,j)}^{(k+1)}$

5:             remove the pair $(P_{(i,j)}^k, C_{(i,j)}^k)$

6:         ELSE

7:             remove the pair $(P_{(i,j)}^{(k+1)}, C_{(i,j)}^{(k+1)})$

8:         END IF

9:     ELSE /* ∀ other pairs with different probabilities of neighboring pairs */

10:         IF the total cost in a lower probability pair is no less than the total cost in a higher probability pair, $C_{(i,j)}^k \geq C_{(i,j)}^{(k+1)}$

11:             remove the pair $(P_{(i,j)}^k, C_{(i,j)}^k)$

12:         END IF

13:     END FOR

The following section gives a detailed example that explains the process of generating a D Table step by step. The illustrated example uses the same values as the B Table shown in Table 7.5. After the D Table is created, we use dynamic programming to search the optimal solutions backward. Since the costs are mapped in D Table, the increase of the execution is linear.

7.3.4 Example of Generating a D Table

Aligning with Algorithm 1, a D Table can be created by the following steps. In the following instruction, symbol ⊙ is also used to represent the operator that combines and compares probabilities and costs. Based on the data given in Table 7.5, there are three steps for producing the list of pairs, including **Path V1 → V2, Path V2 → V3, and Path V3 → V4**.

Creating the D Table for Path V1 → V2

At the beginning of the D Table construction, the rows of the first node V0 are filled up by the data from Table 7.5 directly, referring to Table 7.6. After the columns of V0 are filled up, the path V0 → V1 will be produced under different timing constraints. The selections of neighboring pairs are based on the given timing constraints. The sum of the completion times from two pairs should be no more than the timing constraint. Under timing constraint 2, there is only one probability in this case:

TC 1+1: $(0.8, 9) \odot (0.9, 10) = (0.8 \times 0.9, 9+10) = (0.72, 19)$

This section uses the format "TC *Number a +Number b*" to represent pairs. *Number a* represents the time cost of the preceding nodes. *Number b* represents the time cost of the succeeding nodes. The values of "Number a + Number b" are equal to the corresponding timing constraints.

Details of probabilities under various timing constraints are given as follows:

Under **timing constraint 3**, the following probabilities include:

TC 1+2: $(0.8, 9) \odot (0.9, 10) = (0.8 \times 0.9, 9+10) = (0.72, 19)$

TC 1+2: $(0.8, 9) \odot (0.7, 4) = (0.8 \times 0.7, 9+4) = (0.56, 13)$

TC 2+1: $(0.8, 5) \odot (0.9, 10) = (0.8 \times 0.9, 5+10) = (0.72, 15)$

TC 2+1: $(1.0, 9) \odot (0.9, 10) = (1.0 \times 0.9, 9+10) = (0.9, 19)$

The above operations represent the arithmetic processes with details. According to Definition 1, $(0.72, 19)$ is removed, since the pair $(0.72, 15)$ costs less with the same probability. Other pairs are selected for the pair list, including $(0.56, 13)$, $(0.9, 19)$, and $(0.72, 15)$. The following representations will hide the arithmetic processes and directly show the results.

Under **timing constraint 4**, the probabilities are produced as follows:

TC 1+3: $(0.8, 9) \odot (1.0, 10) = (0.8, 19)$

TC 2+2: $(0.8, 5) \odot (0.9, 10) = (0.72, 15)$

TC 2+2: $(0.8, 5) \odot (0.7, 4) = (0.56, 9)$

TC 2+2: $(1.0, 9) \odot (0.9, 10) = (0.9, 19)$

TC 2+2: $(1.0, 9) \odot (0.7, 4) = (0.7, 13)$

TC 3+1: $(1.0, 5) \odot (0.9, 10) = (0.9, 15)$

According to Definition 1, the following pairs are removed, including $(0.8, 19)$, $(0.9, 19)$, and $(0.72, 15)$. The remain pairs include $(0.7, 13)$, $(0.56, 9)$, and $(0.9, 15)$.

Under **timing constraint 5**, the probabilities are produced as follows:

TC 1+4: $(0.8, 9) \odot (1.0, 4) = (0.8, 13)$

TC 2+3: $(0.8, 5) \odot (1.0, 10) = (0.8, 15)$

TC 2+3: $(1.0, 9) \odot (1.0, 10) = (1.0, 19)$

TC 3+2: $(1.0, 5) \odot (0.9, 10) = (0.9, 15)$

TC 3+2: $(1.0, 5) \odot (0.7, 4) = (0.7, 9)$

According to Definition 1, the pair $(0.8, 15)$ is removed and the remain pairs include $(0.8, 13)$, $(1.0, 19)$, $(0.9, 15)$, and $(0.7, 9)$.

Under **timing constraint 6**, the probabilities include:

TC 2+4: $(0.8, 5) \odot (1.0, 4) = (0.8, 9)$

TC 2+4: $(1.0, 9) \odot (1.0, 4) = (1.0, 13)$

TC 3+3: $(1.0, 5) \odot (1.0, 10) = (1.0, 15)$

According to Definition 1, the pair $(1.0, 15)$ is removed. The gained pairs include $(0.8, 9)$ and $(1.0, 13)$.

Under **timing constraint 7**, there is only one probability for path $V1 \rightarrow V2$:

TC 3+4: $(1.0, 5) \odot (1.0, 4) = (1.0, 9)$

The D Table considering the path $V1 \rightarrow V2$ is produced as represented in Table 7.7.

Creating the D Table for Path $V2 \rightarrow V3$

Leveraging the same approach as the one producing Path $V0 \rightarrow V1$ can create the following probability list.

Table 7.7 D Table Addressing the Path V1 → V2

T	(P, C)	(P, C)	(P, C)	(P, C)
2	(0.72, 19)			
3	(0.56, 13)	(0.72, 15)	(0.9, 19)	
4	(0.56, 9)	(0.7, 13)	(0.9, 15)	
5	(0.7, 9)	(0.8, 13)	(0.9, 15)	(1.0, 19)
6	(0.8, 9)	(1.0, 13)		
7	(1.0, 9)			

1. Under timing constraint 3, one probability is TC 2+1: (0.72, 19) ⊙ (0.9, 9) = (0.648, 28)

2. Under timing constraint 4,

   TC 2+2: (0.72, 19) ⊙ (0.8, 5) = (0.576, 24)

   TC 2+2: (0.72, 19) ⊙ (0.9, 9) = (0.648, 28)

   TC 3+1: (0.56, 13) ⊙ (0.9, 9) = (0.504, 22)

   TC 3+1: (0.72, 15) ⊙ (0.9, 9) = (0.648, 24)

   TC 3+1: (0.9, 19) ⊙ (0.9, 9) = (0.81, 28)

   The selected pairs include (0.504, 22), (0.81, 28), and (0.648, 24). (0.576, 24) is removed from comparing (0.576, 24) with (0.648, 24). (0.648, 28) is removed because (0.648, 24) costs less but with the same probability.

3. Under timing constraint 5,

   TC 2+3: (0.72, 19) ⊙ (0.8, 5) = (0.576, 24)

   TC 2+3: (0.72, 19) ⊙ (0.9, 9) = (0.648, 28)

   TC 3+2: (0.56, 13) ⊙ (0.8, 5) = (0.448, 18)

   TC 3+2: (0.56, 13) ⊙ (0.9, 9) = (0.504, 22)

   TC 3+2: (0.72, 15) ⊙ (0.8, 5) = (0.576, 20)

   TC 3+2: (0.72, 15) ⊙ (0.9, 9) = (0.648, 24)

   TC 3+2: (0.9, 19) ⊙ (0.8, 5) = (0.72, 24)

   TC 3+2: (0.9, 19) ⊙ (0.9, 9) = (0.81, 28)

   TC 4+1: (0.56, 9) ⊙ (0.9, 9) = (0.504, 18)

   TC 4+1: (0.7, 13) ⊙ (0.9, 9) = (0.63, 22)

   TC 4+1: (0.9, 15) ⊙ (0.9, 9) = (0.81, 24)

The optimal pairs include (0.576, 20), (0.63, 22), (0.504, 18), and (0.81, 24). The pairs (0.576,24), (0.648, 24), and (0.72, 24) are removed since (0.81, 24) has a higher probability by the same cost. Using the same method can remove pairs (0.504, 22) and (0.448, 18) because of the pairs (0.63, 22) and (0.504, 18). Pair (0.648, 28) is removed, because it has a lower performance than (0.648, 24) that has already been wiped. Pair (0.81, 28) is removed, since it is worse than the pair (0.648, 28) that is also removed.

4. Under the timing constraint 6, using the same method can obtain the following redundant-pair free list:

$$(0.9, 15) \odot (0.9, 9) = (0.81, 24)$$
$$(0.56, 9) \odot (0.8, 5) = (0.448, 14)$$
$$(0.9, 15) \odot (0.8, 5) = (0.72, 20)$$
$$(1.0, 19) \odot (0.9, 9) = (0.9, 28)$$
$$(0.7, 9) \odot (0.9, 9) = (0.63, 18)$$

The abandoned pairs include (0.72, 28), (0.576, 24), (0.504, 22), (0.81, 28), (0.648, 24), (0.448, 18), (0.72, 24), (0.576, 20), (0.63, 22), and (0.504, 18).

5. Under timing constraint 7,

TC 2+5: $(0.72, 19) \odot (0.8, 5) = (0.576, 24)$

TC 2+5: $(0.72, 19) \odot (1.0, 9) = (0.72, 28)$

TC 3+4: $(0.56, 13) \odot (0.8, 5) = (0.448, 18)$

TC 3+4: $(0.56, 13) \odot (1.0, 9) = (0.56, 22)$

TC 3+4: $(0.72, 15) \odot (0.8, 5) = (0.576, 20)$

TC 3+4: $(0.72, 15) \odot (1.0, 9) = (0.72, 24)$

TC 3+4: $(0.9, 19) \odot (0.8, 5) = (0.72, 24)$

TC 3+4: $(0.9, 19) \odot (1.0, 9) = (0.9, 28)$

TC 4+3: $(0.56, 9) \odot (0.8, 5) = (0.448, 14)$

TC 4+3: $(0.56, 9) \odot (0.9, 9) = (0.504, 18)$

TC 4+3: $(0.7, 13) \odot (0.8, 5) = (0.56, 18)$

TC 4+3: $(0.7, 13) \odot (0.9, 9) = (0.63, 22)$

TC 4+3: $(0.9, 15) \odot (0.8, 5) = (0.72, 20)$

TC 4+3: $(0.9, 15) \odot (0.9, 9) = (0.81, 24)$

TC 5+2: $(0.7, 9) \odot (0.8, 5)$ = $(0.56, 14)$

TC 5+2: $(0.9, 15) \odot (0.9, 9)$ = $(0.81, 24)$

TC 5+2: $(0.7, 9) \odot (0.9, 9)$ = $(0.63, 18)$

TC 5+2: $(1.0, 19) \odot (0.8, 5)$ = $(0.8, 24)$

TC 5+2: $(0.8, 13) \odot (0.8, 5)$ = $(0.64, 18)$

TC 5+2: $(1.0, 19) \odot (0.9, 9)$ = $(0.9, 28)$

TC 5+2: $(0.8, 13) \odot (0.9, 9)$ = $(0.72, 22)$

TC 6+1: $(0.8, 9) \odot (0.9, 9)$ = $(0.72, 18)$

TC 5+2: $(0.9, 15) \odot (0.8, 5)$ = $(0.72, 20)$

TC 6+1: $(1.0, 13) \odot (0.9, 9)$ = $(0.9, 22)$

The selected pairs include (0.56, 14), (0.9, 22), and (0.72, 18).

Pairs (0.72, 28), (0.72, 24), (0.72, 22), and (0.72, 20) are removed because they all have fewer performances than the pair (0.72, 18). Pairs (0.56, 22) and (0.6, 22) are removed, because they have fewer probabilities than the pair (0.9, 22). Pairs (0.448, 18), (0.56, 18), (0.504, 18), (0.64, 18), and (0.63, 18) are removed, because they have less probabilities than the pair (0.72, 18). Pairs (0.576, 24) is removed, because it has less probability than the pair (0.72, 24) that is already removed. Pair (0.576, 20) is removed, because it has less probability than (0.72, 20) that is already removed. Pair (0.9, 28) is removed, because it costs more than pair (0.9, 22). Pair (0.448, 14) is removed, because it has less probability than (0.56, 14). (0.81, 24), and (0.81, 24) are removed because they have less probabilities with more costs than (0.9, 22).

6. Use the same calculation method to gain the results for other timing constraints, until the timing constraint 12.

7. Under timing constraint 12:

   TC 6+6: $(0.8, 9) \odot (1.0, 5) = (0.8, 14)$
   TC 6+6: $(1.0, 13) \odot (1.0, 5) = (1.0, 18)$
   TC 7+5: $(1.0, 9) \odot (0.8, 5) = (0.8, 14)$
   TC 7+5: $(1.0, 9) \odot (1.0, 9) = (1.0, 18)$

   The selected pairs are (1.0, 18) and (0.8, 14).

8. Under timing constraint 13:

   There is only one path: TC 7+6: $(1.0, 9) \odot (1.0, 9) = (1.0, 14)$

Table 7.8 represents a D Table showing the path V2 → V3.

Table 7.8 D Table Showing the Path V2 → V3

T	(P, C)	(P, C)	(P, C)	(P, C)	(P, C)
3	(0.648, 28)				
4	(0.504, 22)	(0.81, 28)	(0.648, 24)		
5	(0.576, 20)	(0.63, 22)	(0.504, 18)	(0.81, 24)	
6	(0.81, 24)	(0.448, 14)	(0.72, 20)	(0.9, 28)	(0.63, 18)
7	(0.56, 14)	(0.9, 22)	(0.72, 18)		
8	(0.64, 14)	(0.9, 18)			
9	(1.0, 28)	(0.8, 14)	(0.9, 18)		
10	(1.0, 22)	(0.9, 18)	(0.8, 14)		
11	(1.0, 18)	(0.8, 14)			
12	(1.0, 18)	(0.8, 14)			
13	(1.0, 14)				

Creating the D Table for Path V3 → V4

Creating the D Table for path V3 → V4 uses the same method of creating the path V2 → V3 of the D Table. In this case, the procedure will not be completed until reaching the longest timing constraint, which is 19.

1. Under timing constraint 4:

   There is only one path, TC 3+1: $(0.65, 28) \odot (0.2, 8) = (0.1296, 36)$

2. Under timing constraint 5:

   TC 3+2: $(0.648, 28) \odot (1.0, 8) = (0.648, 36)$

   TC 4+1: $(0.504, 22) \odot (0.2, 8) = (0.1, 30)$

   TC 4+1: $(0.648, 24) \odot (0.2, 8) = (0.13, 32)$

   TC 4+1: $(0.81, 28) \odot (0.2, 8) = (0.16, 36)$

   The selected pairs include (0.648)

3. Under timing constraint 6:

   TC 3+3: $(0.648, 28) \odot (0.4, 2) = (0.2592, 30)$

   TC 3+3: $(0.648, 28) \odot (1.0, 8) = (0.648, 36)$

   TC 4+2: $(0.504, 22) \odot (1.0, 8) = (0.504, 30)$

TC 4+2: $(0.648, 24) \odot (1.0, 8) = (0.648, 32)$

TC 4+2: $(0.81, 28) \odot (1.0, 8) = (0.81, 36)$

TC 5+1: $(0.504, 18) \odot (0.2, 8) = (0.1152, 26)$

TC 5+1: $(0.576, 20) \odot (0.2, 8) = (0.126, 28)$

TC 5+1: $(0.63, 22) \odot (0.2, 8) = (0.126, 30)$

TC 5+1: $(0.81, 24) \odot (0.2, 8) = (0.162, 32)$

The selected pairs include $(0.1152, 28)$, $(0.1008, 26)$, $(0.504, 30)$, $(0.81, 36)$, and $(0.648, 32)$.

$(0.126, 30)$ and $(0.2592, 30)$ are removed, because they have less probabilities than the pair $(0.504, 30)$. $(0.162, 32)$ is removed, because it has a less probability than the pair $(0.648, 32)$. $(0.648, 36)$ is removed, because it costs more than $(0.648, 32)$.

4. Under timing constraint 7:

TC 3+4: $(0.648, 28) \odot (0.4, 2) = (0.2592, 30)$

TC 3+4: $(0.648, 28) \odot (1.0, 8) = (0.648, 36)$

TC 4+3: $(0.504, 22) \odot (0.4, 2) = (0.2016, 24)$

TC 4+3: $(0.504, 22) \odot (1.0, 8) = (0.504, 30)$

TC 4+3: $(0.648, 24) \odot (0.4, 2) = (0.2592, 26)$

TC 4+3: $(0.648, 24) \odot (1.0, 8) = (0.648, 32)$

TC 4+3: $(0.81, 28) \odot (0.4, 2) = (0.324, 30)$

TC 4+3: $(0.81, 28) \odot (1.0, 8) = (0.81, 36)$

TC 5+2: $(0.504, 18) \odot (1.0, 8) = (0.504, 26)$

TC 5+2: $(0.578, 20) \odot (1.0, 8) = (0.576, 28)$

TC 5+2: $(0.63, 22) \odot (1.0, 8) = (0.63, 30)$

TC 5+2: $(0.81, 24) \odot (1.0, 8) = (0.81, 32)$

TC 6+1: $(0.448, 14) \odot (0.2, 8) = (0.0896, 22)$

TC 6+1: $(0.63, 18) \odot (0.2, 8) = (0.126, 26)$

TC 6+1: $(0.72, 20) \odot (0.2, 8) = (0.144, 28)$

TC 6+1: $(0.81, 24) \odot (0.2, 8) = (0.162, 32)$

TC 6+1: $(0.9, 28) \odot (0.2, 8) = (0.18, 36)$

The selected pairs include $(0.2016, 24)$, $(0.576, 28)$, $(0.63, 30)$, $(0.504, 26)$, $(0.81, 32)$, and $(0.0896, 22)$.

Pairs (0.2592, 30), (0.504, 30), and (0.324, 30) are removed, because they all have fewer probabilities than the pair (0.63, 30). (0.81, 36) is removed, because it costs more than (0.81, 32). (0.126, 32) is removed, because it has a lower probability than (0.81, 32). (0.648, 36) and (0.18, 36) are removed, because they have lower probabilities than the pair (0.81, 36), which has already been removed. (0.648, 36) is removed, because it has a lower probability but a higher level cost than (0.81, 32). Pairs (0.2592, 26) and (0.126, 26) are removed, because they both have lower probabilities than (0.504, 26). (0.144, 28) is removed, because it has a lower probability than (0.576, 28).

5. Under timing constraint 8:

TC 3+5: $(0.648, 28) \odot (0.4, 2) = (0.2592, 30)$

TC 3+5: $(0.648, 28) \odot (1.0, 8) = (0.648, 36)$

TC 4+4: $(0.504, 22) \odot (0.4, 2) = (0.2016, 24)$

TC 4+4: $(0.504, 22) \odot (1.0, 8) = (0.504, 30)$

TC 4+4: $(0.648, 24) \odot (0.4, 2) = (0.2592, 26)$

TC 4+4: $(0.648, 24) \odot (1.0, 8) = (0.648, 32)$

TC 4+4: $(0.81, 28) \odot (0.4, 2) = (0.324, 30)$

TC 4+4: $(0.81, 28) \odot (1.0, 8) = (0.81, 36)$

TC 5+3: $(0.504, 18) \odot (0.4, 2) = (0.2016, 20)$

TC 5+3: $(0.504, 18) \odot (1.0, 8) = (0.504, 26)$

TC 5+3: $(0.576, 20) \odot (0.4, 2) = (0.2304, 22)$

TC 5+3: $(0.576, 20) \odot (1.0, 8) = (0.576, 28)$

TC 5+3: $(0.63, 22) \odot (0.4, 2) = (0.252, 24)$

TC 5+3: $(0.63, 22) \odot (1.0, 8) = (0.63, 30)$

TC 5+3: $(0.81, 24) \odot (0.4, 2) = (0.324, 26)$

TC 5+3: $(0.81, 24) \odot (1.0, 8) = (0.81, 32)$

TC 6+2: $(0.448, 14) \odot (1.0, 8) = (0.448, 22)$

TC 6+2: $(0.63, 18) \odot (1.0, 8) = (0.63, 26)$

TC 6+2: $(0.72, 20) \odot (1.0, 8) = (0.72, 28)$

TC 6+2: $(0.81, 24) \odot (1.0, 8) = (0.81, 32)$

TC 6+2: $(0.9, 28) \odot (1.0, 8) = (0.9, 36)$

TC 7+1: $(0.56, 14) \odot (0.2, 8) = (0.112, 22)$

TC 7+1: $(0.72, 18) \odot (0.2, 8) = (0.144, 26)$

TC 7+1: $(0.9, 22) \odot (0.2, 8) = (0.18, 30)$

The selected pairs include (0.81, 32), (0.2016, 20), (0.448, 22), (0.72, 28), (0.9, 36), and (0.63, 26).

Pairs (0.648, 36) and (0.81, 36) are removed because they both have lower probabilities than pair (0.9, 36). (0.648, 32) is removed, because it has a lower probability than (0.81, 32). Pairs (0.2592, 30), (0.504, 30), (0.324, 30), (0.63, 30), and (0.18, 30) are removed, because they have lower probabilities but higher costs than pair (0.72, 28). (0.576, 28) is removed, because it has a lower probability than (0.72, 28). Pairs (0.2304, 22) and (0.112, 22) are removed, because they have lower probabilities than (0.448, 22). Pairs (0.2592, 26), (0.504, 26), (0.324, 26), and (0.144, 26) are removed, because they have lower probabilities than (0.63, 26). Pairs (0.2016, 24) and (0.252, 24) are removed, because they have lower probabilities but higher costs than pair (0.448, 22).

6. Use the same calculation method to gain the results for other timing constraints, until timing constraint 16.

7. Under timing constraint 16:

TC 10+6: $(0.8, 14) \odot (1.0, 2) = (0.8, 16)$

TC 10+6: $(0.9, 18) \odot (1.0, 2) = (0.9, 20)$

TC 10+6: $(1.0, 22) \odot (1.0, 2) = (1.0, 24)$

TC 11+5: $(0.8, 14) \odot (0.4, 2) = (0.32, 16)$

TC 11+5: $(0.8, 14) \odot (1.0, 8) = (0.8, 22)$

TC 11+5: $(1.0, 18) \odot (0.4, 2) = (0.4, 20)$

TC 11+5: $(1.0, 18) \odot (1.0, 8) = (1.0, 26)$

TC 12+4: $(0.8, 14) \odot (0.4, 2) = (0.32, 16)$

TC 12+4: $(0.8, 14) \odot (1.0, 8) = (0.8, 22)$

TC 12+4: $(1.0, 18) \odot (0.4, 2) = (0.4, 20)$

TC 12+4: $(1.0, 18) \odot (1.0, 8) = (1.0, 26)$

TC 13+3: $(1.0, 14) \odot (0.4, 2) = (0.4, 16)$

TC 13+3: $(1.0, 14) \odot (1.0, 8) = (1.0, 22)$

The selected pairs include (0.9, 20), (0.8, 16), and (1.0, 22).

(1.0, 24) and (1.0, 26) are removed, because they have higher costs than (1.0, 22). (0.8, 22) and (0.2, 22) are removed, because they have lower probabilities than (1.0, 22). (0.4, 20) are removed, because they have lower probabilities than (0.9, 20). (0.32, 16) are removed, because they have lower probabilities than (0.8, 16).

8. Under timing constraint 17:

TC 11+6: (0.8, 14) ⊙ (1.0, 2) = (0.8, 16)

TC 12+5: (1.0, 18) ⊙ (0.4, 2) = (0.4, 20)

TC 11+6: (1.0, 18) ⊙ (1.0, 2) = (1.0, 20)

TC 12+5: (1.0, 18) ⊙ (1.0, 8) = (1.0, 26)

TC 12+5: (0.8, 14) ⊙ (0.4, 2) = (0.32, 16)

TC 13+4: (1.0, 14) ⊙ (0.4, 2) = (0.4, 16)

TC 12+5: (0.8, 14) ⊙ (1.0, 8) = (0.8, 22)

TC 13+4: (1.0, 14) ⊙ (1.0, 8) = (1.0, 22)

The selected pairs include (1.0, 20) and (0.8, 16).

Pairs (1.0, 26) and (1.0, 22)s are removed, because they have higher costs than (1.0, 20). (0.4, 20) is removed, because it has a lower probability than (1.0, 20). (0.8, 22) is removed, because it has a higher cost than (0.8, 16). (0.2, 22) is removed, because it has a lower probability than (0.8, 22), which has already been removed. (0.32, 16) and (0.4, 16) are removed, because they have lower probabilities than (0.8, 16).

9. Under timing constraint 18:

TC 12+6: (0.8, 14) ⊙ (1.0, 2) = (0.8, 16)

TC 12+6: (1.0, 18) ⊙ (1.0, 2) = (1.0, 20)

TC 13+5: (1.0, 14) ⊙ (0.4, 2) = (0.4, 16)

TC 13+5: (1.0, 14) ⊙ (1.0, 8) = (1.0, 22)

The selected pairs include (1.0, 20) and (0.8, 16).

(1.0, 22) is removed because it has a higher cost than (1.0, 20). (0.4, 16) is removed because it has a lower probability than (0.8, 16).

10. Under timing constraint 19:

TC 13+6: (1.0, 14) ⊙ (1.0, 2) = (1.0, 16)

There is only one pair under this timing constraint.

Table 7.9 represents the final results of the D Table for path V3 → V4.

Table 7.9 D Table Showing the Path V3 → V4

T	(P, C)	(P, C)	(P, C)	(P, C)	(P, C)	(P, C)
4	(0.1296, 36)					
5	(0.648, 36)	(0.1008, 30)	(0.1296, 32)			
6	(0.1152, 28)	(0.1008, 26)	(0.504, 30)	(0.81, 36)	(0.648, 32)	
7	(0.2016, 24)	(0.576, 28)	(0.63, 30)	(0.504, 26)	(0.81, 32)	(0.0896, 22)
8	(0.81, 32)	(0.2016, 20)	(0.448, 22)	(0.72, 28)	(0.9, 36)	(0.63, 26)
9	(0.1792, 16)	(0.252, 20)	(0.56, 22)	(0.9, 30)	(0.72, 26)	
10	(0.224, 16)	(0.288, 20)	(0.64, 22)	(0.9, 26)		
11	(0.504, 20)	(0.9, 26)	(0.256, 16)	(1.0, 36)	(0.8, 22)	
12	(0.448, 16)	(0.63, 20)	(0.8, 22)	(0.9, 26)	(1.0, 30)	
13	(0.56, 16)	(0.9, 24)	(0.72, 20)	(1.0, 26)	(0.8, 22)	
14	(0.64, 16)	(0.9, 20)				
15	(0.8, 16)	(0.9, 20)	(1.0, 22)			
16	(0.9, 20)	(0.8, 16)	(1.0, 22)			
17	(1.0, 20)	(0.8, 16)				
18	(1.0, 20)	(0.8, 16)				
19	(1.0, 16)					

According to the table, the shortest timing constraint is 4 units of time, and the longest constraint is 19. The path V1 → V2 → V3 → V4 can be found by the final results. For example, under timing constraint 9, there are five paths, which are (0.1792, 16), (0.252, 20), (0.56, 22), (0.9, 30), and (0.72, 26). The path reaching the pair (0.252, 20) can be found out by the following steps:

1. $(0.63, 18) \odot (0.4, 2) = (0.252, 20)$ when V3 → V4

2. $(0.7, 9) \odot (0.9, 9) = (0.63, 18)$ when V2 → V3

3. $(1.0, 5) \odot (0.7, 4) = (0.7, 9)$ when V1 → V2

4. Therefore, the path V1 → V2 → V3 → V4 ends at pair (0.252, 20) and derives from $(1.0, 5) \odot (0.7, 4) \to (0.7, 9) \odot (0.9, 9) \to (0.63, 18) \odot (0.4, 2) \to (0.252, 20)$.

In summary, the *PTM of HES* has an advantage in solving the

HA problems. The total cost of the system can be reduced by scheduling the guaranteed confidence probabilities under the various timing constraints. The next section briefly introduces the concept of *Nondeterministic Polynomial-Time Problems*, which explains the problem type of this chapter.

7.4 NONDETERMINISTIC POLYNOMIAL-TIME PROBLEMS

Nondeterministic Polynomial-Time Problems (NP-Problem) is a set of decision problems that cannot be solved by a polynomial-time algorithm [93]. A *Decision Problem* is to determine whether there is a route whose cost is no more than K for a given K. One of the examples of NP-Problems is Traveling Salesman Problem (TSP), which is to find the cheapest way of visiting all of the cities and returning to the starting point when given a collection of cities and the cost of travels between each pair of them.

7.4.1 Cook's Theorem

The Propositional Satisfiability Problem (SAT) problem is one of the hardest problems in NP, which is also abbreviated as a *Satisfiability* problem. The problem usually addresses a judgment issue that determines whether there exists a true value assignment to a set of sentences in a propositional logic. A *logic* refers to an assignment value to the *Formal Language* that is a symbolizing approach using symbol strings to represent a set of constraints, rules, or structures. *Cook's Theorem* states that all the problems in NP can be "reduced" to SAT problems by using the given Boolean formula F to determine whether there are assignments for each x_i, such that $F=TRUE$.

Problem A reduces to Problem B, and A is smaller or less than B (A < B). The algorithm solving B can be used to solve A. So Problem B is more difficult or not simpler than Problem B.

Example 1. Problem A: find the medium of a sequence. Problem B: sort a sequence, and A is less or smaller than B (A < B).

B is in NP, and SAT < B →. From Cook's theorem, we know that SAT is hardest in NP, then B is somewhat equivalent to SAT. C is in NP, and B < C, etc. Many problems are like SAT and B; they are called NP-complete problems. Note that this "reduction" must be done in polynomial time. If there is a polynomial time solution for just one NP complete problem, NP == P. How to prove problem B is NP complete: Show that B is in Np. Find an NP complete problem A, and you can make a polynomial time reduction (transformation): A < B.

7.5 EXERCISES

7.5.1 Fundamental Questions

1. What is the concept of *Heterogeneous Embedded Systems*?

2. What are key features of *Heterogeneous Embedded Systems*?

3. What basic models do *Heterogeneous Embedded Systems* have?

4. What is dynamic programing and how does dynamic programming contribute to the *Heterogeneous Embedded Systems*?

5. What are the characteristics of *Functional Units*? What role do *Functional Units* play in *Heterogeneous Embedded Systems*?

6. What is the definition of the *Fixed Time Model of Heterogeneous Embedded Systems*? What does the term *Fixed Time* mean in this concept?

7. Why do we need to accomplish the *Heterogeneous Assignment* for optimizing the *Fixed Time Model*?

8. What does a *Data Flow Graph* mean? In which situation do we need to use this technique?

9. What is the purpose(s) of *Minimum Resource Scheduling* after finishing the *Heterogeneous Assignment* in *Fixed Time Models*?

10. What is the concept of the *Heterogeneous Assignment with Probability* problem?

11. What is a *Guaranteed Confidence Probability*?

12. What does a *Probabilistic Data Flow Graph* mean? What are the differences between *Probabilistic Data Flow Graph* and *Data Flow Graph*?

13. What is a *B Table* in *Heterogeneous Assignment* with *Probability* problems?

14. What is a *D Table* in *Heterogeneous Assignment* with *Probability* problems? What is the relationship between the *B Table* and the *D Table*?

15. What is a *Nondeterministic Polynomial-Time* problem? Give an example.

16. How do you think of the *Propositional Satisfiability Problem*?

7.5.2 Practical Questions

1. **Practice for Fixed Time Model**

   Table 7.10 represents 5 nodes A, B, C, D, and E in a linked list. Each node has two different working modes, which all have different completion times and resource costs. For example, node A has mode A1 and mode A2. Your mission includes:

   (a) You need to calculate the minimum total cost while satisfying timing constraints by using dynamic programming.

   (b) Show and explain **each step**.

   (c) What are the mode assignments for all nodes? Give the details of all paths.

Table 7.10 Nodes with Completion Time and Costs

Nodes	Time	Cost
A1	1	6
A2	2	4
B1	3	8
B2	5	5
C1	4	9
C2	6	7
D1	2	9
D2	5	4
E1	3	7
E2	7	4

2. **Additional Question for Fixed Time Model**

Design an experiment or practical scenario that can use the results of the question *Practice for Fixed Time Model*. Do a comparison between this algorithm and the algorithms taught in other chapters, such as *Chapter Mobile Embedded Systems Architecture*.

3. **Practice for Probabilistic Time Model**

Shown in Table 7.11, there are 4 nodes 0, 1, 2, and 3 in a linked list. Each node has two different working modes, R1 and R2. The table displays the probabilities, time, and costs of each node. Here are your missions:

(a) Convert Table 7.11 into a table showing the **cumulative distribution functions** and the cost at each node by using different functional unit types. (Refer to Table 7.4.)

(b) Produce a **B Table**. (Refer to Section 7.3.2.)

(c) Produce a **D Table**. (Refer to Section 7.3.3 and Section 7.3.4.)

(d) Calculate the minimum total cost while satisfying timing constraints with all guaranteed probabilities by using dynamic programs.

(e) Show and explain **each step**.

(f) For the hard real-time scenario with timing constraint 19, what is the mode assignment for all nodes to get the minimum cost?

Table 7.11 Nodes with Times, Probabilities, and Costs

Nodes	R1			R2		
	T_1	P_1	C_1	T_2	P_2	C_2
0	1	0.7	8	2	0.7	3
	3	0.3	8	4	0.3	3
1	1	0.8	9	2	0.6	4
	2	0.2	9	3	0.4	4
2	1	0.9	7	3	0.2	5
	4	0.1	7	5	0.8	5
3	1	0.4	10	2	0.6	6
	3	0.6	10	5	0.4	6

7.6   GLOSSARY

Dynamic Programming
>   is an approach of solving complicated problems by dividing them into smaller-sized sub-problems.

Heterogeneous Embedded Systems (HESs)
>   are method of deploying multiple functional units in an embedded system for achieving a higher-level performance.

Heterogeneity
>   refers to multiple basic operating units, such as memories, processors, and graphic processing units.

Functional Unit
>   is a low-level component or a group of components that are used for a specific purpose, such as arithmetic functions, assignments, logic operations, or to compare operations.

Fixed Time Model (FTM)
>   is a model consisting of a number of nodes that all have fixed value with the specific execution times.

Probabilistic Time Model
>   is a model consisting of a number of nodes that are restricted by the conditional executive times that are associated with the multiple inputs or hardware usages.

B Table
>   is a tabulation that can represent the costs and probabilities of the node completions under different timing constraints.

D Table
>   is a tabulation that represents optimal solutions with probabilities and costs under different timing constraints, which is generated by using dynamic programming.

Nondeterministic Polynomial-Time Problems (NP-Problem)

>   is a set of decision problems that cannot be solved by a polynomial-time algorithm.

Decision Problem

is to determine whether there is a route whose cost is no more than K for a given K.

Cook's Theorem

state that all the problems in NP can be "reduced" to SAT problems by using the given Boolean formula F to determine whether there are assignments for each x_i, such that $F=TRUE$.

CHAPTER 8

Mobile Optimizations by Loop Scheduling

CONTENTS

Loops OPTIMIZATION is an important and effective technique for achieving a better performance without replacing or enhancing hardware. This chapter introduces another approach for optimizing mobile embedded systems. In some practical scenarios, the performance of the mobile embedded systems can be measured by two parameters, namely time and power. One of the optimal schemas is accomplishing tasks under timing constraints with a lower-level energy consumption. For reaching this goal, this chapter provides students with a method that uses the *Loop Scheduling* technique to increase the working efficiency and power management capability, since completing *loops* is one of the most time-consuming and energy-consuming parts of a mobile application. Optimizing *Loops* is an important and effective technique for achieving a better performance by using the existing mobile infrastructure. The main contents of this chapter include:

1. The concepts related to the loop scheduling optimization

2. Categories of scheduling

3. Optimization methods of loop scheduling

4. Differences between assignments and rotations with timing constraints

5. Using Probability Data Flow Graph (PDFG) technique for loop scheduling optimization

8.1 INTRODUCTION

This chapter aims to instruct students to gain the knowledge of mobile embedded systems using loop scheduling and parallel computing techniques. Students should discern the operating principle of the timing optimizations and understand how to implement the schemas introduced in this chapter. Crucial concepts should be fully cognized from reading this chapter, such as Probabilistic Data-Flow Graph (PDFG), *Retiming, Rotation Scheduling*, and *Parallel Computing*. After reading this chapter, students need to perceive the scenarios of leveraging and implementing the mentioned techniques. Throughout this chapter, students should be able to answer the following questions:

1. What are the differences between *Probabilistic Data-Flow Graph* and *Data-Flow Graph*? Which one is more effective in the real-world context?

2. When and why can *Loop Scheduling* and *Parallel Computing* achieve the time and power optimizations in mobile embedded systems?

3. What are the meanings of *Retiming, Unfolding*, and *Rotation*? How do you use these two techniques in the optimization of time and power?

4. What are the key steps of implementing *Loop Scheduling Optimization*?

8.2 BASIC GRAPH MODELS AND TECHNIQUES

8.2.1 Data-Flow Graph in Loop Scheduling

In prior chapters, we already introduce the Data-Flow Graph (DFG) approach that is using graphic diagrams to represent data dependencies or functional units between operations. In practice, there are a variety of methods for modeling applications with sequencing graphs. Using the graphic-based methodology can consider each application a sequence of activities, functions, and task schedules [94]. For the purpose of optimizations, various phases within an application can be synthesized as a chain of subprocesses with using graph-theoretical methods [95, 62, 96]. This chapter mainly uses techniques derived from the DFG method to represent loop scheduling [97]. The definition of DFG loops is given by Definition 2. Main notations used in this chapter are given in Table 8.1.

Table 8.1 Main Notations Used in This Chapter

G	Data-Flow Graph (DFG)
G_r	Retimed DFG
G_f	Unfolded graph DFG
V	A set of nodes $-A_1, A_2, \ldots, A_n{}''$, A_n refers to nodes
E	A set of edges
d	A function representing delays attached to an edge
d_r	Retimed delay
t	Computation time
$t(v)$	Computation time unit(s) of each node
$r(v)$	Delay time unit(s) of each node
$D(p)$	The total computation time of path p
$T(p)$	The total delay counts of path p
$B(G)$	The iteration bound of the data-flow graph G
$T(l)$	Refers to the summation of all computation times in a cycle.
$D(l)$	Refers to the summation of all delay times in a cycle.
l	Refers to a cycle consisting of both computations and delays.
P	Iteration period
r	Function of retiming
f	Unfolding factor
S	The number of points in design space
c	A cycle period

Definition 2 $G=\langle\ V,\ E,\ d,\ t\ \rangle$ *represents a directed graph with features of node-weighted and edge-weighted; where* $V = -A_1, A_2, \ldots, A_n$ " *representing a set of nodes;* $\exists\ E_i = A_j \to A_k$, *referring to the edge* E_i *that starts at* A_j *and goes toward* A_k; $t(v)$ *refers to the computation time of the node* v.

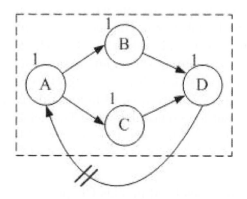

Figure 8.1 An example of a Data-Flow Graph (DFG).

Fig. 8.1 represents an example of DFG in which $V=-$ A, B, C, D". A symbol "$\to$" is used to describe an edge from one node to another. From the example, A $\to$ C refers to the edge from A to C. In Fig. 8.1, there are five edges shown in arrow lines, including A $\to$ C, A $\to$ B, B $\to$ D, C $\to$ D, and D $\to$ A. The edge "D $\to$ A" is marked by two short lines, which means that the edge has two delays. Other edges do not have delays, which are shown by normal arrow lines without marking short lines. The computation time of each node, $t(v)$, is usually stated as a value number beside nodes. According to Fig. 8.1, it depicts the computation time of each node is one time unit. Based on understanding the DFG schema, we introduce the concept of the *Iteration* in the loop scheduling.

The **iteration** represents the process repetitions that have each node in V executed exactly once. An iteration can be associated with a static schedule. A *static schedule* means the nodes must follow the order of precedence defined by the given DFG. The weighted edges are used to represent the inter-iteration dependencies. For instance, as shown in Fig. 8.1, an iteration j has two nodes D and A connected by the edge e. The delay from D to A is $d(e)$. This means that the computation of node v at iteration j is associated with the execution of node n at iteration $j - d(e)$. Other edges in the figure do not have delays, which means the data dependencies attached to those edges are within the same iteration.

Moreover, the **cycle period** refers to the total computation time of the longest zero-delay path in a DFG. We use $c(G)$ to represent the cycle period, use $D(p)$ to represent the total computation time, and use $T(p)$ to represent the total delay count of path, "p." For example, the $c(G)$ of DFG in Fig. 8.1 is 3 time units, if we assume that the computation time is one time unit at each node. The mathematical expression of $c(G)$ is: $c(G) = $ max–$T(p)$: $p \in G$ is a path with $D(p) = 0$".

The purpose of introducing *iteration* and *cycle period* is to design an optimized loop scheduling algorithm. The optimizations can be achieved by optimizing the processes of iterations and minimizing the time costs of cycle periods. In practice, a given DFG consists of a number of cycles that have different timing consumptions. The optimization principle is to minimize the execution time of all tasks in one iteration. Two important approaches for minimizing the total execution time include *retiming* and *unfolding*.

8.2.2 Retiming and Unfolding

Retiming is an optimization approach that transforms a DFG into the polynomial time and minimizes the cycle periods by redistributing registers or delays in a circuit. The principal method of the retiming is to reorganize or restructure the logical positions of the registers or latches in a circuit [98, 69]. Using a graph-based approach can effectively distribute delays among the edges [99, 62]. For example, Fig. 8.2 shows a retimed graph deriving from Fig. 8.1.

As exhibited in Fig. 8.2, a retiming can be considered a function *retiming r*, which redistributes the nodes of the previous DFG from Fig. 8.1. The new DFG is represented as $G_r = \langle V, E, d_r, t \rangle$, with a retimed delay "$d_r$." In this case, the delay time of node A is 1 time unit. B, C, and D nodes do not have any delay times. The retiming results in a new period of cycle $c(G_r)$ that turns into 2 from 3. Considering the dependencies, the retiming functions are various, which depends on the independent situations.

We can abstract a mathematical expression from the descriptions of the retiming mentioned above. Fig. 8.3 illustrates a common situation of the retiming formulation. The figure represents that there is an $r(v)$,

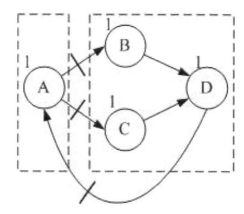

Figure 8.2   An example of Retimed Data-Flow Graph (DFG)

the delay time units following the edge from v to w, $v \rightarrow w$, from which is subtracted the edges from u to v, $u \rightarrow v$. All nodes u, v, and w are within the DFG G. According to the representations in Fig. 8.3, the retiming can be formulated by $d_r(e) = d(e) + r(u) - r(v)$, which is also given in Equation (8.1). The formulation describes the delay time units for each edge $u \rightarrow v$.

$$d_r(e) = d(e) + r(u) - r(v) \tag{8.1}$$

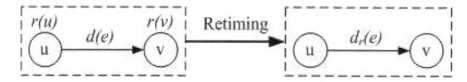

Figure 8.3   Retiming formulation.

Unfolding is another technique that can optimize loop scheduling with improving the average cycle period of a static schedule. The fundamental principle of the *unfolding* is to unroll and flatten the original DFG multiple times in order to gain a certain number of the copies of the original node sets and use the Instruction-Level Parallelism (ILP) to optimize the *Iteration Periods* [77]. ILP is a paradigm that is applied to examine the capability of simultaneous operations in a computing program or an application. An *iteration period* refers to the average computation time of an iteration for a DFG.

This approach can be also translated into mathematic expressions. Students can refer to the following descriptions to further discern the concept of the *unfolding*. As we discussed, the first step of the *unfolding* is to unfold the original graph, DFG G, f times. The unfolded graph is represented as a G_f, and the f is marked as an *unfolding factor*. Each G_f has f copies of the original node set, V. The duplicated f copies makes the schedule contain f iterations of the original DFG. This operation provisions a proposition for using the ILP approach to improve the iteration periods between iterations. The iteration period P can be formulated by $P=c(G_f)/f$.

Based on the *unfolding* approach, the concept of the *Iteration Bound* is introduced for the purpose of the scheduling calculations. An *Iteration Bound* means the maximum ratio of computation time to delay time for all cycles within a DFG. The precondition is that there must be at least one loop in the DFG. The ratio can be gained by calculating the proportions of the total computation time to the total delay time.

For example, we give an example by using the retimed DFG shown in Fig. 8.2. The iteration bound of this DFG is $1\frac{1}{2}$ from $3/2$. In the calculation, 3 derives from the total computation time that is a summation of B, C, and D. 2 is gained from 2 delays attached to B and C. For attaining the optimization of the loop scheduling, the minimum unfolding factor with the retiming function needs to be found. Therefore, understanding this concept is fundamental for students to further explore the timing optimizations with using *retiming* and *unfolding*. The definition of the *iteration bound* is given by Definition 3.

Definition 3 *The **iteration bound** of a DFG is a B(G) that is the maximum ratio of computation time to delay time for all cycles within a DFG. The equation $B(G)=max_{\forall l}\frac{T(l)}{D(l)}$. l refers to a cycle consisting of both computations and delays. T(l) refers to the summation of all computation times in a cycle. D(l) refers to the summation of all delay times in a cycle.*

8.3 FUNDAMENTAL TIMING OPTIMIZATIONS

Considering the conditions of resource restraints, there are two types of scheduling optimization problems. The first type of scheduling problem is improving loop scheduling with resource constraints; the other type is optimization without resource constraints. The determination of the optimization types depends on whether there are parallel operations executed by the parallel-style hardware. For example, multiple processors designed by Very Long Instruction Word (VLIW) architecture can simultaneously support up to eight operations, which implies that resource constraints need to be considered. This chapter introduces an approach Rotation Scheduling Algorithm (RSA), which is a polynomial-time scheduling algorithm that considers the resource constraints. The algorithm uses the *retiming* approach on DFGs and produces an optimal loop schedule in polynomial time with iterations.

Rotation Scheduling is a scheduling schema that is utilized to optimize the performances of loop schedules with multiple resource constraints [100, 30]. Using rotation scheduling technique can offer an approach for compacting iterations of loops and generating a minimum schedule length in a polynomial time [101]. The method of implementing rotation scheduling is given in Section 8.4.

The approach introduced in this section is an advanced optimal algorithm that has a better performance than most other algorithms. For example, prior research had proved that instruction scheduling that parallels hardware pipelining could efficiently optimize loops. In computer science, this type of instruction scheduling is also known as *Modulo Scheduling* or *Software Pipelining*. However, it has been determined that the rotation scheduling algorithm is more superior than modulo scheduling for digital signal processing applications by optimizing the schedule length.

Fig. 8.4 gives an example of assignment for a dual-processor system. The left column represents the execution time, listing from 1 to 13 time units. Five tasks are attached to the corresponding processor with time consumptions. For example, task 1 takes 3 time units, and tasks 2 and 3 are succeeding tasks. According to Fig. 8.4, the accomplishment time is 13 time-unit.

Moreover, using rotation can reduce the accomplishment time of the cycle. Fig. 8.5 represents an example of rotation with using the same system as the one shown in Fig. 8.4. The cycle length is lowered down to 10 time units and processor 2 to execute more tasks, including tasks 1 and 2. The comparison between Fig. 8.4 and Fig. 8.5 describes a clear advantage of using rotation to improve the working efficiency for the given DFG.

Minimizing Unfolding Factors One of the challenging parts of

	Processor 1	Processor 2
1	1	
2		
3		
4	3	2
5		
6	4	
7		
8		
9		
10	5	
11		
12		
13		

Figure 8.4 A template example of assignment.

the rotation scheduling algorithm is that it is hard to find the feasible solution in a large design space in a short period. Addressing the optimization target, a *Design Space* is associated with retiming, unfolding factor, and the number of points. The number of points is represented by S. We define the value of the *Design Space* $=r \times f \times S$. The aim of the optimization is producing **the minimum sets of unfolding factors** to lower down the iteration period constraint with retiming.

The method of producing the minimum cycle periods follows a few steps:

1. Confirm that there is a legal static schedule with retiming for a DFG.

2. Find out the values of variables in the given DFG, including a set of nodes "V", a set of edges "E", delays "d", and computation time "t". Define "c" as a cycle period.

3. The minimum cycle period can be gained when matching two conditions. First, the value obtained by dividing the cycle period

	Processor 1	Processor 2
1	3	2
2		
3	4	1
4		
5		
6		
7	5	
8		
9		
10		
11		
12		
13		

Figure 8.5 A template example of rotation.

by unfolding factor is not smaller than the iteration bound of the DFG. Second, the cycle period is not less than the greatest computation time at nodes.

4. Ceiling the product of unfolding factor and the iteration bound of the DFG.

5. Compare the biggest computation time of all nodes with the outcome generated at step (4). The bigger value is the minimum cycle period.

Fig. 8.6 represents an example of producing the minimum cycle period. According to the figure, there are three nodes in a DFG, namely A, B, and C. The computation times of each node are various, with $t(A)=1$, $t(B)=5$, and $t(C)=1$, which are also given in the figure. Edges A → B and B → C do not have any time delay. The edge C → A has four time units delay, which is marked by four short lines. The cycle period of the given DFG is 7 time units deriving from 1 + 5 + 1. According to Definition 3, the iteration bound is 7/4, since the total computation time units are 7 and the total delay time units are

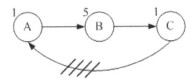

Figure 8.6 An example of the minimum cycle periods using Theorem 8.1.

4. When the unfolding fact is equal to 2, the best feasible cycle period with retiming should be 5, which derives from a bigger value selection from 5 and 4. Moreover, 5 is the longest computation time of the node. 4 is a ceiling of $2\times(7/4)$, which is a product of unfolding factor and the iteration bound of the data-flow graph. This cycle period is considered a minimum cycle period for the given DFG. This result also represents that there is no schedule with a cycle period less than 5 when the unfolding factor is 2.

The above steps can translated into mathematical expressions, which is given in Theorem 8.1.

Theorem 8.1 (Minimum Cycle Period $c_{min}(G_f)$) *There is a legal static schedule with retiming, let $G=\langle V,E,d,t\rangle$, $f \in Z^+$, $c \in R$, if $c/f \geq B(G)$ and $c \geq max_v t(v)$, $\forall v \in V$, then $c_{min}(G_f)=max(max_v t(v), \lceil f \cdot B(G)\rceil)$*

8.4 TIME AND POWER OPTIMIZATIONS WITH LOOP SCHEDULING

Having the knowledge of retiming and unfolding is a basis of learning the advanced optimization method in loop scheduling. This section focuses on introducing the optimal algorithm for time and power optimization with loop scheduling.

8.4.1 Probabilistic Data-Flow Graph

The technique of DFG is a traditional approach for synthesizing mobile embedded systems. However, in real-world implementations, the system behaviors and complexities often require a higher-level DFG. Normal DFG has difficulties in dealing with the system uncertainties. Most current solutions are *Assumption Case-Based* approaches, which are based on the assumption of the computation time at the worst case or the average-level case. Nevertheless, this approach cannot be competent to many practical situations because computation and communication times may become random variables. The unallowable error range caused by the random variables can dramatically decrease the accuracy and eventually result in inefficient schedules.

Probabilistic Data-Flow Graph (PDFG) is introduced to optimize those systems having tasks with uncertain computation times, such as interface systems, fuzzy systems, or artificial intelligence systems [72]. The main objective of PDFG is to make the behaviors of the complex systems understandable. To reach this goal, the optimized graph can be obtained by using a probabilistic approach. The crucial part of the approach is generating cycle periods that are close to optimal status with a high-degree of confidence.

According to the prior research, using a PDFG-based solution is superior to the assumption case-based approach [30, 72, 78]. The improvement of the schedule length using the new probabilistic retiming can reach up to 40% shorter than the worse-case-based and up to 30 % shorter than the average-case-based approaches in the same circumstance. The efficiency of implementing PDFG has a great advantage. For designing an optimization algorithm, a probabilistic model needs to be created in order to keep the outcomes within the allowable error range. An effective probabilistic model should contain all possible values of the event variables.

Fig. 8.7 gives an example of representing complex system behaviors. The corresponding behavior information is displayed by Table 8.2. There are five nodes in the graph, and each node has various attributes when selecting different routes. Three routes are available, including $A{\rightarrow}B{\rightarrow}D$, $A{\rightarrow}C{\rightarrow}D$, and $A{\rightarrow}G{\rightarrow}D$, which are represented as R_1, R_2, and R_3 in Table 8.2. The attribute variables counted in this graph include time, probabilities, and energy consumptions [102], represented as T, P, and E in Table 8.2.

For example, node A performs differently when implementing different routes. When selecting route 1, R_1, node A has two working mode. The first mode needs 1 time unit computation time at 70% probability of accomplishment rate with 10 units of energy consumption. The other mode needs 3 time units computation time at 100% probability of accomplishment rate with the same energy consumption as the first working mode. The 100% probability derives from a sum of 30% and 70%, (0.3+0.7).

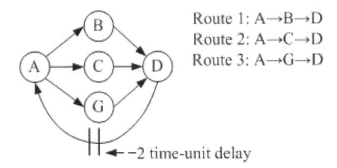

Route 1: A→B→D
Route 2: A→C→D
Route 3: A→G→D

−2 time-unit delay

Figure 8.7 An example of probabilistic DFG corresponding with Table 8.2.

Table 8.2 Table for PDFG with Time, Probabilities, and Energy Consumptions of its Nodes Under Different Routes

Nodes	R_1			R_2			R_3		
	T	P	E	T	P	E	T	P	E
A	1	0.7	10	2	0.8	5	4	0.8	1
	3	0.3		5	0.2		6	0.2	
B	2	1.0	7	3	1.0	5	5	1.0	1
C	1	1.0	9	2	1.0	7	3	1.0	3
G	1	0.8	7	4	0.8	3	5	0.6	2
	2	0.2		5	0.2		6	0.4	
D	1	0.8	9	3	0.9	4	5	0.5	1
	3	0.2		4	0.1		6	0.5	

Moreover, node A has a different performance when going through route 2, referring to R_2. At R_2, there are also two working modes. The first working mode can finish the task within 2 time units at 80% probability and requires 5 units of energy cost. The other working mode can finish the task by 5 time units at 100% probability with 5 units of energy cost. Finally, the last route R_3 offers another choice for node A. The first working mode at R_3 needs 4 time units to complete the task. The probability is 80% and energy cost is 1. The second working mode at R_3 needs 6 time units to complete the task, with 100% probability and 1 unit of energy cost.

The rest nodes represented in Table 8.2 can be operated as the same as the procedures described above. To optimize the loop scheduling, an optimal solution combining the benefits of each route needs to be found out, even though it is a challenging task in practice [103]. The following section can guide students to design a solution using the skills of loop scheduling optimizations.

8.4.2 Loop Scheduling and Parallel Computing

A graph-based approach is usually gained from a loop program in practice. Loop scheduling optimization is usually combined with implementing *Parallel Computing* [72]. Parallel computing is a paradigm for computation that simultaneously executes multiple calculations. The operating principle of parallel computing is dividing bigger-size tasks into smaller-size subtasks and executes divided tasks simultaneously. The implementation of parallel computing enables a loop to complete multiple processes within one cycle. Utilizing retiming techniques in loop scheduling generates an optimal solution, which uses the advantages of parallel computing to maximize the performance of the existing infrastructure [104].

A Parallel Computing System (PCS) is a computer or system that applies multiple processors for completing multiple parallel processes. The legacy technique of multiprocessing systems only allowed each processor to attach to its own processor package. Current multiprocessing technology enables multiple logical processors to work within one package, which is executed by a multicore processor. The emerging technology has introduced various types of PCS. One of the popular methods categorizing PCSs is classifying PCSs by processors and memories [105, 106, 75]. Examples of modern PCSs are the Raw multiprocessor developed by MIT, the Trips multiprocessor developed by the University of Texas, and Power5 developed by IBM.

The following is an example of a loop program named W. Fig. 8.8 represents a corresponding DFG for program W. Assume that there are four processors available for running the program W, involving processors P_1, P_2, P_3, and P_4. This section gives an optimal solution that can obtain the minimum total execution time using retiming. The first step is drawing a DFG according to the given program W. The expressions of program W refers to the following.

The given program W:
For (i∈ N)
{A[i]=D[i-2]+12;

B[i]=A[i]×4;
C[i]=A[i]-10;
G[i]=A[i]+2;
D[i]=B[i]+C[i]+G[i];}

According to the given program W, the edge $D \rightarrow A$ has two time units delay because "A[i] = D[i-2]+12". In this expression, "i-2", means two time units delay from A to D. Other edges do not have any time units delay in this case. The expressions also describe the relationship between nodes and the edge directions. For example, "B[i]=A[i]×4" means the edge $A{\rightarrow}B$. The expression "D[i]=B[i]+C[i]+G[i]" refers to the three edges pointing at node D, including $B{\rightarrow}D$, $C{\rightarrow}D$, and $G{\rightarrow}D$. Combing all expressions can gain a loop that can be distinctly exhibited by a DFG.

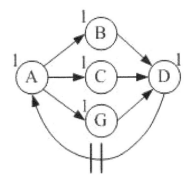

Figure 8.8 The probabilistic data-flow graph for program W.

As exhibited in Fig. 8.8, a DFG is drawn based on program W, in which $V=\{A, B, C, G, D\}$. $u{\rightarrow}v$ represents an edge from node u to node v. In the figure, the edge set consists of seven edges, which are $A{\rightarrow}B$, $A{\rightarrow}C$, $A{\rightarrow}G$, $B{\rightarrow}D$, $C{\rightarrow}D$, $G{\rightarrow}D$, and $D{\rightarrow}A$. As we discussed, the edge $D{\rightarrow}A$ has two time units delay, which is represented by an arrow line marked by two short lines. One short line refers to one time unit delays. Other edges do not have time delay, which are represented by the arrow lines without short lines. The computation time at each node is 1, also marked beside each node. Following this DFG leads to the current iteration time consumption, which needs go through all nodes in set V exactly once.

Fig. 8.9 represents the iterations of the static schedule deriving from Fig. 8.8. In this case, three processors are being used. The arrow

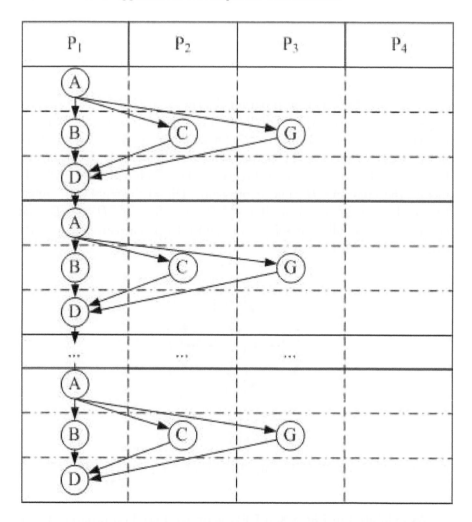

Figure 8.9 Iterations of the static schedule for the given data-flow graph.

lines depict the order of nodes, and the arrow points at the succeeding node. For example, the arrow line between node A and B means node B can be executed after node A. Using this static schedule needs three execution cycles to complete each loop. Therefore, if the program ran 100 times, the number of the total execution cycles would be 300, from 3×100.

In order to optimize the loop scheduling, a shorter loop can be achieved by reducing the number of execution cycles. To reach this goal, both retiming and rotation are needed. The optimization procedure for

PDFG using retiming and rotation is represented in Figures 8.10 –8.13. The main steps are respectively represented in Figures 8.10, 8.11, 8.12, and 8.13.

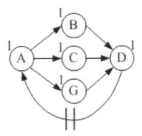

Figure 8.10   The probabilistic data-flow graph for program W.

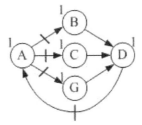

Figure 8.11   The probabilistic data-flow graph after retiming.

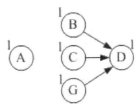

Figure 8.12   The static scheduling probabilistic data-flow graph before regrouping.

1. **Original PDFG**

   Fig. 8.10 illustrates an original PDFG for the given program W,

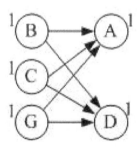

Figure 8.13 The optimization procedure of the probabilistic data-flow graph with retiming.

which is as same as Fig. 8.8. At this stage, the PDFG follows the static schedule and there is no optimization yet. The edge $D{\rightarrow}A$ has two time units delay. Three execution cycles are needed to complete a loop so that the loop schedule length is 3. The PDFG follows the given program W shown as follows.

For (i∈ N)
{A[i]=D[i-2]+12;
B[i]=A[i]×4;
C[i]=A[i]-10;
G[i]=A[i]+2;
D[i]=B[i]+C[i]+G[i];}

2. **Retiming**

Next, Fig. 8.11 represents a PDFG stating a status after retiming. The delays in the circuit are redistributed for the purpose of minimizing the cycle periods. We redistributed a delay from edge $D \rightarrow A$ to the edges starting at A, including edges $A \rightarrow B$, $A \rightarrow C$, and $A \rightarrow G$, due to considering the dependencies of the nodes. The redistributed delays at these three edges are the same, 1 time unit delay, which is shown in Fig. 8.11. At this stage, there are still three execution cycles in the loop. Referring to Equation (8.1) in Section 8.2.1, delays at each node after retiming can also be retrieved by the following calculations.

Calculating d_r for $A \rightarrow B$, $d_r(e) = d(e) + r(u) - r(v) = 0 + 1 - 0 = 1$

Calculating d_r for $A \rightarrow C$, $d_r(e) = d(e) + r(u) - r(v) = 0 + 1 - 0 = 1$

Calculating d_r for $A \rightarrow G$, $d_r(e) = d(e) + r(u) - r(v) = 0 + 1 - 0 = 1$

The loop body can be represented as follows:
```
{B[i]=A[i]×4;
C[i]=A[i]-10;
G[i]=A[i]+2;
D[i]=B[i]+C[i]+G[i];
A[i+1]=D[i-1]+12; }
```

3. **Rotation**

Moreover, the final step of the optimization procedure is using the rotation technique. As discussed in Section 8.3, this step mainly compacts iterations of loops to minimize the schedule length. Fig. 8.12 gives a status before regrouping the loop. Node A is split from the loop, and other nodes follow the static loop schedule. Step (2) shows that node A has one time unit delay to all three succeeding nodes, B, C, and G. Due to the dependencies of the nodes, node A can be rotated so it can be a succeeding node of nodes B, C, and G.

Fig. 8.13 shows the PDFG after rotations. As shown in the figure, the regrouped PDFG **only has two execution cycles**, which means the loop schedule length is 2. The following program is the code of the equivalent loop after regrouping the loop body. The loop body can be represented as follows:
```
B[N]=A[N]×4;
C[N]=A[N]-10;
G[N]=A[N]+2;
D[N]=B[N]+C[N]+G[N];
```

Fig. 8.14 illustrates an optimized iteration of PDFG. This solution also needs three processors. Compared with the solution represented by Fig. 8.9, the optimized loop schedule has shorter execution cycles. The loop schedule length has been reduced from 3 to 2. If the program ran 100 times, the number of the total execution cycles for the loop

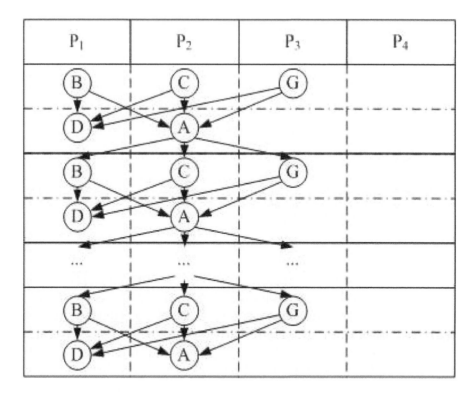

Figure 8.14 Iterations of the probabilistic data-flow graph after retiming.

after optmization would be 200, from 2 × 100. The working efficiency has been increased at least 30% in this case.

8.5 CONCLUSIONS

This chapter focuses on loop scheduling optimizations for mobile apps. The significance of understanding the schemas introduced in this chapter is to overcome two resource-consuming aspects, namely, computation time and energy consumption, by optimizing loop scheduling. After learning this chapter, students should discern key concepts of loop optimizations and be able to design an optimal loop for high performance of mobile apps.

8.6   EXERCISES

8.6.1   Fundamental Questions

1. What is a *Directed Acyclic Graph?*
   What is a *Data-Flow Graph*, then?

2. What does *Static Schedule* mean?

3. Explain the method of determining a *Cycle Period.*

4. Describe the concept of *retiming* and when the retiming technique can optimize a loop schedule.

5. What is an *Unfolding*, and what role does the unfolding play in the loop scheduling optimization?
   What is an *unfolding factor?*

6. Describe your understandings of *Iteration.*

7. What is the concept of the *Iteration Period?*

8. What is the concept of the *Iteration Bound?*
   Try to compare iteration period with iteration bound and explain the differences between these two concepts.

9. What is a static scheduling? What do we need to use static scheduling for?

10. Describe the basic operating principle of using retiming to optimize loop scheduling.

11. What is a Probabilistic Data-Flow Graph (PDFG)?
    Why do we need a PDFG to solve some problems in practice?

12. Two important optimization parameters are considered in this chapter. What are they?
    Use a few simple sentences to describe the importances of those two parameters.

13. What is the definition of *Parallel Architecture?*

14. What is the definition of *Parallel Computing?*

15. Use your own sentences to describe the differences between parallel architecture and parallel computing.

16. Use a few simple sentences to describe the relationship between loop scheduling and parallel computing in mobile optimization.

8.6.2 Practical Questions

The following questions provide students with an opportunity to practice the optimization techniques learned in this chapter. Two crucial parts covered by the questions are drawing a data-flow graph and using retiming.

1. **Drawing Data-Flow Graph Practice**

    Referring to the following given program, draw a data-flow graph. The time delay can be represented by marking short line(s) at the edge. One short line refers to one time unit delay.

    The given program:
    For (i= 1; i<N; i++) {
    A[i]=D[i-3]*3;
    B[i]=A[i]-8;
    C[i]=A[i]+1;
    D[i]=B[i]+C[i];
    E[i]=C[i]*D[i];}

2. **Retiming Technique Practice (a)**

    Fig. 8.15 gives a simple PDFG that has four nodes, including node A, B, C, and D. Assume the computation time at all nodes is 1 time unit. Three processors are available for your optimization. There is one time unit delay at the edge $D \rightarrow A$. Your mission is to use the technique introduced in this chapter to optimize this PDFG and draw a regrouped graph. To explain the analysis procedure, students are required to draw the scheduling maps step by step.

3. **Retiming Technique Practice (b)**

    Fig. 8.16 gives a PDFG that is more complicated than Practical Question 2). There are five nodes in this PDFG, which are nodes

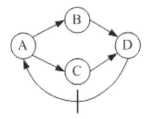

Figure 8.15 Figure for practical question 2).

A, B, C, D, and E. Assume the computation time at all nodes is 1 time unit. Four processors are available for your optimization. There are three time units delay at the edge $E \to A$. Your mission is to use the technique introduced in this chapter to optimize this PDFG and draw a regrouped graph. To explain the analysis procedure, students are required to draw the scheduling maps step by step.

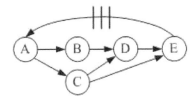

Figure 8.16 Figure for practical question 3).

4. **Loop Scheduling Optimization Practice**

Task 1: Given the below program W, please draw the corresponding *Data-Flow Graph* (DFG).

For (i= 1 to N)
{A[i]=D[i-2]+6;
B[i]=A[i]*2;
C[i]=A[i]-7;
G[i]=A[i]+1
D[i]=B[i]+C[i]+G[i];}

Task 2: We have four processors, P_1, P_2, P_3, and P_4, available. Your **first mission** is finding out the number of total execution cycles without retiming after running the program W 100 times.

Your **second mission** is figuring out the number of the total execution cycles with using retiming after running the program W 100 times. Try to compare two results generated from these two approaches. For explaining the analysis procedure, students are required to draw the scheduling maps step by step.

8.7 GLOSSARY

Directed Acyclic Graph

is an approach that is uses graphic diagrams to represent data dependencies or functional units between operations.

Static Schedule

means the nodes must follow the order of precedence defined by the given DFG.

Cycle Period

refers to the total computation time of the longest zero-delay path in the given DFG.

Retiming

is an optimization approach that transforms a DFG into the polynomial time and minimizes the cycle periods by redistributing registers or delays in a circuit.

Unfolding

is a technique that can optimize loop scheduling with improving the average cycle period of a static schedule.

Instruction-Level Paralleism

is a paradigm that is applied to examine the capability of simultaneous operations in a computing program or an application.

Iteration

represents the process repetitions that have each node in a set of nodes executed exactly once.

Iteration Period

refers to the average computation time of an iteration.

Iteration Bound

means the maximum ratio of computation time to delay time for all cycles within a DFG.

Static Schedule

means the nodes must follow the order of precedence defined by the given data-flow graph.

Unfolding Factor

the number representing how many times the original DFG has been unfolded.

Rotation Scheduling Algorithm

is a polynomial-time scheduling algorithm that considers the resource constraints.

Probabilistic Data-Flow Graph

is an advanced level DFG that is used to optimize those systems having tasks with uncertain computation times.

Parallel Architecture

refers to a type of computing architecture supporting simultaneous multiple operations.

Parallel Computing

is a paradigm for computation that simultaneously executes multiple calculations by using multiple processors.

Parallel Computing System

is a computer or system that applies multiple processors for completing multiple parallel processes.

III

Mobile App Techniques in Emerging Technologies

CHAPTER 9

Mobile Cloud Computing in Mobile Applications Deployment

CONTENTS

M o b i l e CLOUD COMPUTING has become a hot topic in the Android mobile application field. This chapter aims to provide students with a panoramic view about mobile cloud computing and its implementations in mobile apps development. A number of key concepts and techniques related to the filed of mobile cloud computing are introduced in this chapter. Throughout this chapter, students should be able to understand the crucial techniques being employed in mobile cloud and common applied architecture. This learning experience aims to enable students to build up connections between mobile cloud and mobile apps development skills. The main goal of learning this chapter is to facilitate students to gain the ability of developing mobile apps via a cloud-based approach. The main contents of this chapter include:

1. Concepts related to mobile cloud computing

2. Mobile cloud computing architecture

3. Technological structure of mobile cloud

4. Key technologies in mobile cloud

9.1 INTRODUCTION

This chapter instructs students about mobile cloud computing in order to assist students in bridging mobile cloud with the development skills learned in prior chapters. The chapter focuses on introducing the holistic view of mobile cloud with details for each technical dimension. The technological structure of mobile cloud consists of three aspects, mobile computing, mobile Internet, and cloud computing. Essential techniques implemented in each aspect are important instructional contents in this chapter, and are aligned with mobile app development and optimization techniques [107].

The aim of learning this chapter is twofold. First, students should have a good cognition of the implementation of mobile cloud by perceiving various technology selections. Second, students need to have the capability of understanding and using the architecture of mobile cloud computing in a real-world scenario. Throughout this chapter, students should be able to answer the following questions:

1. What are the main differences between mobile cloud computing and cloud computing?

2. What are the key components of the mobile cloud technological structure?
   What relationships do these components have?

3. What are the key technologies being implemented in cloud computing?
   What features do they have?

4. What is the mobile cloud architecture and how does it work?

9.2   CONCEPTS OF MOBILE CLOUD COMPUTING

Mobile Cloud Computing (MCC) is a technological paradigm that uses cloud-based approaches to provide mobile users using multiple services with mobile technologies and devices. This approach delivers cloud-based services to mobile end users by utilizing the benefits of mobile devices and extending the services scope [108, 109, 110, 111]. There are two main workload migrations that leverage the advantages of remote servers, including data processing [104, 99] and data storage [112, 113, 114]. The schema of achieving the operation migrations is to move on-premise data processing and storage onto the remote physical servers. The value of applying MCC-based solutions is to increase the capabilities of mobile devices by outsourcing workloads to the cloud servers. The computations of mobile apps can be completed on remote servers, which provides mobile apps with an approach for producing a higher-level performance [104, 115].

9.2.1   Technological Structure of Mobile Cloud Computing

MCC applications are applied to provision mobile cloud-based services represented by the mobile devices [110, 116]. The service representations require support from a few aspects of technologies. Main technologies involve three dimensions, which are mobile computing, wireless networks, and cloud computing [117, 110]. Most current MCC services can be considered a combination of these three angles. Fig. 9.1 shows a technical structure of MCC with a brief description of corresponding techniques in each dimension.

Fig. 9.2 represents a service flow diagram of leveraging MCC-based

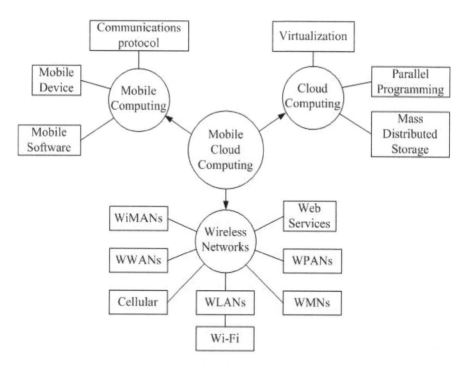

Figure 9.1 Technical structure of mobile cloud computing.

applications running on mobile devices. Three vital components in the diagram are mobile computing, wireless networks, and cloud servers. The communications between mobile devices and cloud servers are carried by various wireless networks. Service presentations are given on mobile devices in which mobile users can access the services. These three parts are three key techniques for generating an MCC-based solution.

9.2.2 Differences between Cloud Computing and Mobile Cloud

In most situations, cloud computing shares most approaches of service models and deployments with MCC [118, 119]. The concept of *Cloud Computing* is defined as a computing paradigm that uses Web-based technologies to provide users with scalable on-demand services with sharing or offering computing resources [120]. Considering the means of service delivery, there are still two differences between cloud computing and MCC, even though MCC originally derives from cloud computing.

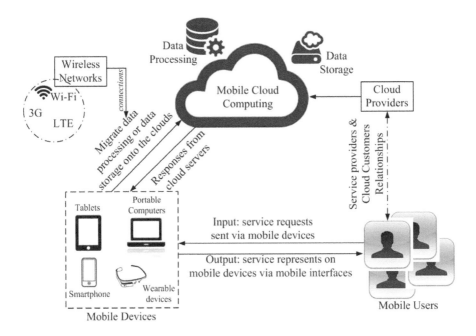

Figure 9.2 A diagram of leveraging mobile cloud computing.

First, the MCC model may have a different focus than general cloud computing does [121]. Both cloud computing and MCC solutions can be carried on both wired and wireless networks. However, MCC services accentuate the role of wireless communications and interconnectivities rather than virtualizing remote computing resources, which is emphasized by cloud computing. Compared with cloud computing, a wireless network is a fundamental component in MCC. MCC-based solutions must be designed, developed, and implemented by considering the usage in a wireless operating environment [122, 123, 124]. Leveraging mobile technologies enables MCC to be a driver of intelligent mobile communications.

Second, MCC service offerings are mobility-oriented services that emphasize the usage of mobile devices, interfaces, and platforms. This requires that MCC-based solutions not only perform the functionality that on-premise solutions can do, but also introduces mobility-based extensions, such as real-time communications, wireless data synchronization, and touch-screen features [125]. These extensions are considered crucial values for generating MCC services. Dissimilar to MCC, cloud computing services spread their service offerings in the broader ranged domains.

9.2.3 Mobile Computing

The term *Mobile Computing* is a group of technologies for building up the connectivity and communications between mobile devices on the Web. The technologies include at least three aspects: communications protocols, mobile devices, and mobile software. Most data communications need an assortative operation combining these three technologies [126]. Fig. 9.3 represents a conceptual structure of key aspects in mobile computing. A number of examples in each aspect are also given in the figure.

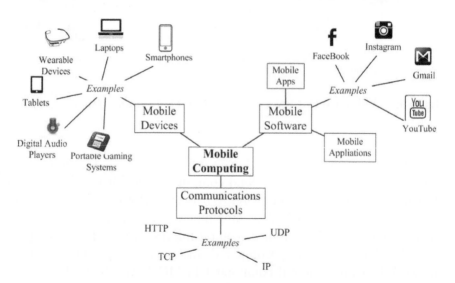

Figure 9.3 Three key aspects of mobile computing and examples.

A *Communications Protocol* is a set of rules that ensure all mobile devices involved in the communication can understand each other when data are transmitted. The rules in communications protocol need to govern the data transmission based on the specified purposes. For example, basic core Internet protocols are the Transmission Control Protocol (TCP) and Internet Protocol (IP), which are often called *TCP/IP Model*. This protocol model aims to provide communicated computing with a reliable and secure data transmission. Instead, another common protocol, Connectionless User Datagram Protocol (UDP), is mainly used for fast communications with lower-level security requirements [127].

The next facet of mobile computing is mobile devices. *Mobile Devices* refer to a set of portable or wearable devices with the capability of wireless communications, on which applications can execute. Common mobile devices include laptops, tablets, smart-phones, wearable devices, digital audio players, and portable gaming systems. Addressing the issue of mobility, mobile devices are also considered a platform in which end-users can acquire Internet-based services or access online database without the limitations of wired networks [128].

Next, *Mobile Software* refers to those applications or apps running on mobile devices that are used to represent mobile services. In the discipline of computer science, the concept of an app is different from an application. Both concepts are used to describe a computer program of service representations running on mobile devices. However, there is a major difference between applications and apps. An application runs directly on the Operating System (OS) but an app runs within the framework, such as Android. For example, those programs running on Android are Android apps. Using the approach of developing apps in the framework can remarkably reduce the app's development time.

There are a few approaches for mobile users to acquire mobile apps or applications. A common way is downloading mobile software from the Application Distribution Platforms (AppDP). Generally speaking, an AppDP is an interface for provisioning software purchases and downloads, which are owned and operated by the OS provider. For instance, current typical AppDPs include App Store, Amazon Appstore, Google Play, Windows Store, Windows Phone Store, and Samsung Apps Store. Some examples of popular mobile apps are Facebook, Google Maps, Gmail, Instagram, and YouTube.

9.2.4 Wireless Networks

Mobile Internet, also known as *Wireless Networking Technologies*, is a set of advanced networking technologies that activate interconnectivity between communicators over the wireless networks by which mobile software is supported. *Communicators* in mobile Internet are a number of *Network Nodes*, which refer to multiple types of processing locations occurring in various digital infrastructures. These network nodes can be seen as a few connective and communicative points with different purposes or functions. All activities taking place at network nodes must follow the networking rules defined by deployed protocols [129]. In essence, a network node itself can acknowledge the succeeding actions by its programming capability. Basic types of network nodes include connection and endpoint nodes, which point out two fundamental movements during the processes of data transmissions.

Moreover, there are a variety of wireless network types for different usage purposes. Currently, common wireless network types include Wireless Personal Area Networks (WPANs), Wireless Local Area Networks (WLANs), Wireless Mesh Networks (WMNs), Wireless Metropolitan Area Networks (WiMANs), Wireless Wide Area Networks (WWANs), and Cellular Network (Cellular). Table 9.1 evaluates a comparison among current main wireless network types. In general, mobile wireless networks still face restrictions of bandwidth when service coverage scope becomes larger and mobility level goes higher. Serving smaller sized area coverage is an efficient approach for mobile users to gain faster communications by using local access points connected to the Internet. Due to the limitations of space, this section mainly introduces three network types that are broadly adopted in current industry, including WLANs, WWANs, and Cellular.

Note: *Wireless Mesh Topology* is a wireless networking type that interconnects all mobile devices.

9.2.4.1 Wireless Local Area Networks (WLANs)

Wireless Local Area Networks (WLANs), also abbreviated to Wirelss LAN or WLAN, is a wireless deployment method for a local small-ranged area usage through a high frequency radio connection [130]. The Internet connection access can be either an existing wired network, such as an *Ethernet* connection, or other wireless sources. The coverage extent usually depends on the capability of equipment. The speed of communications is varied from 1 to 600 Mbps due to different product performances and standards. Currently, this wireless network type is one of the most popular types used in practice because of plenty of advantages.

First, the establishment of WLANs is simple for most users and service providers. A WLAN consists of a number of wireless stations. A *Wireless Station* in WLANs refers to any equipment connecting to the wireless medium within a wireless network. There are mainly two

Table 9.1 Comparison of Current Various Types of Wireless Networks.
T (Type), P (Performance), CC (Coverage Capability)

T	P	Applications	CC
WPANs	Moderate	Personal use purpose	Small
WLANs	High	Community or organization use; connecting mobile devices via an access point connected to Internet (Wi-Fi)	Within an area
WMNs	High	Using radio nodes within a mesh topology to connect mesh clients that are mobile devices	Global
WiMANs	High	Cover larger areas than WLANS; the wireless service is offered and operated by an organization in most situations	Within a city
WWANs	Low	Mobile access to the wireless networks	Global
Cellular	Low	Mobile access to the wireless networks by using cell-style distributed radio networks	Global

sorts of wireless stations: Wireless Access Point Station (WAPS) and Wireless Client Point Station (WCPS). WAPS plays a communicator role that receives and transmits high frequency radio signals for devices involved in wireless communications. A wireless router is an example of WAPS, which is often used to distribute radio signals by connecting with a wired or wireless network. A WCPS means mobile devices or all fixed devices with wireless network interfaces, which are using wireless networking services. For instance, mobile phones, portable laptops, and wireless-connected desktops are all client stations within a WLAN.

Second, WLANs has a high level flexibility so that it can be deployed to meet various demands. Multiple communication methods can be supported by WLANs, which include peer-to-peer and point-to-point. Point-to-Point is a communication method supporting wireless connections between networking nodes or endpoints. For example, a laptop can have a wireless connection to a printer by using the point-to-point communication method. Next, a Peer-to-Peer (P2P) network method is an approach of building up a network by connecting networking nodes that are both networking clients and server. In most situation, a P2P network is established in a Decentralised system. A *Decentralized Network System* is a distributed network model in which each networking node only works on local operations and has equal responsibility to the network. In addition, *Centralized Network System* is a network model consisting of a master node and endpoint nodes, and is suitable for a small group of users who work together in a limited space.

A typical application of WLANs is Wireless Fidelity (Wi-Fi), which has become a popular way to leverage WLANs. The following section describes the main differences between two resemblant concepts: WLANs and Wi-Fi. This section also gives a conceptual map for establishing a Wi-Fi to assist students to further understand the placement of this technology. Fig. 9.4 shows a structure of a Wi-Fi network. According to the representation of the figure, Wi-Fi can gain wireless sources from both wired and wireless Internet sources.

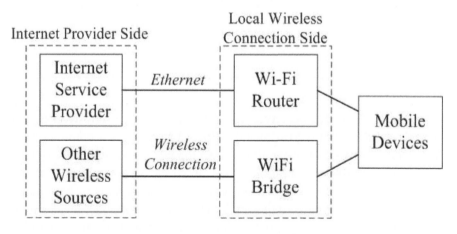

Figure 9.4 A structure of the Wi-Fi network.

9.2.4.2 Comparison between Wireless Local Area Networks and Wireless Fidelity

The meaning of WLANs is different from Wi-Fi, even though these two concepts often refer to the same technologies in our daily life. In a perspective of techniques, they are two different concepts in the subject of computer science. Students should understand the main difference between these two definitions. The main distinction between WLANs and Wi-Fi is that Wi-Fi is only one type of WLANs. WLANs users can have accesses to wireless networks via a radio connection. Wi-Fi refers to a group of products following the 802.11 wireless protocol family in WLANs.

9.2.4.3 Wireless Wide Area Network

Wireless Wide Area Networks (WWANs), also known as Wirelss WAN or Wireless broadband, is a large geographic-usage wireless network in which a great number of cells transmit radio signals to both mobile and on-premise devices. This wireless network model has an efficient performance in transmitting signals to fast moving devices compared with WLANS that can only serve slow-moving equipment within a limited range site [131][132].

Main technologies of WWANs include *Global System for Mobile Communications* (GSM), *Code Division Multiple Access* (CDMA), and *Worldwide Interoperability for Microwave Access* (WiMAX). GSM and CDMA are two legacy cellular technologies, and both leverage High Speed Packet Access (HSPA) and Evolution-Data Optimized (EV-DO) to transmit data.

GSM is a global standard for operating mobile communications, which was developed by European Telecommunications Standards Institute (ETSI). A basic GSM network is composed of a number of subsystems, including Base Station Subsystem (BSS), Network Switching Subsystem (NSS), Operation Support Subsystem (OSS), and Mobile Station. A mobile station is user equipment that communicates with BSS who is responsible for signals transceivers and controllers. NSS connects with BSS via a defined interface in which communications can be carried and switched between different networks. Both NSS and BSS are supported by OSS. In practice, some additional subsystems are added into this GSM structure according to the requirements of database or communications, such as Equipment Identity Register and Chargeback Center.

Next, CDMA is another approach for mobile communications that can transmit multiple digital signals by connecting multiple terminals through the same transmission medium. CDMA is an implementation of the *Channel-Access Schema* that enables different data streams or radio signals to go through or share the same communication channel. This method is also defined as *Multiplexing*. Main technology of this approach is using *Spread-Spectrum* that extends bandwidth capacity by varying the frequency of the transmitted signals. The operational process includes three steps: multiplexing input signals, carrying a multiplexed signals over a high data rate link, and demultiplexing data signals as output data. Multiple channel access facilitates CDMA to execute a better performance than GSM.

Finally, WiMAX is an alternative substitute for GSM and CDMA or a capacity enhancement for the existing networks. The deployment of WiMAX is similar to Wi-Fi, but it offers a larger coverage and supports a greater number of mobile users. The speed of data transmission is up to 1 gigabit/sec, which is based on the IEEE 802.16 standard. WiMAX supports multiple Radio Access Network (RAN) topologies and a typical WiMAX has three parts: Mobile System, Access Service Network (ASN), and Connectivity Service Network (CSN). A mobile system is a platform for users to access the networks, which is similar to the mobile system in GSM. ASN consists of a few BSSs and ASN gateways in which the radio signals can access the networks. CSN is an inter-connectivity component that links all IPs and aligns all attached IP core networks Table 9.2 displays a comparison between WiMAX and Wi-Fi in five perspectives, namely, standard, coverage, bandwidth, mobility, and users.

9.2.4.4 Cellular Network

A *Cellular Network* refers to a mobile network type that is composed of a large number of radio base stations. Each base station covers a specific scope of area that is defined as a "cell". Adjoining cells do not use the same frequency in order to avoid interferences. A cellular network is an efficient approach that supports reusing the same frequency by a few techniques, such as distributed cells, cell signal encoding, or switching call techniques.

A basic cellular network comprises mobile stations, base stations, and Mobile Switching Center (MSC). Each base station is a medium that simultaneously interconnects with all mobile stations within its

Table 9.2 Comparison between WiMAX and Wi-Fi

	WiMAX	Wi-Fi
Standard	IEEE 802.16	IEEE 802.11 standard family
Coverage	Large area (up to 40 miles coverage per WiMAX antenna)	Small area (usually up to a few hundred feet)
Bandwidth	adjustable bandwidth range from 1.25 to 20 MHz	20 or 25 MHz
Mobility	Available (technology is designed for mobile users)	None (slow moving users in a limited space)
User	A large scalability, from one to hundreds of users depending on the demands	Limited number of users depending on the device

coverage scope and carries data transmissions to MSC. An MSC is responsible for routing data by receiving traffic and switching calls between mobile networks. Sometimes, an MSC also plays a management role that governs and controls wireless connections and cells or clusters. A *Cluster* is a group of adjoining cells. Fig. 9.5 illustrates an example of the cellular network structure.

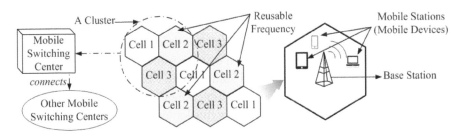

Figure 9.5 An example of the cellular network structure.

As exhibited in the figure, a group of cells represent a cellular network. Cells with the same colors and styles mean the same frequency is used. The adjacent cells use distinct frequencies to avoid interferences with each other. For example, in Fig. 9.5, none of the *Cell 2s* are neighboring cells, which indicates that all *Cell 2s* leverage the same frequency. The same frequency used in a cellular network is called a *Reusable Frequency.* Moreover, a cluster of cells is connecting with an MSC that links to other MSCs.

9.3 MAIN TECHNIQUES OF MOBILE CLOUD COMPUTING

This section introduces main techniques implemented in MCC from varying outlooks. Three main schemas in cloud computing are Virtualization, Parallel Programming Model, and Mass Distributed Storage. These three technologies address three different aspects of delivering MCC services, namely, service delivery and communications between mobile devices and remote servers, remote side data processing, and remote data storage.

9.3.1 Virtualization

Virtualization is a mechanism that virtualizes object computing resources to represent them in a service-based manner by various service levels [133]. A Virtual Machine (VM) is a software-based approach that is broadly used in current cloud solutions. End users can gain cloud services through executing virtualizations by which infrastructure, platform, and software are represented. Three main advantages of applying VMs are cutting costs, saving energy, and facilitating maintenance. Most cloud services can be delivered to cloud customers by using VMs.

A VM is an emulating technique that is used to distribute and virtualize multiple remote computing resources and present the computing acquisitions to end users in a service mode. In cloud computing, users can execute the cloud-based solutions to acquire the same performances as that of on-premise solutions, since the computing services run virtually on the local site. The implementation of VM in MCC is also effective, because data processing and data storage running on the remote servers are represented to cloud customers by a stimuli-presenting mode [134]. Currently, most remote computing resources can turn into cloud services by adopting VM technologies, from apps to operating systems.

Fig. 9.6 represents an example of using VMs to carry cloud services to cloud customers. VMs perform the same functions as the remote

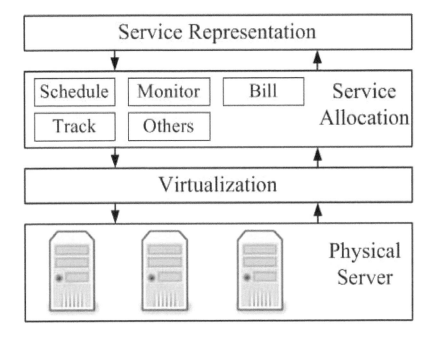

Figure 9.6 An example of using a virtual machine to deliver cloud services.

physical servers via a wireless or wired Internet connection. Service requests are allocated to various VMs depending on the request types, when cloud users try to obtain cloud services. The service request will be sent to physical machines going through VMs in which the service responses will be passed. Cloud users can acquire their service responses once the responses reach the service representation layer, which is usually a user interface followed by an API.

Furthermore, a VM is usually considered a secure schema to protect users' information because the virtualization-based platform has an independent operating circumstance [135]. Most VMs isolate from the rest parts of the system and execute as an application running on the operating system. The main vulnerability of implementing VMs is that attacks to lower layer hypervisor are dynamic. The consistent changing threats result in difficulties of continuous security. Moreover, switching VMs between different physical servers is not secure, as a simulated operating system does not host a firewall to separate VMs.

In short, a VM-based cloud solution is a popular mechanism in current cloud industry. It is a safe approach unless the lower layer hypervisor is attacked and controlled by attackers. Other concerns of using VM-based solutions involve virtualization overuse and reliability, which are related to the users' IT strategies and policies. Technically speaking, a VM is becoming one of the common approaches to present cloud customers services by leveraging simulating technologies.

9.3.2 Parallel Programming Model

Parallel Programming Model (PPM) is a technology used for solving concurrent tasks based on a cloud-based platform. This schema is widely adopted in parallel data processing running on the remote servers. The main purpose of using PPM is generating parallel programs that can be efficiently compiled and operated. PPM is an important mechanism for mobile cloud developers and providers who are usually requested to offer rapid services over a wireless network [136]. It is also an approach to successfully resolve great sized data transmissions. The principle of PPM is to divide a complex problem or process into a few sub-problems or sub-processes [28].

Two typical techniques applied in PPM include *Interacting Processes* and *Decomposing Problems.*

Interacting Processes, also known as *Processes Interactions*, is an approach used for increasing operational efficiency by interacting parallel processes. The crucial part of this method is to find out the interactive proportions between parallel processes [137, 138]. Two common ways addressing this issue are sharing memories and passing messages between programs.

Shared Memory is an interacting process method that supports data passing between programs based on a shared global address space in which all parallel programs can read and write data asynchronously. This means it allows programs to run on one or multiple processors either on the local site or over the remote distributed servers. The other way of achieving processes interactions is to pass messages between programs. *Message Passing* is a term describing a solution of exchanging data between processes, which is achieved by communications between parallel programs [139]. A *Message* in message passing is a type of communication content between parallel programs, which can be generated into a number of forms, such as functions, signals, and some types of data packets. Compared with shared memory, message passing has a higher-level flexibility, since it supports both synchronous and asynchronous communications.

Moreover, the second technique of PPM is decomposing problems. The term *Problem Decomposition* refers to a methodology that formulates parallel programs. Two typical broadly deployed methods in problem decomposition are function parallelism and data parallelism.

Function Parallelism, also known as *Task or Control Parallelism*, is a method of parallel computing between multiple processors that distributes processes or threads between parallel computing nodes. This approach is often used in multiprocessor systems. The following pseudocode gives an example of function parallelism. In addition, *Data Parallelism* is the other approach of problem decomposition that distributes data between parallel computing nodes instead of distributing processes. As distinguishing from function parallelism, data parallelism focusing on assigning data among multiprocessors based on a few conditional statements [104].

1. if (Processor = "A"){
2.   do function "1";
3.   else if (Processor = "B"){
4.   do function "2";
5.   }
6. }

9.3.3 Mass Distributed Storage

Mass Distributed Storage (MDS) is a novel technology that combines two techniques, cloud mass storage and cloud-distributed storage in order to apply multiple storage servers as well as enhance data reliability and infrastructure credibility [140]. This approach can not only support mass data storage, but also prevent data from various physical threats, such as site disasters, as data are stored in a distributed manner [141][142]. Wireless networks enable distributed storage sites to interconnect and communicate with each other. Leveraging mobile solutions can achieve a secure solution for mobile cloud users to store a large amount of data.

Cloud Mass Storage refers to a schema that store users' large-sized data in the remote servers and ensures the data are readable across various interfaces. The concept derives from *Mass Storage* that usually means a solution for on-premise usage. Moreover, *Cloud Distributed Storage* is a means that stores data on multiple remote databases or nodes.

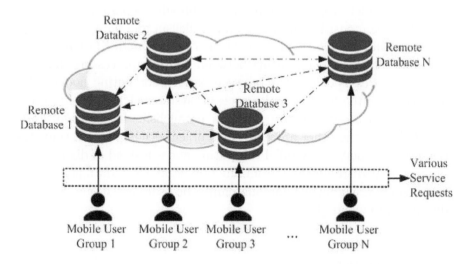

Figure 9.7 A structure of adopting mass distributed storage.

Fig. 9.7 displays a structure of adopting MDS technology in MCC. The figure explains an implementation scenario featuring multiple groups of mobile users who request specific function services as well as some shared services with other groups of mobile users. On the side of remote servers, a few distributed databases are deployed, and each of them has a specific service offering focus. Users can access their target data in a fast way and acquire other service types data through the interconnections within the distributed connected database network.

9.4 MOBILE CLOUD COMPUTING ARCHITECTURE

Mobile Cloud Computing Architecture is a structure of designing, developing, and implementing mobile cloud computing solutions. The architecture consists of a set of technologies that is introduced and evaluated in this chapter. Deploying an MCC-based solution requires three critical supportive aspects, including mobile computing, mobile Internet, and cloud computing. Each aspect is supported by a number

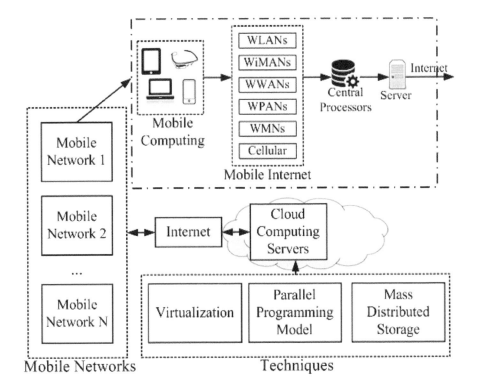

Figure 9.8 Architecture of mobile cloud computing.

of core techniques. Fig. 9.8 illustrates the architecture of MCC, which shows the approach of deploying an MCC solution.

According to the explanation of the figure, mobile cloud users gain mobile cloud services by using access to mobile computing. Mobile devices and Internet communications protocols are two prerequisites [143]. Currently, mobile users have a number of choices of wireless networks that can be used for various demands and mobile equipment [144]. Once users' service requests are received, the requests will go through central processors and mobile network servers to allocate services and connect to cloud servers [145]. Three key technologies support the implementation of cloud computing, involving virtualization, parallel programming model, and mass distributed storage. The service responses will be sent back to mobile users when the physical machines running on the remote servers finish data processing. Mobile cloud users obtain services via a virtual machine that provides cloud users with a service representation.

9.5 EXERCISES

9.5.1 Fundamental Questions

1. What is the concept of Mobile Cloud Computing (MCC)?

2. What are two main workload migrations of implementing mobile cloud computing?

3. Briefly describe the differences between cloud computing and mobile cloud computing.

4. List three key technical aspects of mobile cloud computing.

5. What does the *Mobile Computing* mean?
   What is a communications protocol?

6. Is an app the same as an application? Explain your answer.

7. Give explanations of the following terms: *Wireless Networks*, *Communicators*, and *Network Nodes*. Briefly describe the relationships between these terms.

8. What are main types of wireless networks?

9. Are Wireless LANs different from Wi-Fi? Give your reasons to explain your response.

10. What is the concept of the cellular network?
    What are the main components of the cellular network?
    Explain the meaning of the cluster in a cellular network.

11. Briefly explain the operations of the cellular networks.

12. What are the main techniques for current mobile cloud solutions? List them, and give a short description for each technique.

13. What is a *Virtual Machine*?
    What is the operating principle of the virtual machine?

14. Try to illustrate the process of virtual machine implementations in mobile cloud.

15. Is it secure to use the virtual machine? Please use a few sentences to explain your opinion.

16. What is the concept of *Parallel Programming*? Describe the reasons why cloud providers need to utilize this technology.

17. What is the concept of *Mass Distributed Storage*? Describe an occasion when mass distributed storage is required in mobile cloud computing.

9.5.2 Practical Questions

1. Picture yourself as a Chief Information Officer (CIO) in a company focusing on international trade business. Currently, your company intends to establish a local wireless network for a new-open office site. This project aims to let every employee working in the office access to the Internet with wireless networks. At least have seven employees will work at the office regularly. Meanwhile, a few additional accesses are also needed, since some visitors often ask for Wi-Fi access, such as business partners, guests, or clients. Here is your mission. You need to write a short technical plan and report it to your CIO The technical plan needs to describe which type of wireless networks will be used and the reasons why. A comparison among different types is preferred. Students should use four to five sentences to briefly represent the key points for the plan.

2. Discuss the differences between cloud computing architecture and mobile cloud computing architecture. You can think of this question in a technical perspective, such as whether the architectures are using similar technologies. Try to use four to five sentences to explain your understanding.

9.6 GLOSSARY

Mobile Cloud Computing
is a technological paradigm that uses cloud-based approaches to provide mobile users with multiple services with mobile technologies and devices.

Cloud Computing

is a computing paradigm that uses Web-based technologies to provide users with scalable on-demand services with sharing or offering computing resources.

Mobile Computing

is a technical concept describing a set of technologies for bridging up links and communications between mobile devices.

Mobile Software

represents a group of applications designed for mobile use purposes that run on mobile devices for service representations.

Mobile App

is a set of programs implemented on mobile devices that are normally executed within a framework, such as Android.

Communication Protocol

refers to a set of rules that ensures all mobile devices involved in the communication can understand each other when data are transmitted.

Application Distribution Platforms

are interfaces for provisioning software purchases and downloads, which is owned and operated by OS providers.

Mobile Internet

is a set of of advanced networking technologies that activate interconnectivity between communicators over the wireless networks by which mobile software is supported.

Network Nodes

refers to multiple types of processing locations that occur in various digital infrastructures.

Wireless Local Area Network

is a wireless deployment method for a small-ranged area usage purpose through a high frequency radio connection.

Wireless Station in WLANS

refers to any equipment connecting to the wireless medium within a wireless network.

Point-to-Point

is a communication method supporting wireless connections between networking nodes or endpoints.

Peer-to-Peer (P2P)

is an approach of building up a network by connecting networking nodes that are both networking clients and servers.

Decentralized Network System

is a distributed network model in which each networking node only works on local operations and has equal responsibility to the network.

Centralized Network System

is a network model consisting of a master node and endpoint nodes, which is suitable for a small group of users who work together in a limited space.

Wireless Wide Area Network (WWANS)

also known as *Wirelss WAN* or *Wireless broadband*, is a large geographic-usage wireless network in which a great number of cells transmit radio signals to both mobile and on-premise devices.

Global System for Mobile Communications (GSM)

is a global standard for operating mobile communications, which was developed by the European Telecommunications Standards Institute.

Code Division Multiple Access (CDMA)

is another approach for mobile communications that can transmit multiple digital signals by connecting multiple terminals through the same transmission medium.

Channel-Access Schema

is a mechanism that enables different data streams or radio signals to go through or share the same communication channel.

Spread-Spectrum

is an approach that extends bandwidth capacity by varying the frequency of the transmitted signals.

Virtualization

is a mechanism that virtualizes object computing resources to represent them in a service-based manner by various service levels.

Virtual Machine

is an emulating technique that is used to distribute and virtualize multiple remote computing resources and present the computing acquisitions to end users in a service mode.

Parallel Programming Model (PPM)

is a technology used for solving concurrent tasks based on a cloud-based platform.

Interacting Processes

also known as *Processes Interactions*, is an approach used for increasing operating efficiency by interacting parallel processes.

Shared Memory

is an interacting process method that supports data passing between programs based on a shared global address space in which all parallel programs can read and write data asynchronously.

Message Passing

is a term describing a solution of exchanging data between processes, which is achieved by pass messages.

Message (in Message Passing)

is a type of communication content between parallel programs, which can be generated into a number of forms, such as functions, signals, and some types of data packets.

Problem Decomposition

refers to a methodology that formulates parallel programs.

Function Parallelism

also known as *Task or Control Parallelism*, is a method of parallel computing between multiple processors that distributes processes or threads between parallel computing nodes.

Mass Distributed Storage (MDS)

is a novel technology that combines two techniques, mass storage and distributed storage, in order to apply multiple storage servers as well as enhance data reliability and infrastructure credibility.

Cloud Mass Storage

refers to a scheme that stores users' large-sized data in remote servers and ensures the data are readable across various interfaces.

Cloud Distributed Storage

is a means that stores data on multiple remote databases or nodes.

Mobile Cloud Computing Architecture

is a structure of designing, developing, and implementing mobile cloud computing solutions.

CHAPTER 10

Efficient Data Synchronization on Mobile Devices in Big Data

CONTENTS

Big DATA STORAGE in mobile embedded systems is a critical issue in increasing the performance of mobile apps. In the previous chapter, we introduced mobile cloud computing. It is no doubt that we are in big data era. Big data is a popular term use to describe massive data that are generated and growing by exponential order [146]. Big data brings a lot of benefits to us, but it brings about many challenges as well. Due to the amount of data, all the traditional methods of processing data in relational databases are much more inefficient than before. Furthermore, with the rapid popularity of mobile devices, the big data issues becomes more complicated [147, 148]. In this chapter, we will introduce mobile big data storage, and the main contents of this chapter include:

1. Overview of big data.

2. Mobile big data.

3. Big data processing and analysis.

4. Mobile big data storage.

5. Security and privacy issues of mobile big data.

6. Data Deduplication

10.1 OVERVIEW OF BIG DATA

10.1.1 Understanding Data Type

Big data includes structured, unstructured, and semistructured data. Structured data are data that reside in a fixed field within a record file, and structure data are often managed by *Structured Query Language* (SQL) [149], which is a programming language created for managing and querying data in relational database management systems, such as SQL Server, MySQL, Oralce Rdb, and SQLite [150].

Unstructured data are all those things that cannot be classified and fit into a neat form, such as images, videos, audio, streaming instrument data, webpages, pdf file, emails, and blog entries. Unstructured data mainly indicate unstructured information, which is typically text-heavy [151]. Although unstructured information may contain some formed data, such as numbers, dates, and facts, it cannot be processed easily as structured information [152]. The irregularity and ambiguity of unstructured data make it extremely difficult to process using traditional programs, as compared to structured data in relational databases.

Semistructured data are a form of structured data that do not conform with the formal structure of data models associated with relational databases or other forms of data tables, but nonetheless contain tags or other markers to separate semantic elements and enforce hierarchies of records and fields within the data. Two main types of semistructured data are *Extensible Markup Language* (XML) and *JavaScript Object Notation* (JSON).

Big data are as important to business, society, industrial community, and academia as the Internet has become [153]. More data lead to more accurate analyses, which lead to more confident decision making for greater operational efficiencies, cost reduction, and reduced risk. However, before enjoying the benefits brought by big data, we need to solve some technique problems.

The greatest challenge of big data is the gigantic amount of data. Furthermore the amount is still increasing rapidly [154]. *Computer World* states that unstructured information might account for more than 70% - 80% of all data in an organization [155].

HINT: The zettabyte is a multiple of the unit byte for digital information, and the symbol is ZB. The zebibyte (ZiB) is a related unit with zettabyte. $1ZB = 1000^7 bytes$; $1ZiB = 2^{40}GB = 2^{70}B$.

10.1.2 Categorizing Big Data Models

Big data have some characteristics as follows:

Volume refers to the vast amount of data generates every second. In our daily lives, we produce and share data every second, such as emails, messages, photos, videos, and audio. On Facebook, we send 10 billion messages per day, click the "like" button 4.5 billion times, and upload 350 million new pictures every day. Furthermore, with the rapid development of mobile devices and Internet of Things (IoT), massive sensor data flood servers as well.

Variety refers to the types of data. In the past, we focused on structured data that neatly fit into relational databases. As mentioned above, unstructured data cannot be processed in traditional methods. Moreover, 80% of current data are unstructured.

Big data technology can help us harness different types of data for some specific requirements.

Velocity refers to the speed at which new data are generated and the speed at which data are processed and transmitted to meet the demands. For example, the speed at which credit card transaction are checked must be within milliseconds. Big data technology allows us to analyze data while they are being generated without putting them into databases.

Variability refers to the inconsistency that can be shown by the data at times, thus hampering the process of being able to handle and manage the data effectively.

Veracity refers to the messiness or trustworthiness of the data. Accuracy of analysis depends on the veracity of the source data. With many forms of big data, quality, and accuracy are less controllable than before, but big data and analytic technology can help us work with these types of data, Furthermore, the volumes can be used to make up for the lack of quality or accuracy.

Complexity refers to the difficulties of data management. Data management becomes a very complex process, especially when huge volumes of data come from various sources. To get the information hidden on these data, they need to be linked and correlated, which forms the "complexity" of big data.

We can form data as a table with N columns and T rows, as shown in Figure 10.1. N indicates the dimension of each vector, and T indicates the number of training samples. Based on this table, big data is with large T, or large N, or both. We can separate big data into three models, which are large T with small N, infinite T with small N, and small T with large N.

10.1.3 Current Challenges in Big Data

Facing such massive data, every traditional method is much less efficient than it was before. The challenges of big data include analysis, capture, curation, search, sharing, storage, transfer, visualization, and privacy.

Data sets grow in size in part because they are increasingly being gathered by mobile devices. There are 4.6 billion mobile phone subscriptions worldwide and between 1 billion and 2 billion people

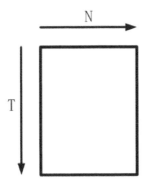

Figure 10.1 The modeling table of big data.

accessing the Internet. Besides mobile phones, thousand kinds of mobile sensors generate and use massive data every second, especially in Smart City.

With billions of mobile devices in the world today, mobile big data is becoming the most significant challenge to be solved. The rise of big data demands that we be able to access data resources anytime and anywhere about every daily thing. Furthermore, these kinds of data are invaluable and profitable if used well. However, to make big data possible to analyze, several challenges must be addressed. More specifically, instead of being restricted to single computers, ubiquitous applications must be able to execute on an ecosystem of networked devices, each of which may join or leave the shared ubiquitous space at any time. Furthermore, there exist analytic tasks that are too computationally expensive to be performed on a mobile device ecosystem. Also, how can we harness the specific capabilities of each device, including varying display size, input modality, and computational resources? In this chapter, we mainly introduce mobile big data storage.

10.2   BIG DATA PROCESSING

Before storing big data, we need to preprocess these data. Methods that scale to big data are of particular interest in data science, although the discipline is not generally considered to be restricted to such data [156, 75, 157]. Data science is the extraction of knowledge from data [126, 158, 159]. It employs techniques and theories drawn from many fields within the broad areas of mathematics, statistics, information theory, and information technology, including signal processing, probability models, machine learning, statistical learning, computer programming, data engineering, pattern recognition and learning, visualization, predictive analytic, uncertainty modeling, data warehousing, data compression, and high performance computing. Data science is emerging to meet the challenges of processing big data [160].

Figure 10.2 is the Data Science Venn Diagram presented by Drew Conway [161, 162]. The primary colors of data are hacking skills, math and stats knowledge, and substantive expertise [163, 164]. Each of these skills are very valuable on their own, but when combined with only one other are at best data science, or at worst downright dangerous. As the hacker is among the most skilled information technology disciplines, it requires a wide knowledge of IT technologies and techniques. Combined with math and statistics knowledge, hacking skills can be used for machine learning. However, some substantive experts can use hacking skills to do some illegal things, and that is the danger zone. Finally, the hacking skills, math and statistics knowledge, and substantive expertise constitute the data science.

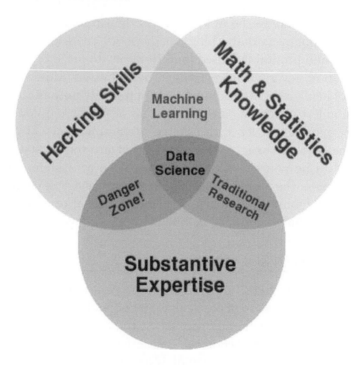

Figure 10.2 Data science venn diagram.

10.2.1 Machine Learning

The development of machine learning, a branch of artificial intelligence used to uncover patterns in data from which predictive models can be developed, has enhanced the growth and importance of data science. Traditional mobile apps do not focus on machine learning because of the restrictions caused by limited capacities of mobile devices. However, using mobile cloud computing has enabled mobile apps to utilize machine learning techniques. The heavy workloads can be migrated to the cloud side by which the mobile devices can save energy and achieve high performance.

Moreover, machine learning is typically classified into three broad categories: supervised learning, unsupervised learning, and semi-supervised learning. We introduce these three types of machine learning in details,

10.2.1.1 Supervised Learning

In supervised learning, the training data are always with features and labels. A supervised learning algorithm analyzes the training data and produces an inferred function. The objective of supervised learning is prediction, ranking, and classification.

Naive Bayes Naive Bayes is surprisingly widely used in supervised learning. The Navie Bayes classifier is based on applying Bayes theorem with naive independence assumptions between the features.

$$classify(f_1, \ldots, f_n) = \arg\max p(C = c) \prod_{i=1}^{n} p(F_i = f_i | C = c) \quad (10.1)$$

We generally estimate $P(f_i|c) using m - estimates:$

$$P(f_i|c) = (n_c + m_p)/(n + m) \quad (10.2)$$

Where: n = the number of training examples for which $C = c$; n_c = the number of examples for which $C = c$ and $F_i = f_i$; p = a priori estimate for $P(f_i|c)$, and m = the equivalent sample size.

For instance, we will use the Naive Bayes method to determine whether a red domestic SUV is stolen. In Bayes' Theorem, $P(A|B) = P(B|A) * P(A)/P(B)$, and if all the events are independent each other, it must be right that: $P(A, B, C|D) = P(A|D) * P(B|D) * P(C|D)$. In this example, we can know that: $P(Yes|red, domestic, SUV) = P(red, domestic, SUV|Yes) * P(Yes)/P(red, domestic, SUV)$, $P(red, dom, SUV|Yes) = P(red|Yes) * P(dom|Yes) * P(SUV|Yes)$, and $P(red, dom, SUV|No) = P(red|No) * P(dom|No) * P(SUV|No)$. We have ten examples, as shown in Figure 10.3, in which we can get the value of n, n_c, p, and m, as shown in Table 10.1. Note that there is no example of a *Red Domestic SUV* in our data set.

Table 10.1 Basic Values

		Yes	No
Red		$n = 5$ $n_c = 3$ $p = 0.5$ $m = 3$	$n = 5$ $n_c = 2$ $p = 0.5$ $m = 3$
SUV		$n = 5$ $n_c = 1$ $p = 0.5$ $m = 3$	$n = 5$ $n_c = 3$ $p = 0.5$ $m = 3$
Domestic		$n = 5$ $n_c = 2$ $p = 0.5$ $m = 3$	$n = 5$ $n_c = 3$ $p = 0.5$ $m = 3$

Example No.	Color	Type	Origin	Stolen?
1	Red	Sports	Domestic	Yes
2	Red	Sports	Domestic	No
3	Red	Sports	Domestic	Yes
4	Yellow	Sports	Domestic	No
5	Yellow	Sports	Imported	Yes
6	Yellow	SUV	Imported	No
7	Yellow	SUV	Imported	Yes
8	Yellow	SUV	Domestic	No
9	Red	SUV	Imported	No
10	Red	Sports	Imported	Yes

Figure 10.3 An example table for Bayes.

From Figure 10.3, we can calculate that:

$$P(Red|Yes) = (3 + 3 * 0.5)/(5 + 3) = 0.5625,$$

$$P(Red|No) = (2 + 3 * 0.5)/(5 + 3) = 0.4375,$$

$$P(SUV|Yes) = (1 + 3 * 0.5)/(5 + 3) = 0.3125,$$

$$P(SUV|No) = (3 + 3 * 0.5)/(5 + 3) = 0.5625,$$

$$P(Domestic|Yes) = (2 + 3 * 0.5)/(5 + 3) = 0.4375,$$

$$P(Domestic|No) = (3 + 3 * 0.5)/(5 + 3) = 0.5625.$$

Then we can calculate the probability of a red domestic SUV is stolen: $P(Yes) * P(Red|Yes) * P(SUV|Yes) * P(Domestic|Yes) = 0.5 * 0.5625 * 0.3125 * 0.4375 = 0.03845$, and the probability of a red domestic SUV isn't stolen: $P(No) * P(Red|No) * P(SUV|No) * P(Domestic|No) = 0.5 * 0.4375 * .5625 * 0.5625 = 0.06921$. Because $0.06921 > 0.037845$, a the red domestic SUV isn't stolen.

Decision Tree

Decision tree learning is a method commonly used in data mining. The goal is to create a model that predicts the value of a target variable based on several input variables. A tree can be "learned" by splitting the source set into subsets based on an attribute value test. This process is repeated on each derived subset in a recursive manner called recursive partitioning. The recursion is completed when the subset at a node has all the same values of the target variable, or when splitting no longer adds value to the predictions. This process of *Top-Down Induction of Decision Trees* (TDIDT) is an example of a greedy algorithm, and it is by far the most common strategy for learning decision trees from data.

Regression

Linear regression is an approach for modeling the relationship between a scalar dependent variable y and one or more explanatory variables denoted X. As shown in Figure 10.4, in linear regression, data are modeled using linerar predictor functions, and unknown model parameters are estimated from the data.

The statistical relationship between the error terms and the regressors plays an important role in determining whether an estimation procedure has desirable sampling properties, such as being unbiased and consistent. Furthermore, the arrangement, or probability distribution of the predictor variables x, has a major influence on the precision

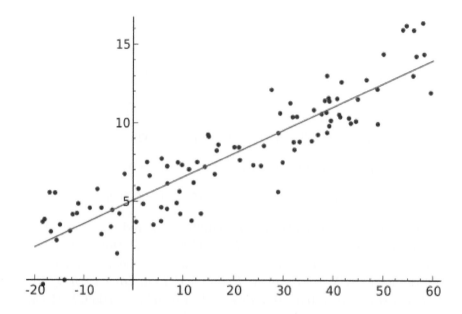

Figure 10.4   Regression analysis.

of estimates of β. Sampling and design of experiments are highly developed subfields of statistics that provide guidance for collecting data in such a way to achieve a precise estimate of β.

Gradient Boosted Decision Tree

Boosting is a machine learning ensemble meta-algorithm for reducing bias primarily and also variance in supervised learning. Gradient boosting is a machine learning technique for regression problems, which produces a prediction model in the form of an ensemble of weak prediction models. While boosting is not algorithmically constrained, most boosting algorithms consist of iteratively learning weak classifiers with respect to a distribution and adding them to a final strong classifier. When they are added, they are typically weighted in some way that is usually related to the weak learners' accuracy. After a weak learner is added, the data is reweighted: examples that are misclassified gain weight, and examples that are classified correctly lose weight. Thus, future weak learners focus more on the examples that previous weak learners misclassified.

10.2.1.2   Unsupervised Learning

Unsupervised learning tasks are always with features but no labels. Since the examples given to the learner are unlabeled, there is no error or reward signal to evaluate a potential solution. This distinguishes unsupervised learning from supervised learning and reinforcement learning. The objectives of unsupervised learning are clustering, feature engineering/discovery, and dimension reduction.

Principle Component Analysis

Principal component analysis (PCA) is a statistical procedure that uses an orthogonal transformation to convert a set of observations of possibly correlated variables into a set of values of linearly uncorrelated variables called principal components. PCA is the simplest of the true eigenvector-based multivariate analyses. Its operation can be thought of as revealing the internal structure of the data in a way that best explains the variance in the data. If a multivariate dataset is visualized as a set of coordinates in a high-dimensional data space, PCA can supply the user with a lower-dimensional picture, a projection or "shadow" of this object when viewed from its most informative viewpoint. This is done by using only the first few principal components so that the dimensionality of the transformed data is reduced.

Figure 10.5 is the PCA of a multivariate Gaussian distribution centered at (1,3) with a standard deviation of 3 in roughly the (0.878, 0.478) direction and of 1 in the orthogonal direction. The vectors shown are the eigenvectors of the covariance matrix scaled by the square root of the corresponding eigenvalue, and shifted so their tails are at the mean.

Clustering

Clustering is the task of grouping a set of objects in such a way that objects in the same group are more similar to each other than to those in other groups. It is a main task of exploratory data mining, and a common technique for statistical data analysis, used in many fields, including machine learning, pattern recognition, image analysis, information retrieval, and bioinformatics.

The left two pictures of Figure 10.6 is a easy progress of clustering, while the right two pictures is a hard one. Furthermore, for Big Data, the challenges will be much more complicated. There are too many examples and features in big data, which makes the processing of clustering extremely slow. Furthermore, due to the variety of devices which generate data, we must consider the hardware fault-tolerance for the

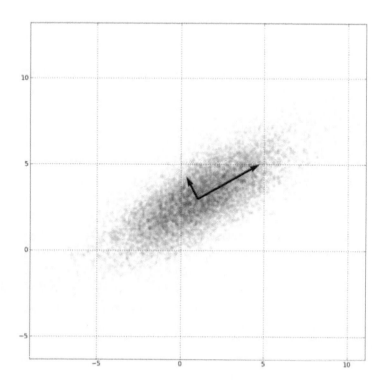

Figure 10.5 PCA of a multivariate Gaussian distribution.

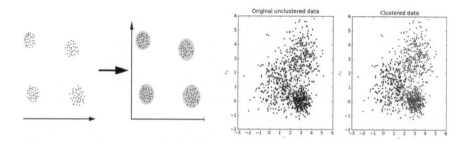

Figure 10.6 Two examples of clustering.

data labels. As a result, how to process big data efficiently is the main goal of mobile big data, which will be introduced in latter sections.

10.2.1.3 Semisupervised Learning

Semi-supervised learning is a class of supervised learning tasks and techniques that also makes use of unlabeled data for training, typically a small amount of labeled data with a large amount of unlabeled data. Semi-supervised learning falls between unsupervised learning and supervised learning. Semi-supervised learning tasks are only with positive labels. Unlabeled data can produce considerable improvement in learning accuracy, when used in conjunction with a small amount of labeled data.

10.3   MOBILE BIG DATA STORAGE

After preprocessing big data, we need to determine how to store and use these data. Normally, we have several choices to deal with these data, such as storing them all onto servers, storing part of them onto servers and leaving others on devices, and storing them all onto devices. Due to the limitations of time and space, we can store the most recent data on devices, and store others onto remote servers. In this section, we mainly focus on mobile big data storage.

10.3.1   Introduction and Basic Concepts

Figure 10.7 is the famous "Moore's Law", which observes that the number of transistors in a dense integrated circuit doubles approximately every 18 months. Currently, the developing of Central Processing Unit (CPU) is much faster than that of memory, which forms the memory wall. CPU speed improved at an annual rate of 55%, while memory speed only improved 10%. Memory latency becomes an overwhelming bottleneck in computer performance. Offering more ways to meet the requirement of memory becomes increasingly important to improve performance and reduce costs.

Currently, heterogenous system with hybrid memory is the trend for not only embedded systems, but also mobile cloud applications. A heterogenous system is a platform that has multiple heterogeneous processing elements, such as memory hierarchy and Input/Output (I/O). There are two kinds of memory, which are volatile memory and non-volatile memory. Volatile memory is the traditional memory includ-

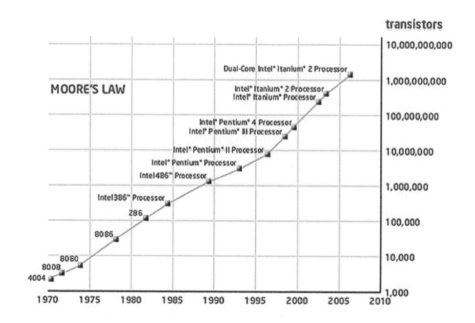

Figure 10.7   Moore's Law. Retrieved from http://archive.isgtw.org/ images/mooreslaw.jpg.

ing *Static Random-Access Memory* (SRAM) and *Dynamic Random-Access Memory* (DRAM). Meanwhile, non-volatile memory is a revolution of memory technologies and it consists of *Phase Change Memory* (PCM), *Magnetoresistive RAM* (MRAM), and Flash Memory. Non-volatile memory is one kind of computer memory that can get back stored information even when the computer is not powered.

Table 10.2 shows the difference between SRAM and DRAM, and Table 10.3 shows the difference between MRAM, PCM, and Flash Memory. SRAM has some pros, such as low cost of read and write, but has some cons, such as high leakage power. Meanwhile, DRAM has some pros, including high density and low price, but has some cons such as high cost of read and write. MRAM has low read cost, low leakage, and high density, but high write costs, including energy and latency. PCM has high memory density and capacity, while it has high write costs and finite endurance, from 10^8 to 10^9. Flash Memory has high durability but very limited endurance, about 10^5.

Table 10.2   Difference between SRAM and DRAM

	R/W Cost	Density	Price
SRAM	Low	Low	High
DRAM	High	High	Low

Table 10.3   Difference between MRAM, PCM, and Flash Memory

	R/W Cost	Density	Capacity	Durability	Endurance
MRAM	Low Read, High Write	High	High	High	Unlimited
PCM	High Write	High	High	Limited	Finite
Flash Memory	Low	High	High	High	Very Limited

10.3.2   Heterogeneous Memory Architecture

To achieve high performance and reduce costs, we can combine different kinds of memories, and that forms heterogeneous memory architecture. As shown in Figure 10.8, we can combine MRAM and SRAM and form a *Scratchpad Memory* (SPM), which can be considered as an on-chip memory. SPM is a high-speed internal memory used for temporary storage of calculations, data, and other work in progress. It can be considered similar to the L1 cache in that it is the next closet memory to the arithmetic logic unit after the internal registers, with explicit instructions to transmit data to and from the main memory. Furthermore, we can combine DRAM and PCM and form an off-chip memory. In this heterogeneous memory architecture, the DRAM is considered as the L2 cache, while the PCM is considered as the main memory.

On-chip memory refers to the memory that physically exists on the micro-controller itself. Meanwhile, off-chip memory refers to the external memory outside the micro-controller. The on-chip memory and the off-chip memory constitute the heterogeneous multi-level memory. Figure 10.10 is the architecture for *Chip Multiprocessor* (CMP). A CMP is a single computing component with two or more independent actual processing units, which are the units that read and execute program instructions [165]. The upper part, surrounded by a bashed line, is the on-chip memory, and the small dashed rectangles are microprocessors.

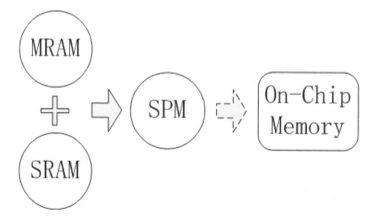

Figure 10.8 Combine MRAM and SRAM into on-chip memory.

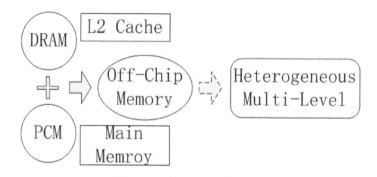

Figure 10.9 Combine DRAM and PCM into off-chip memory.

The blue line in the on-chip memory indicates local access. The red line indicates remote access, and the green line indicates main memory access.

In practices, CMP systems with heterogeneous SPMs are widely used in embedded systems, especially in mobile devices. In CMP systems, putting the same data into different memory units has different costs, which can be defined as power and latency. The power is proportional to latency. Furthermore, there are various kinds of tasks, including fine granularity and coarse granularity. Different tasks use different kinds of data and at different frequencies, which makes big data processing and storage more complicated than traditional data.

To improve the performance and reduce the cost, we need to determine how to allocate data to different memory units.

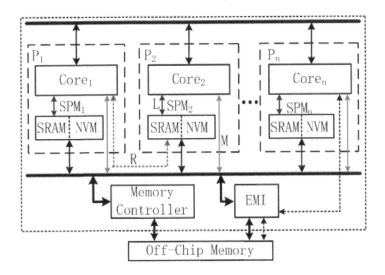

Figure 10.10   Heterogeneous SPM architecture for CMP.

10.3.3   Multi-dimensional Dynamic Programming Data Allocation

In this section, we introduce a hybrid SPM on-chip memory architecture that incorporates SRAM and MRAM to enhance the overall performance of memory systems, as mentioned in Figure 10.8. A challenging problem is that a hybrid SPM architecture must resolve how to reduce energy consumption, memory access latency, and the number of write operations to MRAM. To take advantage of the benefits of each type of memory, we must strategically allocate data on each memory module so that the total memory access cost can be minimized. Recall that SPMs are software controllable, which means the datum on it can be managed by programmers or compilers [166, 167].

For example, there are seven pieces of data, which are A, B, C, D, E, F, and G. In these data, only G is SRAM, while others are main memory. Based on the reference, we assume the memory access cost and moving cost are shown in Table 10.4 for demonstration purposes. Generally, we can use CACTI (developed by HP) to model cache and memory access time, cycle time, area, leakage, and dynamic power. CACTI is an integrated cache and memory access time, cycle

Table 10.4 Cost for Different Memory Operations

Operation		SRAM	MRAM	Main
Read		2	4	80
Write		2	10	80
Move	SRAM	0	7	70
	MRAM	5	0	70
	Main	65	80	0

Table 10.5 Number of Memory Access

Data	Reads	Writes
A	7	1
B	6	2
C	5	3
D	4	4
E	3	5
F	2	6
G	1	7

time, area, leakage, and dynamic power model. In Table 10.4, the row of "Move" indicates the cost of moving data from one memory to another. For example, 7 represents the cost of moving data from SRAM to MRAM.

The total cost of the whole system is the sum of cost of read, write, and move, and it can be formulated as:

$$Total_{cost} = \sum_{i=0}^{n}(\#R_i \times \$R_i + \#W_i \times \$W_i + \$M_i). \qquad (10.3)$$

In Equation 10.3, the $\#R$ indicates the amount of read operations, and the $\#W$ indicates the amount of write operations. The $\$R$ indicates the cost of read operation, and the $\$W$ indicates the cost of write operation. The $\$M$ indicates the cost of data move. For example, the total cost of allocating G to SRAM is: $Cost_{GS} = 1*2+7*2 = 16$. The amount of reading G is 1, and the cost of reading SRAM is 2; thus, the total cost of reading G is 1*2. Similarly, the total cost of writing G is 7*2. G uses SRAM; thus, the cost of allocating G to SRAM is 0; The total cost of allocating A to MRAM is: $Cost_{AM} = 7 * 4 + 1 * 10 + 80 = 118$. The amount of reading A is 7, and the cost of reading MRAM is 4, thus the cost of reading A is 7*4. Meanwhile, the total cost of writing A is 1*10. A is in the main memory; thus, the cost of moving A from the main memory to MRAM is 80.

Table 10.6 The Cost of Allocating Each Data to Different Memory Units

Data	SRAM	MRAM	Main
A	81	118	640
B	81	124	640
C	81	130	640
D	81	136	640
E	81	142	640
F	81	148	640
G	16	81	710

Using Equation 10.3, we can calculate the costs of allocating data to different memory units, as shown in Table 10.6. Then we set x and y as the amount of **unavailable** MRAM units and **unavailable** SRAM units. Assume that there are four MRAM blocks and two SRAM blocks. Figure 10.11 shows all the costes when $x = 4, y = 0, 1, 2$. If $x = 4, y = 2$, which means that all MRAM and SRAM cannot be used, all data are in the main memory:

The total cost is $4550 = 640 + 640 + 640 + 640 + 640 + 640 + 710$.

If $x = 4, y = 1$, which means that all MRAM cannot be used, but one SRAM can be used:

If we allocate A to SRAM, the total cost is $3991 = 4550$ C (640 - 81).

If we allocate B, C, D, E, and F to SRAM, the total costs are $3991 = 4550$ C (640 - 81).

If we allocate G to SRAM, the total cost is $3856 = 4550 - (710 - 16)$.

If $x = 4, y = 0$, which means all MRAM cannot be used, but two SRAM can be used:

If allocating B to SRAM, and A is already allocated to SRAM, the total cost is $3432 = 3991 - (640 - 81)$.

If we allocate G to SRAM, the total cost is $3297 = 3856 - (640 - 81)$.

x = 4							
y	A	B	C	D	E	F	G
0	3432	3432	3432	3432	3432	3432	3297
1	3991	3991	3991	3991	3991	3991	3856
2	4550						

Figure 10.11 The first step of dynamic programming.

Figure 10.12 shows all the costs when $x = 3$, $y = 0, 1, 2$. If $x = 3, y = 2$, which means that one MRAM space can be used:

If allocating A to MRAM, the total cost is: $4028 = 4550 - (640 - 118)$.

If allocating B to MRAM, the total cost is: $4034 = 4550 - (640 - 124)$; however, this cost is bigger than allocating A to MRAM, thus we still allocating A to MRAM, when the total cost is: $4028 = 4550 - (640 - 118)$.

If allocating C to MRAM, the total cost is: $4040 = 4550 - (640 - 130)$; however, this cost is bigger than allocating A to MRAM, thus we still allocating A to MRAM, when the total cost is: $4028 = 4550 - (640 - 118)$.

If allocating D to MRAM, the total cost is: $4046 = 4550 - (640 - 136)$; however, this cost is bigger than allocating A to MRAM, thus we still allocating A to MRAM, when the total cost is: $4028 = 4550 - (640 - 118)$.

If allocating E to MRAM, the total cost is: $4052 = 4550 - (640 - 142)$; however, this cost is bigger than allocating A to MRAM, thus we still allocating A to MRAM, when the total cost is: $4028 = 4550 - (640 - 118)$.

If allocating F to MRAM, the total cost is: 4058 = 4550 - (640 - 148); however, this cost is bigger than allocating A to MRAM, thus we still allocating A to MRAM, when the total cost is: 4028 = 4550 - (640 - 118).

If allocate G to MRAM, the total cost is: 3921 = 4550 - (710 - 81).

If $y = 1$, which means that one MRAM and one SRAM space can be used

Assuming that A uses MRAM, if B uses SRAM, the total cost is 3469 = 4028 - (640 - 81).

Assuming that A uses MRAM, if C uses SRAM, the total cost is 3469 = 4028 - (640 - 81).

Assuming that A uses MRAM, if D uses SRAM, the total cost is 3469 = 4028 - (640 - 81).

Assuming that A uses MRAM, if E uses SRAM, the total cost is 3469 = 4028 - (640 - 81).

Assuming that A uses MRAM, if F uses SRAM, the total cost is 3469 = 4028 - (640 - 81).

Assuming that A uses MRAM, if G uses SRAM, the total cost is 3334 = 4028 - (710 - 16). Assuming that A uses SRAM, if G uses MRAM, the total cost is 3399 = 3921 - (640 - 118). 3334 < 3399; thus, we choose 3334 as the lowest total cost, which indicates that A uses MRAM, while G uses SRAM.

If $y = 0$, which means that one MRAM and two SRAM space can be used:

Assuming that A uses MRAM and B uses SRAM, if C uses SRAM, the total cost is 2910 = 3469 - (640 - 81).

Assuming that A uses MRAM and B uses SRAM, if D uses SRAM, the total cost is 2910 = 3469 - (640 - 81).

Assuming that A uses MRAM and B uses SRAM, if E uses SRAM, the total cost is 2910 = 3469 - (640 - 81).

Assuming that A uses MRAM and B uses SRAM, if F uses SRAM, the total cost is 2910 = 3469 - (640 - 81).

Assuming that G uses MRAM, other two kinds of data use SRAM, and the total cost is: 2803 = 3921 - 2*(640-81). Assuming that G uses SRAM, any two other kinds of data use one MRAM and one SRAM, and the total cost is: 2775 = 3469 - (710 - 16). The cost of the second strategy is lower than the first one, thus we select 2775 as the alternative choice.

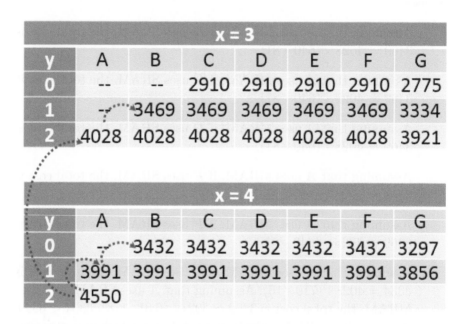

x = 3							
y	A	B	C	D	E	F	G
0	--	--	2910	2910	2910	2910	2775
1	--	3469	3469	3469	3469	3469	3334
2	4028	4028	4028	4028	4028	4028	3921

x = 4							
y	A	B	C	D	E	F	G
0	--	3432	3432	3432	3432	3432	3297
1	3991	3991	3991	3991	3991	3991	3856
2	4550						

Figure 10.12 The second step of dynamic programming.

Figure 10.13 shows all the costs when $x = 2$, $y = 0, 1, 2$. If $x = 2, y = 2$, which means that two MRAM space can be used:

Assuming that A uses MRAM, if allocating B to MRAM, the total cost is: 3512 = 4028 - (640 - 124).

Assuming that A uses MRAM, if allocating C to MRAM, the total cost is: 3518 = 4028 - (640 - 130). Assuming that A uses MRAM, if allocating B to MRAM, the total cost is: 3512 = 4028 - (640 - 124). As a result, we select 3512 as the choice, which means $A \rightarrow MRAM, B \rightarrow MRAM$.

D, E,s and F are the same as the C; thus, the costs of them are all 3512.

Assuming that A uses MRAM, if allocating B to MRAM, the total cost is: 3512 = 4028 - (640 - 124). Assuming that A uses MRAM, and allocating G to MRAM, the total cost is 3399 = 4028 - (710 - 81). As a result, we select 3399 as the choice, which means $A \rightarrow MRAM, G \rightarrow MRAM$.

If $x = 2, y = 1$, which means that two MRAM and one SRAM space can be used:

Assuming that A uses MRAM and B uses MRAM, if allocating C to SRAM, the total cost is: 2953 = 3512 - (640 - 81). The strategy is $A \rightarrow MRAM, B \rightarrow MRAM, C \rightarrow SRAM$.

Assuming that A uses MRAM and B uses MRAM, if allocating D to SRAM, the total cost is: 2953 = 3512 - (640 - 81). The strategy is $A \rightarrow MRAM, B \rightarrow MRAM, D \rightarrow SRAM$.

Assuming that A uses MRAM and B uses MRAM, if allocating E to SRAM, the total cost is: 2953 = 3512 - (640 - 81). The strategy is $A \rightarrow MRAM, B \rightarrow MRAM, E \rightarrow SRAM$.

Assuming that A uses MRAM and B uses MRAM, if allocating F to SRAM, the total cost is: 2953 = 3512 - (640 - 81). The strategy is $A \rightarrow MRAM, B \rightarrow MRAM, F \rightarrow SRAM$.

Assuming that A uses MRAM and B uses MRAM, if allocating G to SRAM, the total cost is: 2818 = 3512 - (710 - 16). Assuming that A uses SRAM, B and G use MRAM, the total cost is 2846 = 4550 - (640 - 81) - (640 - 124) - (710 - 81). As a result, we select 2818 as the choice, which means $A \rightarrow MRAM, B \rightarrow MRAM, G \rightarrow SRAM$.

Then we can calculate the costs when $x = 0, 1$, and all the results are shown in Figure 10.13. The calculating progress is similar to the previous ones in Chapter 9.

After calculating all the results, we can back trace the lowest cost of every table for every data from the strategy when $x = 0, y = 0$. As shown in Figure 10.14, we get the trace as following:

G: 1245 = 1939 - (710 - 16), $G \rightarrow SRAM$

x = 0						
y	A	B	C	D	E	F	G
0	--	--	--	--	--	1380	1245
1	--	--	--	--	1939	1939	1804
2	--	--	--	2498	2498	2498	2373

x = 1						
y	A	B	C	D	E	F	G
0	--	--	--	--	1884	1884	1749
1	--	--	--	2443	2443	2443	2308
2	--	--	3002	3002	3002	3002	2883

x = 2						
y	A	B	C	D	E	F	G
0	--	--	--	2394	2394	2394	2259
1	--	--	2953	2953	2953	2953	2818
2	--	3512	3512	3512	3512	3512	3399

Figure 10.13 The third step of dynamic programming.

F: $1939 = 1939$, $F \rightarrow$ Main memory

E: $1939 = 2498 - (640 - 81)$, $E \rightarrow$ SRAM

D: $2498 = 3002 - (640 - 136)$, $D \rightarrow$ MRAM

C: $3002 = 3512 - (640 - 130)$, $C \rightarrow$ MRAM

B: $3512 = 4028 - (640 - 124)$, $B \rightarrow$ MRAM

A: $4028 = 4550 - (640 - 118)$, $A \rightarrow$ MRAM

x = 0							
y	A	B	C	D	E	F	G
0	--	--	--	--	--	1380	1245
1	--	--	--	--	1939	1939	1804
2	--	--	--	2498	2498	2498	2373

x = 1							
y	A	B	C	D	E	F	G
0	--	--	--	--	1884	1884	1749
1	--	--	--	2443	2443	2443	2308
2	--	--	3002	3002	3002	3002	2883

x = 2							
y	A	B	C	D	E	F	G
0	--	--	--	2394	2394	2394	2259
1	--	--	2953	2953	2953	2953	2818
2	--	3512	3512	3512	3512	3512	3399

x = 3							
y	A	B	C	D	E	F	G
0	--	--	2910	2910	2910	2910	2775
1	--	3469	3469	3469	3469	3469	3334
2	4028	4028	4028	4028	4028	4028	3921

x = 4							
y	A	B	C	D	E	F	G
0	--	3432	3432	3432	3432	3432	3297
1	3991	3991	3991	3991	3991	3991	3856
2	4550	4550	4550	4550	4550	4550	4550

Figure 10.14 The fourth step of dynamic programming.

We can formulate the total cost as follows:

$Cost[d_i, m_1, m_2, \ldots, m_M] =$

$$
\begin{cases}
\sum_{i=1}^{N} C(d_i, MM_i), & \text{SRAM and MRAM are full} \\
\infty, & \text{there is not enough space for data } i \\
min \begin{pmatrix} Cost[d-1, m_1, m_2, \ldots, m_M] \\ Cost[d_i, m_1+1, m_2, \ldots, m_M] - (C(d_i, MM_i) - C(d_i, m_1)) \\ Cost[d_i, m_1, m_2+1, \ldots, m_M] - (C(d_i, MM_i) - C(d_i, m_2)) \\ \cdots \\ Cost[d_i, m_1, m_2, \ldots, m_M+1] - (C(d_i, MM_i) - C(d_i, m_M)) \end{pmatrix}, & \text{else}
\end{cases}
$$

$$(10.4)$$

Table 10.7 shows the compared result of multi-dimensional dynamic programming with a heuristic algorithm. It is easy to prove that this multi-dimensional dynamic programming algorithm is optimal, and the time complexity of it is under polynomial time, which is O(N*sizeof(SRAM)*sizeof(MRAM)). However, this algorithm has a disadvantage, which is that the space complexity of it is overhead, especially for multi-core processors.

Table 10.7 The Compared Result with a Heuristic Algorithm

Allocation	Heuristic	Multi-dimensional dynamic programming
SRAM	A,B	E,G
MRAM	C,D,E,F	A,B,C,D
Main	G	F
Cost	1428	1245

10.4 SECURITY AND PRIVACY ISSUES

There are now more than six billion smartphones in use out there generating data. Information about every text, every search, every phone call, every email, and every picture or video users upload or store is stored. Every smartphone user will generate about 60 gigabytes of data each year. Then multiply that by six billion devices, we generate and store more than 335 exabytes of information every year with smartphones alone. These data are big data without a doubt, and they do benefit our work, study, and life. However, these data contain our private information and bring about unpredictable potential safety hazards.

Location data is the most frequently used data in smartphones. It can be used in apps whose main function are maps, photo organization, *social networking service* (SNS), shopping and restaurant recommendations, and weather. As mentioned in the first chapter, 50% of the top iOS free apps and 24% of the top iOS paid apps to track users' location. Although users are warned whenever an app intends to capture the location, they usually choose to allow the permission for the functions offered by the app. The first and the most direct risk is physical security concerns. Users' tracks are easily exposed to someone who has their real-time and accurate location data. Using some simple data mining methods, users' habits and customs are easy to infer. Stalking, burglary, even murder are more possible to happen to them. The second risk is about corporate, government, and martial espionage concerns.

Album is also widely used in smartphones. Users not only take photos for memory, but also for convenience, such as taking photos instead of writing them down and printscreening the route found by Maps. As a result, smartphones with large storage capacities hold increasing an amount of pictures, including life photos and information pictures. Meanwhile, due to the popularity of SNS, people form a habit of posting a photo showing what they are doing using SNS apps. Almost all SNS apps successfully get permission to users' Album. There are some other kinds of apps that also access users' Album, such as cloud storage app, wallpaper app, customized album app, and picture decorating app. In fact, users use these apps to deal with just several or parts of their photos, not all of them.

However, current smartphone operating systems just provide coarse-grained permission authorization, all or none. Furthermore, this kind of permission authorization is always one-time operation, and almost always appears during the first-time use. If a user authorizes an app to access their album once, this app will have this permission forever. The iOS gives users a way of escape, where users can manually disable the permission of an app to their photos in the Privacy Settings. What's worse, in Android, users have no ways to disable the permission of some apps unless the apps are uninstall. Users' daily photos reveal their daily lives. The over collection of photos not only infringes users' right, such as portrait, but also may damage users' reputations. In addition, users' photos about information are much more valuable than daily ones. With the help of data over-collection apps, third party organizations can get some photos collected from users' smartphones and use them for commerce. This kind of behavior is equivalent to stealing assets from users. For example, one designer sprouts a novel idea and draws a draft, then he takes photos for the record. There will be direct loss to him if his photos are collected by some app and sold to his/her competitors. More generally, it is infuriating to find a photo of oneself shown on some advertisement or somewhere exceeding one's expectations.

To contact others more conveniently, users are willing to create new contacts, replenish existing contacts with email addresses, new phone number, and remarks. The functionality of address books does provide users convenience for communication and work. However, over-collection of users' address books brings serious potential security hazards. The address book includes user names, physical addresses, phone numbers, email addresses, and other notes. Similar to photos, current smartphones operation systems fail to provide fine-grained permission authorization. Once an app get the permission to user's address book, it can collect all information in this address book. The data about address book is usually captured by SNS apps, online game apps, commercial apps and apps which have the function of "sharing with your friend". The contacts of users have great worth. These data can be used by the app developers to expand their customer base, and used by third party organizations to market additional mobile apps or services to those in the contact list. Furthermore, the data over-collection of contacts may bring potential corporate espionage. If a user plugs his/her smartphones into his/her corporate desktop at work, it will give them the option to sync with contacts from email software, such as Outlook, which always include both personal and enterprise contacts. However, the app only asks the user whether to give the permission to access the address book, even though the contacts belong to the enterprise. That extremely reduces security of enterprise data.

Calendar apps are used in aim of organizing users' schedules, tracking events and reminding users of impending events. Users store the names and phone numbers for meeting attendees, meeting dates, and times and attachments within the remark section. Both iOS and Android have their calendar apps attached in the operating system, and it is impossible to uninstall them unless jailbreak. These calendar apps can easily get permission to users' calendars because their main function is managing users' calendars. As a result, users do not usually deny the permission of calendar apps to their calendars. Furthermore, there are some other kinds of apps, offered in the markets that also use calendars as their auxiliary functions, such as lifestyle apps, travel apps, and business apps. Once getting the permission to a user's calendar, all these apps will access every line of information stored within that calendar. The main risk of calendar data over collection is corporate espionage. Calendar data includes information about users' meetings and events. Information about meetings is commercial secrets. It will be a tremendous loss to one corporation if calendar information like call-in information, call passwords, folks attending, and topics discussed was divulged to its competitors. To say the least, divulgence of information about users' personal events also brings harassments to users, if this information came into possession of third party organizations, such as advertising agencies.

Both International Mobile Station Equipment Identity (IMEI) and Unique Device Identifier (UDID) are the unique IDs of one's phone, and they are like cookies on websites that users cannot delete. Although Apple has prohibited iOS developers from using UDID as a method to track and identify users, this rule is only enforced on devices with the latest version of iOS. In fact, iOS 8 adoption rate just inched up to around 50 percent. Furthermore, Apple has encouraged app developers to use new methods of user identification, and to track user behavior on an app-by-app basis. As we all know, the importance of Primary Key in databases, IMEI/UDID is equally significant as Primary Key. It identifies data in phones and makes all data categorized by device. That makes data closer to the real world and more valuable for data mining. The main concern of accessing IMEI/UDID is that user behavior can be correlated across multiple apps and matched to a unique user. Even if a user has various usernames and passwords for each app, his/her data can easily be integrated by the unique ID of his/her device. Moreover, the IMEI/UDID may also be used to match with real user data, such as names, passwords, locations, and others. It allows app developers and advertisement networks to create a complete profile of a user across multiple apps and profiles and combine it with other over collected data for an in-depth view of users.

Some SNS apps, such as Facebook and Twitter, can access data of location, photos, address book, and even UDID. For example, a photo taken and shared by an SNS app is embedded with the location, data, and time, and where and when this photo was taken. The behavior of taking and clicking to share a photo is manually finished by the user, while uploading or sending is automatically done by apps. Furthermore, uploading or sending is mainly run in the background, and most users would not even actively know which photos are being uploaded and when. Even worse, photos with embedded location information uploaded by different apps can be labeled with the same IMEI/UDID, which indicates they are sent from the same device and deprive users of all their privacy. We discuss the apps' behaviors of data over collecting in two aspects as follows.

Due to the locked developing environment and manual auditing, iOS seems more secure than other smartphone operating systems. However, these two constraints mainly work in solving malwares, but not data over collection. From the report of Appthority, 93% of iOS apps exhibited at least one risky behavior, as compared to 89% of Android apps. As a result, data over-collection by apps is a concern to all smartphone users.

Almost all current operating systems of smartphones only provide coarse-grained permissions to apps. Users only have two choices, yes or no, when an app asks for permission to access users' data. Users normally choose yes to give permissions to an app for the function it offers. However, that means this app gets the permission to access every line of this data. This kind of permission is obviously too excessive and need to be detailed. However, it is so complicated to figure out what data on earth a user allows an app to access. Most current smartphone operating systems cannot provide fine-grained permissions. Thankfully, Apple first provided multiple permissions about location data to apps in iOS 8, which are "when-in-use" and "always". Unfortunately, other data in iOS or all data in non-iOS is still suffering the crisis of being over-collected. Furthermore, providing multiple permissions is not a user-friendly solution, which burdens users with higher operation complexity.

10.5 DATA DEDUPLICATION

With the unstoppable increase of big data, the storage industry is in a race to provide higher and higher densities of data storage devices at lower costs, and data deduplication technology is becoming even more important. Data deduplication is a technique for reducing the amount of storage space needed, as shown in Figure 10.15. In most organizations, the file systems contain duplicate copies of many pieces of data for safety, availability, reliability, and performance. However, the amount of data is increasing so fast that it becomes the bottleneck of the total performance itself. Fortunately, data deduplication techniques can help eliminate extra copies with pointers that lead back to the original copy.

One of the most common forms of data deduplication implementation works by comparing chunks of data to detect duplicates.

> Chunking. In some systems, chunks are defined by physical layer constraints. Other systems only complete files are compared, which is called single-instance storage. The most intelligent method of chunking is sliding block. In sliding block, a window is passed along the file stream to seek out more naturally occurring internal file boundaries.

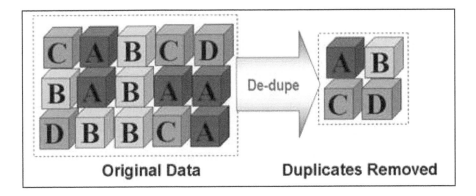

Figure 10.15 Data deduplication.

Client backup deduplication. This is the process where the deduplication hash calculations are initially created on the source machines. Files that have identical hashes to files already in the target device are not sent, the target device just creates appropriate internal links to reference the duplicated data. The benefit of this is that it avoids data being unnecessarily sent across the network, thereby reducing traffic load.

Primary storage and secondary storage. By definition, primary storage systems are designed for optimal performance, rather than lowest-possible cost. The design criteria for these systems is to increase performance, at the expense of other considerations. Moreover, primary storage systems are much less tolerant of any operation that can negatively impact performance. Secondary storage systems contain primarily duplicate, or secondary, copies of data. These copies of data are typically not used for actual production operations and, as a result, are more tolerant of some performance degradation in exchange for increased efficiency.

10.6 EXERCISES

10.6.1 Fundamental Questions

1. What is structured data?

2. What is unstructured data?

3. What is semi-structured data?

4. Please describe the *Volume of Big Data*.

5. What is the *Veracity of Big Data*?

6. What is supervised learning in machine learning?

7. In Bayes Theorem, how do you calculate $P(A|B)$, when you have known $P(B|A), P(A)$, and $P(B)$?

8. What is decision tree?

9. What is unsupervised learning?

10. What is *Clustering* used for in unsupervised learning?

11. What is semi-supervised learning?

12. What is Moore's Law?

13. What is memory wall?

14. What is non-volatile memory?

15. What is Scratch Pad Memory?

16. What is CMP systems?

17. Are the data generated by mobile devices big data?

18. What is chunk in data deduplication?

10.6.2 Practical Questions

1. In Section 10.3, we calculated the results from $x = 4$ to $x = 2$. Please calculate all the results when $x = 1, y = 0, 1, 2$. The cost of allocating each data to different memory units is shown in Table 10.6. The result is shown in Figure 10.14. Please give the detailed progress of calculating.

IV

Appendices

IV

Appendices

Appendix 1: Project 1

PROJECT DESCRIPTION

In this course project, students will be assigned into about 20 groups (2–3 students in each group), and each group needs to complete the Android project followed by the requirements of the project. There are three phases, *Initial, Basic,* and *Advanced*. At the midterm of this semester, students need to submit their Android project.

PROJECT OBJECTIVE

The objective of the projects is to assist students in having a better understanding of mobile application development from a perspective of practice. Instructors will facilitate students to build up their knowledge scaffold through a constructivism-based instructional method. Students need to be able to bridge the gap between theoretical knowledge and operating skills after this real-world-based learning experience. Each team is encouraged to accomplish the project via collaborative group work. The project will be followed by an order of three phases.

PROJECT GUIDELINES

Basic requirement: Develop a mini game in Android.

The role: There are three kinds of animals, which are mouse, cat and elephant. The mouse can be eaten by the cat, and the cat can be crumpled by the elephant. However, the mouse can beat the elephant. Design a mini game: player can choose an animal to fight against the animal chosen by the computer. The result of the fight must be shown in the application.

Advanced requirement: Additional functions and User Interface (UI) will get extra points. Students can improve the basic project by adding more functions and beautifying UIs.

Meanwhile, students are encouraged to design their own project, but they must submit their proposal about what projects they plan to develop by a specific date.

PROJECT PLAN

Phase 1 Initial

Each team should study Chapter 3 to understand every steps of downloading and installing Integrated Development Environment (IDE) and Android Software Development Kit (SDK). In this assignment, students are encouraged to download and install the latest version of Java and Android SDK.

Before starting the project, each team should elect a leader who is responsible for coordinating project activities and communicating with the instructor. The due date of submitting title of the project with the name of the team leader is *Month, Day, Year.*

Phase 2 Basic

In this phase, each team should study the Rock-Paper-Scissors Game Design Tutorial and accomplish the basic function of this project. The due date of submitting the basic version of the Android project is October 19th, 2015. The basic function may cover the following aspects:

1. Basic UI of this Android Project

2. Basic functions of this Android Project

There is no report submission for this phase.

Phase 3 Advanced

In this phase, each team can design and implement some additional functions or improve the User Interface of this Android project. The due date of submitting the basic version of the Android project is *Month, Day, Year.* Every team should submit the source code and report.

Appendix 2: Project 2

PROJECT DESCRIPTION

In this course project, students will be assigned into about 20 groups (2–3 students in each group) and each group needs to complete the Android project followed by the requirements of the project. This project is divided into three steps, and at the end of this semester, students need to submit their Android projects.

PROJECT OBJECTIVE

The objective of the projects is to assist students to have a better understanding of energy consumption topics on mobile systems from a perspective of practice. Instructors will facilitate students to build up their knowledge scaffold through a constructivism-based instructional method. Students need to be able to bridge the gap between theoretical knowledge and operating skills after this real-world-based learning experience. Each team is encouraged to accomplish the project via collaborative group work. The project will be followed by an order of two basic phases and one advanced phase.

PROJECT REQUIREMENTS

1. Develop an Android app to monitor resource usage for running processes.

2. Analyze the relations between energy consumption and tasks.

3. Design methods to reduce the energy consumption.

PROJECT PLAN

Phase 1

Each team should develop an Android app to show usages for every running process about CPU, memory, and battery. Fig. 10.16 is a sample from OS Monitor to give student a brief understanding of the requirement of the first requirement.

The interfaces and the functions of this project are not required to be as the same as those from the sample. However, students should implement the function of monitoring of Central Processing Unit (CPU), memory, and battery. Students can ignore other information, such as process ID, thread information, PPID, and others. Students can find some useful information on:

1. https://code.google.com/p/android-os-monitor/

2. https://github.com/eolwral/OSMonitor

Figure 10.16   Print-screens of OS Monitor as samples.

Phase 2

In this phase, each team should submit a report about the analysis of the relations between energy consumption and tasks. Students can list all the energy consumption information about tasks using the app they developed in the first phase, then they can analyze the reasons. Students should give details about the scenarios of their analysis, including the configuration of emulators or real devices, the information of tasks, the information of Android system, and the statistics methods they used.

Phase 3 Advanced

In this phase, each team can design its own approach to reducing the energy consumption of mobile devices. Students can use some scheduling algorithms learned in class to schedule tasks based on the energy consumption information; design and implement the dynamic programming algorithm introduced in class to allocate tasks; or propose an approach to stop useless services. Follows are some hints to implement the function of saving energy consumption.

1. There are a number of tasks running on a mobile device, and it is unnecessary for some of them to keep running, such as data synchronization. Students can design algorithms to reduce the times of data transmission to reduce the communication cost. Furthermore, some useless services or previous apps can be terminated to reduce the usage of CPU.

2. From the analysis in phase 2, students can obtain detailed information about the energy consumption of running tasks. The energy consumption can be considered as the cost, while the performance constraint can be used to quantify the time constraint. With these two constraints, the goal is to find the solution with the lowest cost while satisfying the time constraint requirement.

Appendix 3: BirthProvider.java. Codes

BIRTHPROVIDER.JAVA. CODES

```java
import java.util.HashMap;
import android.content.ContentProvider;
import android.content.ContentUris;
import android.content.ContentValues;
import android.content.Context;
import android.content.UriMatcher;
import android.database.Cursor;
import android.database.SQLException;
import android.database.sqlite.SQLiteDatabase;
import android.database.sqlite.SQLiteOpenHelper;
import android.database.sqlite.SQLiteQueryBuilder;
import android.net.Uri;
import android.text.TextUtils;
import android.util.Log;

    public class BirthProvider extends ContentProvider {
// fields for my content provider
static final String PROVIDER_NAME = "example.android.my.cptester";
static final String URL = "content://" + PROVIDER_NAME + "/friends";
static final Uri CONTENT_URI = Uri.parse(URL);

    // fields for the database
static final String ID = "id";
static final String NAME = "name";
```

```
static final String BIRTHDAY = "birthday";

    // integer values used in content URI
static final int FRIENDS = 1;
static final int FRIENDS_ID = 2;

    DBHelper dbHelper;
    // projection map for a query
private static HashMap<String, String> BirthMap;

    // maps content URI "patterns" to the integer values that were set
above
static final UriMatcher uriMatcher;
static-
uriMatcher = new UriMatcher(UriMatcher.NO_MATCH);
uriMatcher.addURI(PROVIDER_NAME, "friends", FRIENDS);
uriMatcher.addURI(PROVIDER_NAME, "friends/#", FRIENDS_ID);
}
    // database declarations
private SQLiteDatabase database;
static final String DATABASE_NAME = "BirthdayReminder";

    static final String TABLE_NAME = "birthTable";
static final int DATABASE_VERSION = 1;
static final String CREATE_TABLE =
" CREATE TABLE " + TABLE_NAME +
" (id INTEGER PRIMARY KEY AUTOINCREMENT, " +
" name TEXT NOT NULL, " +
" birthday TEXT NOT NULL);";

    // class that creates and manages the provider's database
private static class DBHelper extends SQLiteOpenHelper {

    public DBHelper(Context context) {
super(context, DATABASE_NAME, null, DATABASE_VERSION);
// TODO Auto-generated constructor stub
}

    @Override
public void onCreate(SQLiteDatabase db) {
```

```
// TODO Auto-generated method stub
db.execSQL(CREATE_TABLE);
}
```

```
    @Override
public void onUpgrade(SQLiteDatabase db, int oldVersion, int newVer-
sion) {
// TODO Auto-generated method stub
Log.w(DBHelper.class.getName(),
"Upgrading database from version " + oldVersion + " to "
+ newVersion + ". Old data will be destroyed");
db.execSQL("DROP TABLE IF EXISTS " + TABLE_NAME);
onCreate(db);
}
```

```
    }
```

```
    @Override
public boolean onCreate() {
// TODO Auto-generated method stub
Context context = getContext();
dbHelper = new DBHelper(context);
// permissions to be writable
database = dbHelper.getWritableDatabase();
```

```
    if(database == null)
return false;
else
return true;
}
```

```
    @Override
public Cursor query(Uri uri, String[] projection, String selection,
String[] selectionArgs, String sortOrder) {
// TODO Auto-generated method stub
SQLiteQueryBuilder queryBuilder = new SQLiteQueryBuilder();
// the TABLE_NAME to query on
queryBuilder.setTables(TABLE_NAME);
```

```
    switch (uriMatcher.match(uri)) {
```

```java
// maps all database column names
case FRIENDS:
queryBuilder.setProjectionMap(BirthMap);
break;
case FRIENDS_ID:
queryBuilder.appendWhere( ID + "=" + uri.getLastPathSegment());
break;
default:
throw new IllegalArgumentException("Unknown URI" + uri);
}
if (sortOrder == null || sortOrder == " "){
// No sorting → sort on names by default
sortOrder = NAME;
}
Cursor cursor = queryBuilder.query(database, projection, selection,
selectionArgs, null, null, sortOrder);
/**
* register to watch a content URI for changes
*/
cursor.setNotificationUri(getContext().getContentResolver(), uri);

    return cursor;
}


    @Override
public Uri insert(Uri uri, ContentValues values)
// TODO Auto-generated method stub
long row = database.insert(TABLE_NAME, " ", values);

    // If record is added successfully
if(row > 0)
Uri newUri = ContentUris.withAppendedId(CONTENT_URI, row);
getContext().getContentResolver().notifyChange(newUri, null);
return newUri;
}
throw new SQLException("Fail to add a new record into " + uri);
}


    @Override
public int update(Uri uri, ContentValues values, String selection,
```

```java
String[] selectionArgs) {
// TODO Auto-generated method stub
int count = 0;

    switch (uriMatcher.match(uri)){
case FRIENDS:
count = database.update(TABLE_NAME, values, selection, selectionArgs);
break;
case FRIENDS_ID:
count = database.update(TABLE_NAME, values, ID +
" = " + uri.getLastPathSegment() +
(!TextUtils.isEmpty(selection) ? " AND (" +
selection + ')' : ""), selectionArgs);
break;
default:
throw new IllegalArgumentException("Unsupported URI " + uri );
}
getContext().getContentResolver().notifyChange(uri, null);
return count;
}

    @Override
public int delete(Uri uri, String selection, String[] selectionArgs) {
// TODO Auto-generated method stub
int count = 0;

    switch (uriMatcher.match(uri)){
case FRIENDS:
// delete all the records of the table
count = database.delete(TABLE_NAME, selection, selectionArgs);
break;
case FRIENDS_ID:
String id = uri.getLastPathSegment(); //gets the id
count = database.delete( TABLE_NAME, ID + " = " + id +
(!TextUtils.isEmpty(selection) ? " AND (" +
selection + ')' : ""), selectionArgs);
break;
default:
throw new IllegalArgumentException("Unsupported URI " + uri);
```

```
}

    getContext().getContentResolver().notifyChange(uri, null);
return count;

    }
    @Override
public String getType(Uri uri) {
// TODO Auto-generated method stub
switch (uriMatcher.match(uri)){
// Get all friend-birthday records
case FRIENDS:
return "vnd.android.cursor.dir/vnd.example.friends";
// Get a particular friend
case FRIENDS_ID:
return "vnd.android.cursor.item/vnd.example.friends";
default:
throw new IllegalArgumentException("Unsupported URI: " + uri);
}
}
}
```

In this file, the DBHelper is with the same function with the DatabaseHandler in the previous section. As a result, we still need to override onCreate() and onUpgrade() methods in DBHelper class.

Then we need to register our content provider in AndroidManifest.xml file to allow other applications to read and write our provider. We add a <provider> tag pair for our own content provider.

```
    <provider
android:name="BirthProvider"
android:authorities="example.android.my.cptester">
</provider>
```

When an application wants to access the data of a ContentProvider, it makes a request. These requests are handled by the ContentResolver object, which communicates with the ContentProvider as a client. We add three methods, which are deleteAllBirthdays(), addBirthday(), and showAllBirthdays(), to have user interface with the application. In MainActivity.java file, we add these three methods as following:

```
    public void deleteAllBirthdays (View view) {
// delete all the records and the table of the database provider
String URL = "content://example.android.my.cptester/friends";
Uri friends = Uri.parse(URL);
int count = getContentResolver().delete(
friends, null, null);
String countNum = count +" records are deleted.";
Toast.makeText(getBaseContext(),
countNum, Toast.LENGTH_LONG).show();
}

    public void addBirthday(View view) {
// Add a new birthday record
ContentValues values = new ContentValues();

    values.put(BirthProvider.NAME,
((EditText)findViewById(R.id.name)).getText().toString());

values.put(BirthProvider.BIRTHDAY,
((EditText)findViewById(R.id.birthday)).getText().toString());

    Uri uri = getContentResolver().insert(
BirthProvider.CONTENT_URI, values);

    Toast.makeText(getBaseContext(),
uri.toString() + " inserted!", Toast.LENGTH_LONG).show();
}
    public void showAllBirthdays(View view) {
// Show all the birthdays sorted by friend's name
String URL = "content://example.android.my.cptester/friends";
Uri friends = Uri.parse(URL);
Cursor  c  =  getContentResolver().query(friends, null, null, null,
"name");
String result = "Results:";

    if (!c.moveToFirst()) {
Toast.makeText(this, result+" no content yet!", Toast.LENGTH_LONG).show();
}else{
do{
result = result + "\n" + c.getString(c.getColumnIndex(BirthProvider.NAME))
```

```
+
" with id " + c.getString(c.getColumnIndex(BirthProvider.ID)) +
" has birthday: " + c.getString(c.getColumnIndex(BirthProvider.BIRTHDAY));
} while (c.moveToNext());
Toast.makeText(this, result, Toast.LENGTH_LONG).show();
}
```

Bibliography

[1] Y. Li, W. Dai, Z. Ming, and M. Qiu. Privacy protection for preventing data over-collection in smart city. *IEEE Transactions on Computers*, 65:1339–1350, 2015.

[2] K. Gai, M. Qiu, H. Zhao, and W. Dai. Anti-counterfeit schema using monte carlo simulation for e-commerce in cloud systems. In *The 2nd IEEE International Conference on Cyber Security and Cloud Computing*, pages 74–79, New York, USA, 2015. IEEE.

[3] H. Jean-Baptiste, L. Tao, K. Gai, and M. Qiu. Understanding model risk management - model rationalization in financial industry. In *The 2nd IEEE International Conference on Cyber Security and Cloud Computing*, pages 301–306, New York, USA, 2015. IEEE.

[4] G. Wu, H. Zhang, M. Qiu, Z. Ming, J. Li, and X. Qin. A decentralized approach for mining event correlations in distributed system monitoring. *Journal of Parallel and Distributed Computing*, 73(3):330–340, 2013.

[5] H. Zhao, M. Chen, M. Qiu, K. Gai, and M. Liu. A novel pre-cache schema for high performance android system. *Future Generation Computer Systems*, 2015.

[6] H. Liang and K. Gai. Internet-based anti-counterfeiting pattern with using big data in China. In *The IEEE International Symposium on Big Data Security on Cloud*, pages 1387–1392, New York, USA, 2015. IEEE.

[7] S. Jayaraman, L. Tao, K. Gai, and N. Jiang. Drug side effects data representation and full spectrum inferencing using knowledge graphs in intelligent telehealth. In *The 2nd IEEE International Conference of Scalable and Smart Cloud*, page PP, Beijing, China, 2016. IEEE.

[8] K. Gai, M. Qiu, S. Jayaraman, and L. Tao. Ontology-based knowledge representation for secure self-diagnosis in patient-centered telehealth with cloud systems. In *The 2nd IEEE International Conference on Cyber Security and Cloud Computing*, pages 98–103, New York, USA, 2015. IEEE.

[9] M. Sette, L. Tao, K. Gai, and N. Jiang. A semantic approach to intelligent and personal tutoring system. In *The 2nd IEEE International Conference of Scalable and Smart Cloud*, page PP, Beijing, China, 2016. IEEE.

[10] G. Alipui, L. Tao, K. Gai, and N. Jiang. Reducing complexity of diagnostic message pattern specification and recognition on in-bound data using semantic techniques. In *The 2nd IEEE International Conference of Scalable and Smart Cloud*, page PP, Beijing, China, 2016. IEEE.

[11] RJ. Destefano, L. Tao, and K. Gai. Improving data governance in large organizations through ontology and linked data. In *The 2nd IEEE International Conference of Scalable and Smart Cloud*, page PP, Beijing, China, 2016. IEEE.

[12] K. Thakur, M. Qiu, K. Gai., and M. Ali. An investigation on cyber security threats and security models. In *The 2nd IEEE International Conference on Cyber Security and Cloud Computing*, pages 307–311, New York, USA, 2015. IEEE.

[13] K. Yu, Y. Gao, P. Zhang, and M. Qiu. Design and architecture of Dell acceleration appliances for database (DAAD): A practical approach with high availability guaranteed. In *The 17th IEEE International Conference on High Performance Computing and Communications*, pages 430–435, New York, USA, 2015. IEEE.

[14] J. Wang, B. Guo, M. Qiu, and Z. Ming. Design and optimization of traffic balance broker for cloud-based telehealth platform. In *2013 IEEE/ACM 6th International Conference on Utility and Cloud Computing*, pages 147–154. IEEE, 2013.

[15] M. Qiu and E. Sha. Energy-aware online algorithm to satisfy sampling rates with guaranteed probability for sensor applications. In *High Performance Computing and Communications*, pages 156–167. Springer, 2007.

[16] M. Ali, K. Thakur, J. Monaco, and M. Qiu. An approach to minimize crossings in phylogenetic trees. In *The 2nd IEEE International Conference on Cyber Security and Cloud Computing*, pages 42–47, New York, USA, 2015. IEEE.

[17] M. Qiu, D. Cao, H. Su, and K. Gai. Data transfer minimization for financial derivative pricing using Monte Carlo simulation with GPU in 5G. *International Journal of Communication Systems*, 2015.

[18] M. Qiu, G. Song, J. Kong, and K. Zhang. Spatial graph grammars for web information transformation. In *Human Centric Computing Languages and Environments, 2003. Proceedings. 2003 IEEE Symposium on*, pages 84–91. IEEE, 2003.

[19] J. Xiong, M. Qiu, L. Gui, and X. Li. On resource scheduling of wireless converged broadcasting and cellular networks with popular services being preferentially delivered. In *The 17th IEEE International Conference on High Performance Computing and Communications*, pages 509–514, New York, USA, 2015. IEEE.

[20] Meikang Qiu and Edwin H-M Sha. Cost minimization while satisfying hard/soft timing constraints for heterogeneous embedded systems. *ACM Transactions on Design Automation of Electronic Systems (TODAES)*, 14(2):25, 2009.

[21] Man Lin, Li Xu, Laurence Tianruo Yang, Xiao Qin, Nenggan Zheng, Zhaohui Wu, and Meikang Qiu. Static security optimization for real-time systems. *Industrial Informatics, IEEE Transactions on*, 5(1):22–37, 2009.

[22] Meikang Qiu and Jiayin Li. *Real-Time Embedded Systems: Optimization, Synthesis, and Networking*. CRC Press, 2011.

[23] J. Wang, M. Qiu, B. Guo, Y. Shen, and Q. Li. User-level side channel attack on workflow system in data-center. In *The 17th IEEE International Conference on High Performance Computing and Communications*, pages 1430–1435, New York, USA, 2015. IEEE.

[24] H. Jean-Baptiste, L. Tao, M. Qiu, and K. Gai. Model risk management systems-back-end, middleware, front-end and analytics. In *The 2nd IEEE International Conference on Cyber Security*

and Cloud Computing, pages 312–316, New York, USA, 2015. IEEE.

[25] A. Butowsky, K. Gai, M. Coakley, M. Qiu, and C. Tappert. City of white plains parking app: Case study of a smart city web application. In *The 2nd IEEE International Conference on Cyber Security and Cloud Computing*, pages 278–282, New York, USA, 2015. IEEE.

[26] K. Gai and A. Steenkamp. A feasibility study of Platform-as-a-Service using cloud computing for a global service organization. *Journal of Information System Applied Research*, 7:28–42, 2014.

[27] K. Gai and S. Li. Towards cloud computing: A literature review on cloud computing and its development trends. In *The 4th IEEE International Conference on Multimedia Information Networking and Security*, pages 142–146, Nanjing, China, 2012. IEEE.

[28] K. Gai, M. Qiu, H. Zhao, L. Tao, and Z. Zong. Dynamic energy-aware cloudlet-based mobile cloud computing model for green computing. *Journal of Network and Computer Applications*, 2015.

[29] X. Liu, M. Qiu, X. Wang, W. Li, and K. Cai. Energy optimization of air-based information network with guaranteed security protection. In *The 2nd IEEE International Conference on Cyber Security and Cloud Computing*, pages 218–223, New York, USA, 2015. IEEE.

[30] M. Qiu, L. Yang, Z. Shao, and E. Sha. Dynamic and leakage energy minimization with soft real-time loop scheduling and voltage assignment. *IEEE Transactions on Very Large Scale Integration (VLSI) Systems*, 18(3):501–504, 2010.

[31] H. Jean-Baptiste, M. Qiu, K. Gai, and L. Tao. Meta meta-analytics for risk forecast using big data meta-regression in financial industry. In *The 2nd IEEE International Conference on Cyber Security and Cloud Computing*, pages 272–277, New York, USA, 2015. IEEE.

[32] H. Han, R. Li, J. Hu, and M. Qiu. Context awareness through reasoning on private analysis for android application. In *The*

2nd IEEE International Conference on Cyber Security and Cloud Computing, pages 150–156, New York, USA, 2015. IEEE.

[33] J. Niu, D. Wang, C. Tong, and M. Qiu. Inferring information propagation over online social networks: Edge asymmetry and flow tendency. In *The 17th IEEE International Conference on High Performance Computing and Communications*, pages 629–634, New York, USA, 2015. IEEE.

[34] Data, data everywhere. http://www.economist.com/node/15557443, February 25, 2011.

[35] M. Qiu, Z. Shao, Q. Zhuge, C. Xue, M. Liu, and E. H. Sha. Efficient assignment with guaranteed probability for heterogeneous parallel dsp. In *12th International Conference on Parallel and Distributed Systems (ICPADS)*, pages 623–630, Minneapolis, Minnesota, USA, 2006.

[36] K. Gai, M. Qiu, B. Thuraisingham, and L. Tao. Proactive attribute-based secure data schema for mobile cloud in financial industry. In *The IEEE International Symposium on Big Data Security on Cloud; 17th IEEE International Conference on High Performance Computing and Communications*, pages 1332–1337, New York, USA, 2015. IEEE.

[37] S. Elnagdy, M. Qiu, and K. Gai. Understanding taxonomy of cyber risks for cybersecurity insurance of financial industry in cloud computing. In *The 2nd IEEE International Conference of Scalable and Smart Cloud*, page PP, Beijing, China, 2016. IEEE.

[38] K. Gai, M. Qiu, L. Tao, and Y. Zhu. Intrusion detection techniques for mobile cloud computing in heterogeneous 5G. *Security and Communication Networks*, PP:1–10, 2015.

[39] L. Chen, M. Qiu, and J. Xiong. An SDN-based fabric for flexible data-center networks. In *The 2nd IEEE International Conference on Cyber Security and Cloud Computing*, pages 121–126, New York, USA, 2015. IEEE.

[40] K. Gai, M. Qiu, and H. Zhao. Security-aware efficient mass distributed storage approach for cloud systems in big data. In *The 2nd IEEE International Conference on Big Data Security on Cloud*, pages 140–145, New York, USA, 2016.

[41] S. Elnagdy, M. Qiu, and K. Gai. Cyber incident classifications using ontology-based knowledge representation for cybersecurity insurance in financial industry. In *The 2nd IEEE International Conference of Scalable and Smart Cloud*, page PP, Beijing, China, 2016. IEEE.

[42] C. Asamoah, L. Tao, K. Gai, and N. Jiang. Powering filtration process of cyber security ecosystem using knowledge graph. In *The 2nd IEEE International Conference of Scalable and Smart Cloud*, page PP, Beijing, China, 2016. IEEE.

[43] K. Gai, M. Qiu, and S. Elnagdy. A novel secure big data cyber incident analytics framework for cloud-based cybersecurity insurance. In *The 2nd IEEE International Conference on Big Data Security on Cloud*, pages 171–176, New York, USA, 2016.

[44] K. Gai, M. Qiu, and S. Elnagdy. Security-aware information classifications using supervised learning for cloud-based cyber risk management in financial big data. In *The 2nd IEEE International Conference on Big Data Security on Cloud*, pages 197–202, New York, USA, 2016.

[45] L. Ma, L. Tao, Y. Zhong, and K. Gai. RuleSN: Research and application of social network access control model. In *IEEE International Conference on Intelligent Data and Security*, pages 418–423, New York, USA, 2016.

[46] K. Gai, M. Qiu, H. Zhao, and J. Xiong. Privacy-aware adaptive data encryption approach of big data in cloud computing. In *The 2nd IEEE International Conference of Scalable and Smart Cloud*, page PP, Beijing, China, 2016. IEEE.

[47] Manuel Egele, Christopher Kruegel, Engin Kirda, and Giovanni Vigna. PiOS: Detecting privacy leaks in iOS applications. In *Proceedings of the 18th Annual Network & Distributed System Security Symposium (NDSS)*, February 2011.

[48] William Enck, Peter Gilbert, Byung-Gon Chun, Landon P. Cox, Jaeyeon Jung, Patrick McDaniel, and Anmol N. Sheth. Taintdroid: An information-flow tracking system for realtime privacy monitoring on smartphones. In *Proceedings of the 9th USENIX Conference on Operating Systems Design and Implementation,*

OSDI'10, pages 1–6, Berkeley, CA, USA, 2010. USENIX Association.

[49] William Enck, Damien Octeau, Patrick McDaniel, and Swarat Chaudhuri. A study of android application security. In *Proceedings of the 20th USENIX Conference on Security*, SEC'11, pages 21–21, Berkeley, CA, USA, 2011. USENIX Association.

[50] Abhijit Bose, Xin Hu, Kang G. Shin, and Taejoon Park. Behavioral detection of malware on mobile handsets. In *Proceedings of the 6th International Conference on Mobile Systems, Applications, and Services*, MobiSys '08, pages 225–238, New York, NY, USA, 2008. ACM.

[51] App reputation report. https://www.appthority.com/app-reputation-report/report/AppReputationReportSummer14.pdf, 2014.

[52] H. Zhao, M. Qiu, K. Gai, J. Li, and X. He. Maintainable mobile model using pre-cache technology for high performance android system. In *The 2nd IEEE International Conference on Cyber Security and Cloud Computing*, pages 175–180, New York, USA, 2015. IEEE.

[53] App reputation report. http://blog.tahoepartners.com/index.php/gartner-summit-the-difference-between-apps-and-applications/, 2014.

[54] L. Tao, S. Golikov, K. Gai, and M. Qiu. A reusable software component for integrated syntax and semantic validation for services computing. In *IEEE Symposium on Service-Oriented System Engineering*, pages 127–132, San Francisco, CA, USA, 2015. IEEE.

[55] Y. Liu, P. Zhang, and M. Qiu. Fast numerical evaluation for symbolic expressions in java. In *The 17th IEEE International Conference on High Performance Computing and Communications*, pages 559–604, New York, USA, 2015. IEEE.

[56] M. Qiu, K. Zhang, and M. Huang. An empirical study of web interface design on small display devices. In *Proceedings of the 2004 IEEE/WIC/ACM International Conference on Web Intelligence*, pages 29–35. IEEE Computer Society, 2004.

[57] K. Zhang, J. Kong, M. Qiu, and G. Song. Multimedia layout adaptation through grammatical specifications. *Multimedia Systems*, 10(3):245–260, 2005.

[58] V. Aggarwal, V. Gopalakrishnan, R. Jana, K. Ramakrishnan, and V. Vaishampayan. Optimizing cloud resources for delivering IPTV services through virtualization. *IEEE Transactions on Multimedia*, 15(4):789–801, 2013.

[59] J. Kong, M. Qiu, and K. Zhang. Authoring multimedia documents through grammatical specifications. In *Multimedia and Expo, 2003. ICME '03. Proceedings. 2003 International Conference on*, volume 2, pages II–629. IEEE, 2003.

[60] P. Panda, N. Dutt, and A. Nicolau. On-chip vs. off-chip memory: The data partitioning problem in embedded processor-based systems. *ACM Transactions on Design Automations of Electronic Systems*, 5(3):682–704, 2000.

[61] M. Qiu, J. Wu, C. Xue, J. Hu, W. Tseng, and E. Sha. QoS for networked heterogeneous real-time embedded systems. In *ISCA PDCCS*, pages 135–140, 2008.

[62] M. Qiu, J. Niu, F. Pan, Y. Chen, and Y. Zhu. Peak temperature minimization for embedded systems with DVS transition overhead consideration. In *2012 IEEE 14th International Conference on High Performance Computing and Communication & 2012 IEEE 9th International Conference on Embedded Software and Systems (HPCC-ICESS)*, pages 477–484, Liverpool, UK, 2012.

[63] X. Zhu, D. Liu, L. Liang, K. Zhong, M. Qiu, and E. H.-M. Sha. SwapBench: The easy way to demystify swapping in mobile systems. In *The 17th IEEE International Conference on High Performance Computing and Communications*, pages 497–502, New York, USA, 2015. IEEE.

[64] M. Qiu, H. Li, and E. Sha. Heterogeneous real-time embedded software optimization considering hardware platform. In *Proceedings of the 2009 ACM Symposium on Applied Computing*, pages 1637–1641. ACM, 2009.

[65] M. Qiu, Z. Chen, and M. Liu. Low-power low-latency data allocation for hybrid scratch-pad memory. *IEEE Embedded Systems Letters*, 6:69–72, 2014.

[66] M. Qiu, G. Wu, J. Hu, W. Tseng, and E. Sha. Energy minimization and latency hiding for heterogeneous parallel memory. In *Parallel and Distributed Systems (ICPADS), 2009 15th International Conference on*, pages 503–510. IEEE, 2009.

[67] Y. Gao, S. Iqbal, P. Zhang, and M. Qiu. Performance and power analysis of high-density multi-GPGPU architectures: A preliminary case study. In *The 17th IEEE International Conference on High Performance Computing and Communications*, pages 66–71, New York, USA, 2015. IEEE.

[68] K. Mao, J. Niu, X. Wang, L. Wang, and M. Qiu. Cross-domain sentiment analysis of product reviews by combining lexicon-based and learn-based techniques. In *The 17th IEEE International Conference on High Performance Computing and Communications*, pages 351–356, New York, USA, 2015. IEEE.

[69] J. Niu, C. Liu, Y. Gao, and M. Qiu. Energy efficient task assignment with guaranteed probability satisfying timing constraints for embedded systems. *IEEE Transactions on Parallel and Distributed Systems*, 25(8):2043–2052, 2014.

[70] W. Dong, X. Li, Y. Li, M. Qiu, L. Dou, L. Ju, and Z. Jia. Minimizing update bits of NVM-based main memory using bit flipping and cyclic shifting. In *The 17th IEEE International Conference on High Performance Computing and Communications*, pages 290–295, New York, USA, 2015. IEEE.

[71] X. Dong, R. Li, H. H, X. Gu, M. Sarem, M. Qiu, and K. Li. An efficient data selection policy for search engine cache management. In *The 17th IEEE International Conference on High Performance Computing and Communications*, pages 122–127, New York, USA, 2015. IEEE.

[72] M. Qiu and E. H. Sha. Cost minimization while satisfying hard/soft timing constraints for heterogeneous embedded systems. *ACM Transactions on Design Automation of Electronic Systems (TODAES)*, 14(2):25, 2009.

[73] M. Qiu and J. Li. *Real-time Embedded Systems: Optimization, Synthesis, and Networking.* CRC Press, 2011.

[74] S. Hua and G. Qu. Approaching the maximum energy saving on embedded systems with multiple voltages. In *Proceedings of the 2003 IEEE/ACM International Conference on Computer-aided Design*, pages 26–29, Washington, DC, USA, 2003. IEEE Computer Society.

[75] Y. Guo, Q. Zhuge, J. Hu, M. Qiu, and E. Sha. Optimal data allocation for scratch-pad memory on embedded multi-core systems. In *IEEE 2011 International Conference on Parallel Processing*, pages 464–471, Taipei City, 2011.

[76] Y. Li, J. Niu, M. Qiu, and X. Long. Optimizing tasks assignment on heterogeneous multi-core real-time systems with minimum energy. In *The 17th IEEE International Conference on High Performance Computing and Communications*, pages 577–582, New York, USA, 2015. IEEE.

[77] Z. Chen, M. Qiu, L. Zhang, F. Hu, and L. Zhang. ILP security optimization method for embedded systems with timing constraints. In *Proceedings of the Seventh Annual Workshop on Cyber Security and Information Intelligence Research*, pages 38–42, Oak Ridge, TN, USA, 2011. ACM.

[78] M. Qiu, C. Xue, Z. Shao, and E. Sha. Energy minimization with soft real-time and DVS for uniprocessor and multiprocessor embedded systems. In *Proceedings of the conference on Design, automation and test in Europe*, pages 1641–1646, Grenoble, France, 2007. EDA Consortium.

[79] X. Liu, M. Qiu, X. Wang, W. Liu, and J. Zhang. Optimization for communication energy efficiency of air-based information network while satisfying timing constraints. In *The 17th IEEE International Conference on High Performance Computing and Communications*, pages 533–558, New York, USA, 2015. IEEE.

[80] M. Qiu, Y. Jiang, and W. Dai. Cost minimization for heterogeneous systems with Gaussian distribution execution time. In *The 17th IEEE International Conference on High Performance Computing and Communications*, pages 547–582, New York, USA, 2015. IEEE.

[81] Y. Chen, M. Alghamdi, X. Qiu, J. Zhang, M. Jiang, and M. Qiu. TERN: A self-adjusting thermal model for dynamic resource provisioning in data centers. In *The 17th IEEE International Conference on High Performance Computing and Communications*, pages 479–490, New York, USA, 2015. IEEE.

[82] M. Qiu, Z. Ming, J. Li, and et. al. Three-phase time-aware energy minimization with DVFS and unrolling for chip multiprocessors. *J. of Syst. Architecture*, 58(10):439–445, 2012.

[83] M. Qiu, E. Sha, M. Liu, M. Lin, S. Hua, and L. Yang. Energy minimization with loop fusion and multi-functional-unit scheduling for multidimensional DSP. *Journal of Parallel and Distributed Computing*, 68(4):443–455, 2008.

[84] M. Qiu, J. Deng, and E. Sha. Failure rate minimization with multiple function unit scheduling for heterogeneous WSNs. In *Global Telecommunications Conference, 2008. IEEE GLOBECOM 2008. IEEE*, pages 1–5. IEEE, 2008.

[85] M. Qiu, J. Niu, L. Yang, X. Qin, S. Zhang, and B. Wang. Energy-aware loop parallelism maximization for multi-core DSP architectures. In *Proceedings of the 2010 IEEE/ACM International Conference on Green Computing and Communications & International Conference on Cyber, Physical and Social Computing*, pages 205–212. IEEE Computer Society, 2010.

[86] M. Qiu, L. Yang, and E. Sha. Rotation scheduling and voltage assignment to minimize energy for SoC. In *Int'l Conf. on Computational Sci. and Engineering*, volume 2, pages 48–55, Vancouver, BC, Canada, 2009.

[87] M. Qiu, W. Gao, M. Chen, J. Niu, and L. Zhang. Energy efficient security algorithm for power grid wide area monitoring system. *IEEE Transactions on Smart Grid*, 2(4):715–723, 2011.

[88] M. Qiu, H. Su, M. Chen, Z. Ming, and L. Yang. Balance of security strength and energy for a PMU monitoring system in smart grid. *IEEE Communications Magazine*, 50(5):142–149, 2012.

[89] J. Li, M. Qiu, J. Niu, L. Yang, Y. Zhu, and Z. Ming. Thermal-aware task scheduling in 3D chip multiprocessor with real-time

constrained workloads. *ACM Trans. on Embedded Computing Systems (TECS)*, 12(2):24, 2013.

[90] M. Qiu, M. Zhong, J. Li, K. Gai, and Z. Zong. Phase-change memory optimization for green cloud with genetic algorithm. *IEEE Transactions on Computers*, 64(12):1–13, 2015.

[91] M. Qiu, J. Wu, F. Hu, S. Liu, and L. Wang. Voltage assignment for soft real-time embedded systems with continuous probability distribution. In *Embedded and Real-Time Computing Systems and Applications, 2009. RTCSA '09. 15th IEEE International Conference on*, pages 413–418. IEEE, 2009.

[92] M. Qiu, Z. Jia, C. Xue, Z. Shao, and E. Sha. Voltage assignment with guaranteed probability satisfying timing constraint for real-time multiproceesor DSP. *The Journal of VLSI Signal Processing Systems for Signal, Image, and Video Technology*, 46(1):55–73, 2007.

[93] S. Krantz and H. Parks. The P/NP problem. In *A Mathematical Odyssey*, pages 217–254. Springer, 2014.

[94] S. Liu and M. Qiu. Thermal-aware scheduling for peak temperature reduction with stochastic workloads. In *16th IEEE Real-Time and Embedded Technology and Applications Symposium, Stockholm: WIP*, pages 59–62. Citeseer, 2010.

[95] P. Zhang, Y. Gao, and M. Qiu. A data-oriented method for scheduling dependent tasks on high-density multi-GPU systems. In *The 17th IEEE International Conference on High Performance Computing and Communications*, pages 694–699, New York, USA, 2015. IEEE.

[96] M. Qiu, L. Zhang, and E. Sha. ILP optimal scheduling for multi-module memory. In *Proceedings of the 7th IEEE/ACM international conference on Hardware/software codesign and system synthesis*, pages 277–286. ACM, 2009.

[97] M. Qiu, C. Xue, Q. Zhuge, Z. Shao, M. Liu, and E. Sha. Voltage assignment and loop scheduling for energy minimization while satisfying timing constraint with guaranteed probability. In *Application-Specific Systems, Architectures and Processors,*

2006. ASAP '06. International Conference on, pages 178–181. IEEE, 2006.

[98] C. Leiserson and J. Saxe. Retiming synchronous circuitry. *Algorithmica*, 6(1-6):5–35, 1991.

[99] M. Qiu, Z. Chen, L. Yang, X. Qin, and B. Wang. Towards power-efficient smartphones by energy-aware dynamic task scheduling. In *2012 IEEE 14th International Conference on High Performance Computing and Communication & 2012 IEEE 9th International Conference on Embedded Software and Systems (HPCC-ICESS)*, pages 1466–1472, Liverpool, UK, 2012.

[100] L. Chao, A. LaPaugh, and E. Sha. Rotation scheduling: A loop pipelining algorithm. *IEEE Transactions on Computer-Aided Design of Integrated Circuits and Systems*, 16(3):229–239, 1997.

[101] L. Chao and E. Sha. Static scheduling for synthesis of DSP algorithms on various models. *Journal of VLSI Signal Processing Systems for Signal, Image and Video Technology*, 10(3):207–223, 1995.

[102] J. Wang, M. Qiu, B. Guo, Y. Shen, and Q. Li. Low-power sensor polling for context-aware services on smartphones. In *The 17th IEEE International Conference on High Performance Computing and Communications*, pages 617–622, New York, USA, 2015. IEEE.

[103] M. Alghamdi, X. Jiang, X. Qin, J. Zhang, M. Jiang, and M. Qiu. TOPS: Two-phase scheduling for distributed real-time systems. In *IEEE Computing, Communications and Applications Conference*, pages 22–22, Beijing, China, 2014. IEEE.

[104] J. Li, M. Qiu, J. Niu, W. Gao, Z. Zong, and X. Qin. Feedback dynamic algorithms for preemptable job scheduling in cloud systems. In *2010 IEEE/WIC/ACM International Conference on Web Intelligence and Intelligent Agent Technology*, volume 1, pages 561–564, Toronto, ON, Canada, 2010.

[105] W. Cesario, A. Baghdadi, L. Gauthier, D. Lyonnard, G. Nicolescu, Y. Paviot, S. Yoo, A. Jerraya, and M. Diaz-Nava. Component-based design approach for multicore SoCs. In *ACM*

Proceedings of the 39th annual Design Automation Conference, pages 789–794, San Francisco, CA, 2002.

[106] G. Nicolescu, S. Yoo, A. Bouchhima, and A. Jerraya. Validation in a component-based design flow for multicore SoCs. In *ACM Proceedings of the 15th international symposium on System Synthesis,* pages 162–167, Kyoto, Japan, 2002.

[107] K. Gai, M. Qiu, H. Zhao, and M. Liu. Energy-aware optimal task assignment for mobile heterogeneous embedded systems in cloud computing. In *The 3rd IEEE International Conference on Cyber Security and Cloud Computing,* page PP, Beijing, China, 2016. IEEE.

[108] L. Wu, S. Garg, S. Versteeg, and R. Buyya. SLA-Based resource provisioning for hosted Software-as-a-Service applications in cloud computing environments. *IEEE Transactions on Services Computing,* 7(3):465–485, 2014.

[109] C. Alcaraz and J. Aguado. MonPaaS: an adaptive monitoring Platform as a Service for cloud computing infrastructures and services. *IEEE Transactions on Services Computing,* 8(1):65–78, 2015.

[110] F. Hu, M. Qiu, J. Li, T. Grant, D. Taylor, S. McCaleb, L. Butler, and R. Hamner. A review on cloud computing: Design challenges in architecture and security. *Journal of Computing and Information Technology,* 19(1):25–55, 2011.

[111] J. Espadas, A. Molina, G. Jimenez, M. Molina, R. Ramjrez, and D. Concha. A tenant-based resource allocation model for scaling Software-as-a-Service applications over cloud computing infrastructures. *Future Generation Computer Systems,* 29(1):273–286, 2013.

[112] M. Qiu, Z. Chen, Z. Ming, X. Qin, and J. Niu. Energy-aware data allocation with hybrid memory for mobile cloud systems. *IEEE Systems Journal,* PP(99), 2014.

[113] J. Wang, B. Guo, M. Qiu, and Z. Ming. Design and optimization of traffic balance broker for cloud-based Telehealth platform. In *2013 IEEE/ACM 6th International Conference on Utility and Cloud Computing,* pages 147–154, Dresden, Germany, 2013.

[114] D. W. Ng, E. Lo, and R. Schober. Energy-efficient resource allocation in OFDMA systems with large numbers of base station antennas. *IEEE Transactions on Wireless Communications*, 11(9):3292–3304, 2012.

[115] W. Dai, H. Chen, W. Wang, and X. Chen. RMORM: A framework of multi-objective optimization resource management in clouds. In *IEEE 9th World Congress on Services*, pages 488–494, Santa Clara, CA, USA, 2013. IEEE.

[116] J. Li, M. Qiu, Z. Ming, G. Quan, X. Qin, and Z. Gu. Online optimization for scheduling preemptable tasks on IaaS cloud systems. *Journal of Parallel and Distributed Computing*, 72(5):666–677, 2012.

[117] Y. Li, K. Gai, Z. Ming, H. Zhao, and M. Qiu. Intercrossed access control for secure financial services on multimedia big data in cloud systems. *ACM Transactions on Multimedia Computing Communications and Applications*, PP:1, 2016.

[118] K. Gai. A review of leveraging private cloud computing in financial service institutions: Value propositions and current performances. *International Journal of Computer Applications*, 95(3):40–44, 2014.

[119] D. Qi, M. Liu, M. Qiu, and S. Zhang. Exponential synchronization of general discrete-time chaotic neural networks with or without time delays. *IEEE Transactions on Neural Networks*, 21(8):1358–1365, 2010.

[120] F. Gu, J. Niu, Z. He, M. Qiu, and C. Fu. CLMRS: Designing cross-LAN media resources sharing based on DLNA. In *The 2nd IEEE International Conference on Cyber Security and Cloud Computing*, pages 133–140, New York, USA, 2015. IEEE.

[121] Y. Tao, H. Dai, B. Sun, S. Zhao, M. Qiu, and Z. Yu. A head record cache structure to improve the operations on big files in cloud storage servers. In *The 17th IEEE International Conference on High Performance Computing and Communications*, pages 46–51, New York, USA, 2015. IEEE.

[122] M. Qiu, Z. Ming, J. Wang, L. Yang, and Y. Xiang. Enabling cloud computing in emergency management systems. *IEEE Cloud Computing*, 1(4):60–67, 2014.

[123] J. Peng, Y. Dai, Y. Rao, X. Zhi, and M. Qiu. Modeling for CPU-intensive applications in cloud computing. In *The 17th IEEE International Conference on High Performance Computing and Communications*, pages 20–25, New York, USA, 2015. IEEE.

[124] A. Steenkamp, A. Alawdah, O. Almasri, K. Gai, N. Khattab, C. Swaby, and R. Abaas. Enterprise architecture specification case study. *Journal of Information System Education*, 24(2):105, 2013.

[125] C. He, X. Fan, and Y. Li. Toward ubiquitous healthcare services with a novel efficient cloud platform. *IEEE Transactions on Biomedical Engineering*, 60(1):230–234, 2013.

[126] M. Sookhak, A. Gani, M. Khan, and R. Buyya. Dynamic remote data auditing for securing big data storage in cloud computing. *Information Sciences*, 2015.

[127] M. Qiu, K. Gai, B. Thuraisingham, L. Tao, and H. Zhao. Proactive user-centric secure data scheme using attribute-based semantic access controls for mobile clouds in financial industry. *Future Generation Computer Systems*, PP:1, 2016.

[128] Z. Wei, G. Pierre, and C. Chi. CloudTPS: Scalable transactions for Web applications in the cloud. *IEEE Transactions on Services Computing*, 5(4):525–539, 2012.

[129] K. Gai, Z. Du, M. Qiu, and H. Zhao. Efficiency-aware workload optimizations of heterogenous cloud computing for capacity planning in financial industry. In *The 2nd IEEE International Conference on Cyber Security and Cloud Computing*, pages 1–6, New York, USA, 2015. IEEE.

[130] B. Crow, I. Widjaja, J. Kim, and P. Sakai. IEEE 802.11 wireless local area networks. *IEEE Communications Magazine*, 35(9):116–126, 1997.

[131] K. Pahlavan. *Principles of wireless networks: A unified approach.* John Wiley & Sons, Inc., 2011.

[132] B. Latre, B. Braem, I. Moerman, C. Blondia, and P. Demeester. A survey on wireless body area networks. *Wireless Networks*, 17(1):1–18, 2011.

[133] L. Chen, Y. Duan, M. Qiu, J. Xiong, and K. Gai. Adaptive resource allocation optimization in heterogeneous mobile cloud systems. In *The 2nd IEEE International Conference on Cyber Security and Cloud Computing*, pages 19–24, New York, USA, 2015. IEEE.

[134] A. Younge, R. Henschel, J. Brown, L. Laszewski, J. Qiu, and G. Fox. Analysis of virtualization technologies for high performance computing environments. In *2011 IEEE International Conference on Cloud Computing*, pages 9–16, Washington, DC, USA, 2011.

[135] D. Zissis and D. Lekkas. Addressing cloud computing security issues. *Future Generation computer systems*, 28(3):583–592, 2012.

[136] D. Kirk and W. Wen-mei. *Programming massively parallel processors: a hands-on approach*. Newnes, 2012.

[137] D. Warneke and O. Kao. Exploiting dynamic resource allocation for efficient parallel data processing in the cloud. *IEEE Transactions on Parallel and Distributed Systems*, 22(6):985–997, 2011.

[138] C. Wang, N. Cao, K. Ren, and W. Lou. Enabling secure and efficient ranked keyword search over outsourced cloud data. *IEEE Transactions on Parallel and Distributed Systems*, 23(8):1467–1479, 2012.

[139] L. Song, D. Niyato, Z. Han, and E. Hossain. Game-Theoretic resource allocation methods for device-to-device communication. *IEEE Wireless Communications*, 21(3):136–144, 2014.

[140] Y. Zheng, Z. Dong, F. Luo, K. Meng, J. Qiu, and K. Wong. Optimal allocation of energy storage system for risk mitigation of DISCOs with high renewable penetrations. *IEEE Transactions on Power Systems*, 29(1):212–220, 2014.

[141] S. Brandt, E. Miller, D. Long, and L. Xue. Efficient metadata management in large distributed storage systems. In *2013 IEEE 10th International Conference on Mobile Ad-Hoc and Sensor Systems*, pages 290–290, Hangzhou, China, 2003.

[142] F. Zhang, Z. Zhou, and W. Xu. Distributed storage and processing method for big data sensing information of machine operation condition. *Journal of Software*, 9(10):2598–2606, 2014.

[143] J. Yu, Y. Zhu, L. Xia, M. Qiu, Y. Fu, and G. Rong. Grounding high efficiency cloud computing architecture: Hw-sw co-design and implementation of a stand-alone web server on FPGA. In *2011 Fourth International Conference on the Applications of Digital Information and Web Technologies*, pages 124–129, Stevens Point, WI, USA, 2011.

[144] H. Dai, Q. Li, M. Qiu, Z. Yu, and Z. Jia. A cloud trust authority framework for mobile enterprise information system. In *2014 IEEE 8th International Symposium on Service Oriented System Engineering*, pages 496–501, Oxford, UK, 2014.

[145] J. Li, M. Qiu, J. Niu, Y. Chen, and Z. Ming. Adaptive resource allocation for preemptable jobs in cloud systems. In *2010 10th International Conference on Intelligent Systems Design and Applications*, pages 31–36, Cairo, Egypt, 2010.

[146] Z. Yu, Q. Wang, Y. Fan, H. Dai, and M. Qiu. An improved classifier chain algorithm for multi-label classification of big data analysis. In *The 17th IEEE International Conference on High Performance Computing and Communications*, pages 1298–1301, New York, USA, 2015. IEEE.

[147] K. Gai, M. Qiu, L. Chen, and M. Liu. Electronic health record error prevention approach using ontology in big data. In *The 17th IEEE International Conference on High Performance Computing and Communications*, pages 752–757, New York, USA, 2015. IEEE.

[148] H. Yin and K. Gai. An empirical study on preprocessing high-dimensional class-imbalanced data for classification. In *The IEEE International Symposium on Big Data Security on Cloud*, pages 1314–1319, New York, USA, 2015. IEEE.

[149] Introduction to SQL. http://www.w3schools.com/sql/sql'intro.asp, 2015.

[150] T. Muzaffar, X. Jiang, X. Qin, and M. Qiu. iTad: I/O thermal aware data center model. In *IEEE International Conference on*

Green Computing and Communications, pages 502–509, Taipei, China, 2014. IEEE.

[151] H. Yin, K. Gai, and Z. Wang. A classification algorithm based on ensemble feature selections for imbalanced-class dataset. In *The 2nd IEEE International Conference on High Performance and Smart Computing*, pages 245–249, New York, USA, 2016.

[152] H. Yin and K. Gai. An empirical study on preprocessing high-dimensional class-imbalanced data for classification. In *The IEEE International Symposium on Big Data Security on Cloud*, pages 1314–1319, New York, USA, 2015.

[153] X. Yu, T. Pei, K. Gai, and L. Guo. Analysis on urban collective call behavior to earthquake. In *The IEEE International Symposium on Big Data Security on Cloud*, pages 1302–1307, New York, USA, 2015. IEEE.

[154] X. He, C. Wang, T. Liu, K. Gai, D. Chen, and L. Bai. Research on campus mobile model based on periodic purpose for opportunistic network. In *The IEEE International Symposium on Big Data Security on Cloud*, pages 782–785, New York, USA, 2015. IEEE.

[155] A. Holzinger, C. Stocker, B. Ofner, G. Prohaska, A. Brabenetz, and R. Hofmann-Wellenhof. Combining HCI, natural language processing, and knowledge discovery-potential of IBM content analytics as an assistive technology in the biomedical field. In *Human-Computer Interaction and Knowledge Discovery in Complex, Unstructured, Big Data*, pages 13–24. Springer, 2013.

[156] C. Liu, J. Chen, L. T. Yang, X. Zhang, C. Yang, R. Ranjan, and K. Rao. Authorized public auditing of dynamic big data storage on cloud with efficient verifiable fine-grained updates. *IEEE Transactions on Parallel and Distributed Systems*, 25(9):2234–2244, 2014.

[157] M. Qiu, E. Khisamutdinov, Z. Zhao, C. Pan, J. Choi, N. Leontis, and P. Guo. RNA nanotechnology for computer design and in vivo computation. *Philosophical Transactions of the Royal Society of London A: Mathematical, Physical and Engineering Sciences*, 371(2000):20120310, 2013.

[158] Vasant Dhar. Data science and prediction. *Communications of the ACM*, 56(12):64–73, 2013.

[159] M. Qiu, J. Liu, J. Li, Z. Fei, Z. Ming, and E. Sha. A novel energy-aware fault tolerance mechanism for wireless sensor networks. In *2011 IEEE/ACM International Conference on Green Computing and Communications*, pages 56–61, Sichuan, China, 2011. IEEE.

[160] M. Qiu, Z. Chen, Z. Ming, X. Qin, and J. Niu. Energy-aware data allocation with hybrid memory for mobile cloud systems. *IEEE Systems Journal*, PP:1–10, 2014.

[161] The data science venn diagram. http://drewconway.com/zia/2013/3/26/the-data-science-venn-diagram, 2010.

[162] D. Neacsu. Novel microcontrollers with direct access to flash memory benefit implementation of multi-optimal space vector modulation. *IEEE Transactions on Industrial Informatics*, 8(3):528–535, 2012.

[163] B. Atitallah, E. Senn, D. Chillet, M. Lanoe, and D. Blouin. An efficient framework for power-aware design of heterogeneous MP-SoC. *IEEE Transactions on Industrial Informatics*, 9(1):487–501, 2013.

[164] R. Bambang, A. Rohman, C. Dronkers, R. Ortega, and A. Sasongko. Energy management of fuel cell/ battery/ super-capacitor hybrid power sources using model predictive control. *IEEE Transactions on Industrial Informatics*, 10(4):1992–2002, 2014.

[165] J. Hu, C. Xue, W. Tseng, Y. He, M. Qiu, and Edwin E. Sha. Reducing write activities on non-volatile memories in embedded CMPs via data migration and recomputation. In *2010 47th ACM/IEEE Design Automation Conference (DAC)*, pages 350–355, Anaheim, CA, USA, 2010.

[166] M. Qiu, Z. Chen, Z. Ming, X. Qin, and J. Niu. Energy-aware data allocation with hybrid memory for mobile cloud systems. *IEEE Systems Journal*, PP(99):1–10, 2014.

[167] R. Fan, H. Jiang, Q. Guo, and Z. Zhang. Joint optimal cooperative sensing and resource allocation in multichannel cognitive radio networks. *IEEE Transactions on Vehicular Technology*, 60(2):722–729, 2011.